alibris

ONCE UPON A TIME
100 COROZAL SHOP CTR
STE. 104 UNIT 401
COROZAL, PR 00783
UNITED STATES

AF770455

To: ALIBRIS APEX DC 76926387-81
APEX
800 AVONDALE AVE.
GRANDVIEW HEIGHTS, OH 43212-3473

Shipping Instructions for JUNEAU88

Print this Packing Slip and enclose inside the front cover of the book.

Please ship this item no later than Fri Sep 25, 2026.

Ship to:

ALIBRIS APEX DC 76926387-81
APEX
800 AVONDALE AVE.
GRANDVIEW HEIGHTS, OH 43212-3473
UNITED STATES

PN #	Item ID	Alibris ID	Media Type	Title / Author	Seller List Price	Order Date
76926387-81	038843	B084322631	BOOK	Beyond the Billable Hour: an Anthology of Alternative Billing Methods Richard C. Reed	$76.97	Sep, 15 2026

Very Good paperback Size: 11x9x1; Lightly used, text and pages clean and unmarked, slight discolor to coverl ship WORLDWIDE From PUERTO RICO, USA. Listing Includes Books Image. Please email me if you need to see more pictures! The orders are processed pro

76926387-81

BEYOND THE BILLABLE HOUR
An Anthology of Alternative Billing Methods

Edited by Richard C. Reed

ABA

Section of Economics of Law Practice

The material contained herein represents the opinions of the authors and editor and should not be construed to be the action of either the American Bar Association or the Economics of Law Practice Section unless adopted pursuant to the Bylaws of the Association.

Printed in the United States of America.
Library of Congress Catalog Card Number 89-45318
ISBN #: 89707-428-9

89 90 91 92 93 5 4 3 2 1

Discounts are available for books ordered in bulk. Special consideration is given to state bar associations, CLE programs and other bar-related nonprofit organizations. Inquire at Publications Planning & Marketing, American Bar Association, 750 North Lake Shore Drive, Chicago, Illinois 60611.

Foreword

How do you set fees to be charged clients for legal services that are fair to the clients and to the lawyer?

This topic has been discussed with increasing frequency of late. Many questions are being raised; some answers are beginning to emerge.

The problem to be dealt with stems from the predominant practice of billing on an hourly basis aggravated by the perception of clients that the cost of legal services is too high.

Client dissatisfaction exists with respect to hourly billing. The courts in making fee awards have expressed a desire for an objective system for setting fees illustrated by the "lodestar" method, yet have increasingly disallowed portions of fees based on time spent and have moved away from the use of subjective factors in making fee awards. Sophisticated purchasers of legal services acting through in-house counsel have attempted to set up policies for outside counsel to contain legal expense and to predict at the outset the legal expense budget.

Perceptive lawyers have long realized that hourly billing often rewards the inefficient practitioner and penalizes the well-organized efficient lawyer. With the increased use of computers and other technology in law practice, the time of the lawyer is a less reliable measure of value. The cost of purchasing hardware and software, developing systems, training personnel and operating the computerized office has added a new dimension to the cost of operating a law office, even though the proper use of technology can result in an improved product at a lower cost to the client.

To wrestle with these problems, Charles F. Robinson, Chairman of the Economics of Law Practice Section, created a special task force to study the complex issues and to find solutions. Active members of the Task Force have been Robert J. Arndt, Luther J. Avery, Ezra Tom Clark, Jr., William C. Cobb, Demetrios Dimitriou and Milton W. Zwicker.

The Task Force issued personal and public invitations for members of the profession to submit their ideas and solutions. Those who have contributed include:

Martha Fay Africa, Donald S. Akins, Mary Ann Altman, Edna R.S. Alvarez, Robert J. Arndt, Luther J. Avery, Paul F. Bellows, Joel P. Bennett, Robert P. Bigelow, Ezra Tom Clark, Jr., William C. Cobb, Alberta I. Cook, Charles R. Coulter, Richard P. Delaney, Ronald W. Del Sesto, Demetrios Dimitriou, Mark A. Dombroff, James Eidelman, Harold A. Feder, Roger Fisher, Jay G. Foonberg, Geoffrey Furlonger, Charles Hansen, Prince A. Hawkins, Geoffrey C. Hazard, Jr., Robert S. Hochdorf, W. William Hodes, John G. Iezzi, Cecilia I. Johnstone, Edward P. Liebensperger, Leonard L. Loeb, Kathryn S. Marshall, James W. McRae, Jesse D. Miller, J. Harris Morgan, Rees Morrison, Theodore P. Orenstein, Richard C. Reed, Samuel L. Reed, Kenneth Roberts, Richard T. Rodgers, Lowell E. Rothschild, A.W. SoRelle III, Jeffrey L. Tolman, Paul G. Ulrich, Sidney C. Volinn, Robert P. Wilkins, Richard A. Williams, and Milton W. Zwicker.

While the work of the Task Force is continuing, stimulated by seminars and programs, it was decided that there should be an early sharing of some of the work products developed to date supplemented by already published articles, all with the hope that additional people would become involved. From the research done to date, certain principles have emerged and some specific patterns of billing methods are being developed that at the very least should promote critical self-evaluation by all practitioners.

This anthology will not be the last word on the subject, if indeed a definitive solution is ever found, for like many conundrums, there may be no perfect solution.

Chapter 1 explains how the profession got where it is today where the clients are billed to a great extent on the basis of hours spent by the lawyers and their fee-charging legal assistants.

The next chapters include materials submitted to the Task Force or articles gathered by the Task Force. At the start of each of these chapters there is an editorial comment that will explain why the material included in that chapter seems important or is innovative or thought-provoking. There will be comments about the author where pertinent so that you will know a bit about the author's perspective.

On the last pages, you will find a bibliography that will enable the curious to study further.

What is an anthology? The dictionary defines it as "a collection." That's what we have collected and published with the hope that your thoughts will be stimulated, your own approaches to billing reexamined, your practice enriched, your client needs better met.

The materials sometimes are contradictory, oftentimes contentious. The authors are expressing their own views, not any official view or policy of the Economics of Law Practice Section or the American Bar Association.

The Task Force thanks the 1987 – 88 Chairman, Charles F. Robinson, for starting this exciting examination of billing ideas and the 1988 – 89 Chairman, Warren L. Tomlinson, for seeing that the project continues.

So peruse, pick and choose, agree or disagree, but most of all, come THINK with us.

Richard C. Reed
Chairman, Special Task Force

Contents

Contents

CHAPTER 1

***Richard C. Reed**, a past chairman of the Economics of Law Practice Section and the editor of this anthology, begins the colloquy by reviewing the evolution of billing practices, and raising questions as to what constitutes "value." His chapter serves as an introduction to the issues addressed throughout the text and is a springboard to the discussion that follows. He is senior lawyer in The Reed McClure Law Firm in Seattle, Washington, where he has practiced for forty years.*

How Did We Get to Where We Are—And What Are We Going to Do About It?

by Richard C. Reed

In yesteryear, law practice was, perhaps, more simple. Firms generally were smaller and more local; there were fewer lawyers; the typical working unit in any size firm was the lawyer and the secretary, both in direct relationship with the client. Capital outlay primarily was for a typewriter, several desks and chairs, a library and possibly an adding machine so someone could balance the simple books of account. Space cost was relatively lower and young lawyers started their careers with little or no salaries.

When it came to billing, lawyers working without time records would review the file and make a judgment, taking into account the impact of the fee on the client who most times was someone who the lawyer knew both as a client and as a friend.

This is not nostalgia; this is fact.

Lawyers when charging and the courts when awarding fees looked to minimum-fee schedules as a guide.

Lawyer advertising was not condoned, and the term *marketing* was not within the lawyer's vocabulary. Lawyers were less mobile and long-term commitments and lawyer's loyalty were more characteristic. In still earlier times, no direct charge was made for the service of young associates, law clerks or legal assistants.

The copy machine had not yet been perfected and discovery was quite limited in scope.

The methods of practicing law have changed enormously at a seemingly ever-increasing pace.

Full service, boutique, specialization and *leveraging* were not terms of art in the practice of law.

But as the mode of practice changed, society also changed at an accelerating rate.

Legal Environmental Changes and Trends

Consider several of the legal environmental changes and trends (many of which have occurred in the past ten years) that have influenced the profession. Among them are:

(a) Increased number of lawyers (more lawyers to compete);
(b) Consumerism;
(c) Elimination of minimum-fee schedules;
(d) Court decisions (e.g., permitting lawyer advertising);
(e) Nationalization of law firms;
(f) Legal clinics;
(g) Proliferation of statutes permitting fee awards (fee shifting);
(h) Increased number of permitted causes of action;
(i) Increased number of governmental regulations, i.e., greater complexity;
(j) Greater tendency to litigate;
(k) Increased discovery (adding cost);

Portions of this article are reprinted with permission of ***Legal Economics.***

- (l) Expansion of in-house legal staffs;
- (m) Increased number of fee-chargers (associates, legal assistants) used for leveraging;
- (n) Use of lodestar (based on time records);
- (o) Declining profitability;
- (p) Court delays;
- (q) Increased specialization;
- (r) Tendency to hire specialists rather than law firms; and
- (s) Increased malpractice liability claims and soaring cost of malpractice insurance (if available)

TECHNOLOGICAL CHANGES

Simultaneously, both lawyers and society have been affected dramatically by technology. The computer has impacted the practice of law with respect to the following:

- (a) More efficient time-record keeping;
- (b) Easier billing procedures;
- (c) Legal research application;
- (d) Personal computers on the lawyer's desk used by the lawyer;
- (e) Greater use of systems;
- (f) Lawyer's use of word processing (at the keyboard);
- (g) Expense of obtaining and developing technology;
- (h) Data-base access;
- (i) Litigation support; and
- (j) Telecommunications.

Today's setting reflects the convergence of (a) changes in the way that law is practiced, (b) the socioeconomic pressures of contemporary society and (c) the impact of technology.

What does all this have to do with alternative billing methods?

Charging for a service reflects the combined effect of all the external and internal pressures to which the lawyer and the law firm are subject.

Twenty or thirty years ago, lawyers were urged to keep time records. Surveys indicated that lawyers who kept time records earned more than those who did not. The lawyers, however, remembered only part of the advice. What the lawyers disregarded was that the reason for keeping time records was to enable the lawyers to know *the cost* of providing the service. No one said that billing solely or primarily on an hourly basis without regard to other relevant but subjective factors was the way to go.

As time-record keeping became more sophisticated, influenced enormously by the computer, lawyers followed the growing trend for calculating billing on an hourly basis without much regard for the exercise of judgment or the weighing of subjective criteria and, particularly, without consideration of the value or benefit to the client of those services.

The courts, too, fell into the time-record trap perhaps for the same reason that lawyers did. Fee setting by the lawyer and fee approval by the courts are difficult tasks. The use of time records provides a superficial appeal of being objective and more automatic and requiring less difficult judgment making.

As we shall see in the chapters that follow, the need for time-record keeping still exists as part of the cost-accounting process that is a necessary part of fee setting for every practitioner. As a matter of fact, even more extensive cost accounting is needed, for a precise knowledge of costs is essential no matter what method of billing is used.

Many variables exist in any representation, some of which can be anticipated by the experienced lawyer and others that are client-caused or the result of actions by opposing counsel, or the courts or other external causes.

Part of the billing process involves the issue of who bears the risks of these uncertainties. Billing on an hourly basis to a considerable extent places the risk on the client, but it also is perceived by clients to encourage inefficiency on the part of the lawyer and to eliminate the incentive for a speedy solution.

To effectively utilize technology in the law office, a great deal of research, development and training time and capital outlay is required. Utilization of technology permits a task to be performed with less time expended by the lawyers. Thus, hourly billing by the lawyer may become an even less reliable index of value as the use of systems and technology expands.

Today, consideration of billing methods is very much on the minds of lawyers, clients and the courts. Perceptive lawyers recognize that hourly billing can penalize the efficient lawyer. Clients are questioning not only the amount of the fee but also the billing methods and appear to be thinking more in terms of value or the benefits received. The courts in making fee awards are wrestling with primarily time-based approaches reduced by negatives and not often enhanced by positives.

Society is more complex; the cost of legal services is high, yet lawyers are in a profit squeeze; the techniques of modern law practice have changed.

Today's realities have prompted the activities of the Special Task Force with the hope that throughout the profession there will be a lot of thought and innovation to devise appropriate methods of billing that will be fair to the lawyers and to their clients, for without clients there would be no need for legal services.

Value Billing

At the outset of the work of the Special Task Force, *value billing* was the first billing method examined in detail. It now appears that there are several creative approaches can be applied to billing, one of which is "Value Billing."

At the Council Meeting of the Economics of Law Practice Section in Philadelphia in October of 1986, Mack Hanan, a consultant, offered several thought-provoking comments on ways lawyers can enhance their practices by adding value to their clients. He suggested that it is necessary to quantify the value the lawyer can give to others, that is, the value to clients. One must ask, "Who are the people we [lawyers] can help grow and what value [in dollars] will be added?"

Hanan suggested that a sophisticated client is perceptive in choosing a lawyer based on which lawyer can provide services that will enable the client to grow and which lawyer is best able to add to the value of the client's assets. Two ways to add value are by obtaining for the client a benefit to which the client is entitled (e.g., recovering damages for a contract that has been breached or successfully completing a transaction that the client perceives will be of benefit, such as an acquisition of a business) or by avoiding a risk or exposure that, if not avoided, would diminish the client's assets. The former is the positive benefit; the latter is the avoidance of the negative impact of a loss of opportunity to the client. Both are within the broad definition of benefit—to accentuate the positive and to eliminate the negative. Both address the issue of whether the total efforts of the lawyer helped in the solution of the client's problem or fulfilled the requirements of the client that the lawyer undertook to perform.

Hanan also suggested that the client who perceives that the attorney has added to the client's value, rather than subtracted from the client's value by charging a fee, will regard the legal services as an investment, not a cost. This is the valuation of legal services in terms of benefit to the client.

Real Life Valuations

Rather than discuss value in the abstract, let us consider certain real-life situations where we feel that we get a good deal in buying a service or product.

1. "I didn't know how to fix it, so I was pleased to pay." Example: My television set didn't work and the television repairman fixed it.
2. "The quality [of the product or service] was good." Example: I wanted and got the best.
3. "I needed an expert who really was the best." Example: My daughter was hit by a car and needed brain surgery.
4. "I really got a bargain." Example: The same model stove sells at most stores for 40 percent more than at my favorite discount house.
5. "Even though the price was high, the quality and service were superb." Example: I dined at the most expensive restaurant, and the food, beverage, atmosphere and service made it the meal of my lifetime.
6. "He knew exactly what to do to get me out of the mess I was in." Example: I had made a lot of mistakes and the deal was going sour. He turned it around for me.
7. "She kept me out of trouble. I am glad I went to her." Example: I was about to invest in a new limited partnership. When I talked to my investment adviser, she gave me the facts and convinced me that it would be a big mistake.
8. "I was really scared when I got sued for $10 million, but my lawyer won the case." Example: My lawyer's knowledge,

skill and hard work resulted in a defense verdict.

9. "He made me a lot of money when he closed the deal and we were able to complete the purchase of the new factory." Example: A wanted acquisition that will produce benefits was the result of skilled efforts.
10. "I'd rather pay someone to do it, so I can do what I want to do." Example: If I pay a gardener to mow the lawn, I can play golf on weekends.
11. "The product or service truly was unique." Example: Only 1,400 coins were ever made.
12. "What I bought will appreciate in value, even though it cost me a lot." Example: Paying a high market price for land that can be zoned for a shopping center.
13. "They stuck to and performed their agreements." Example: The estimate was accurate, they performed when they said they would and built the house well within my range of expectations as to service, quality and price.
14. "You can count on this store's dependability." Example: Shop where you can count on a good product and if there is any problem, just return what you bought for full credit.
15. "They certainly treated me well." Example: When I went to the clinic, the receptionist greeted me warmly, the doctor was available promptly for my appointment and all the staff were caring, interested and helpful.
16. "He is the best person around for that kind of work." Example: Of all the housepainters in town, he does the best work.
17. "They give timely service." Example: I always know my pictures will be ready when they promise.
18. "My lawyer makes me feel like I am her most important client." Example: The lawyer respects me as an individual, understands my problem, works hard to solve it and gives me the impression that he is competent, confident, and cares about me.
19. "I was a basket case when I went in." Example: I was upset, nervous and scared, and feared the worst. My lawyer was calm, reassuring and self-confident, and gave me the feeling that things would turn out all right.
20. "He really went out of his way to help me." Example: It was the middle of the night, the weather was foul and he had to drive thirty miles to where my car was stranded to tow me to where I could get the necessary repairs.

In each of these examples, the person who purchased the product or service had a reason to feel good about the transaction. Each example has an analogy in the practice of law. The purchaser or client received *value* or *benefit* for some perceived reason. The amount to be paid should reflect the value to the purchaser or client of what was received. In all of the examples, a minimum range of quality is implicit in the transaction, for if the quality level falls below the acceptable minimum level, other factors cease to be relevant.

Each of the examples shows why you and I might feel good about paying for the product or service. The negative of each example creates a negative reaction on the part of the user regarding the price that was charged. Obviously, not all factors influencing how we feel about the price charged apply to any specific situation, although several of the examples could be applicable to any one relationship.

If you think in the context of delivering legal services as you go through these examples, you can perceive the situation in which the client may feel the benefits have been conferred.

In the chapters that follow, several lawyers will explain how they are billing their clients. So read on.

We tend to think of this as a current topic, as indeed it is. More than thirty years ago, however, George D. Hornstein said it well in an article, "Legal Therapeutics: The 'Salvage' Factor in Counsel Fee Awards," 69 *Harvard Law Review*, 658 (1956), at page 660:

"One thousand plodding hours may be far less productive than one imaginative, brilliant hour. A surgeon who skillfully performs an appendectomy in seven minutes is entitled to no smaller fee than one who takes an hour; many a patient would think he is entitled to more. The dubious value of the time factor as a standard for legal services has been recognized by many courts:

The value of a lawyer's services is not measured by time or labor merely. The practice of law is an art in which success depends as much as in any other art on the application of imagination—and sometimes inspiration—to the subject matter.

Another fact to be borne in mind is that when hours become a criterion, economy of time may cease to be a virtue. Inexperience, inefficiency, even incompetence will be rewarded. Expeditious termination of litigation will be discouraged—to the great cost of all concerned, including the state."

CHAPTER 2

Mary Ann Altman, *a lawyer, has long been active as a principal in the consulting firm of Altman & Weil, counseling with lawyers concerning the changing methods of law practice. This background enables her to provide perspective to the current issues affecting billing methods. Note the emphasis on the importance of educating clients to understand billing based on value to those clients by the projection of effort and lawyer expertise into an end result that provides a benefit to the client. Her thoughtful observations include helpful suggestions as the profession moves to a new phase.*

A Perspective—From Value Billing to Time Billing and Back to Value Billing

by Mary Ann Altman

Because I was involved personally in the introduction of time records to the legal profession approximately thirty years ago, I can attest to the fact that one of the reasons that time records were instituted originally was to determine the cost of providing legal services. At that time, lawyers had, for many decades, produced bills to clients that were based on the value of the services rather than on the time involved, although time certainly was a mental factor in determining value. Once time records became available to lawyers, lawyers quickly began to use these time records as a billing, rather than as a cost-accounting, tool. It was much easier to ask the bookkeeping department to multiply the time record by a dollar factor and prepare a bill than it was for the lawyer to exercise judgment in a determination of the value of the case.

Personally, I always have felt that pure hourly billing, particularly where a lawyer bills all the work that he or she does at one hourly rate, does not make any sense. Lawyers, at all stages in their careers, are required to master new and different areas of law. To say that a lawyer is worth, for example, $150 an hour for everything that he or she does, does not reflect learning time, work in little-known areas of law and, conversely, expertise gained from multiple experiences in a specific area of law or fact situation. Some lawyers realize this and may establish for themselves as many as five or six different rates. The lowest rate may reflect the learning time needed for new areas of law, while the top rate may reflect a particular recognized expertise. Using multiple rates does not equal the value-billing process, but it is a step in that direction.

Another problem with time billing is that very few lawyers keep truly accurate time records. Some may charge every bit of work, no matter how brief, as a quarter or a half of an hour. Others may underestimate their time and continually end days with three or four hours of billable time when, in fact, they have been active in practice for the entire day. I occasionally have met that rare lawyer who virtually uses a stopwatch to maintain completely accurate time records, but only once or twice over three decades.

Hourly Time Billing—Initial Reaction

Hourly time billing was well received quickly by clients because by using it their bills were based on something tangible that they could understand rather than on a "value of services" concept. Business clients, rather than individual clients, could, in particular, correlate the "product" that they were buying to the products that they themselves produced and sold, and within large corporations local managers and others receiving bills could, in turn, justify the payment of those bills to their superiors at corporate headquarters. The corporate headquarters financial officer, for example, may be unaware of the overall value of the legal services to his or her employer but could clearly comprehend hours and time billing.

Court-approved fees also quickly became subject to time and hourly billing. Many judges may be far removed from the actual practice of law and, in fact, may be unaware of the total long-range value of certain legal services to a client, for they are involved primarily with one fact situation. In situations where the lawyer and the client do not agree on the value of the services, it would be extremely difficult for the court to exclusively use value-basis billing. A logical approach for the court to take would be to examine the time records in order to determine the energy that went into the handling of a matter and the attention that was paid to the client and at the same time to question the long-range value of the services and make a combination time and value assessment.

Courts and some clients have questioned the separate billing of legal assistants, word processing and the like. In the case of legal assistants, a reluctance to pay hourly bills probably is directly related to the newness of the position and the fact that no nationwide or state standards exist that describe the practice of legal assistantship. Because no exclusivity exists within the class of persons performing these services, those persons receiving billings for legal-assistant services may not specifically comprehend what those services are. In order to achieve better acceptance of billings for legal assistants, the attorney must explain what the legal assistant does and how this, in fact, reduces the final bill to the client.

The introduction of word processing brought another dimension to the billing process. Word processing became popular at about the time when lawyers' hourly rates had become a matter of public knowledge, through the legal press and the general press, and resistance to raising those hourly rates was becoming prevalent. Lawyers using word processing soon realized that they had made expensive investments in equipment and clerical support and that they, in fact, had reduced their time in document production through the introduction of that equipment. Because of a reluctance to include word processing as a general overhead item and increase hourly rates, word processing sometimes was billed as a separate disbursement. Unlike copying and duplicating and messenger services that for years were billed as payments to outside service vendors (which, in fact, they were) before duplicating, copying and messenger service became part of the internal law-firm operation, clients became more used to paying these as disbursements and objections to copying, duplicating and messenger charges were rare. Word processing, however, entered the law firm as a part of its internal operation with very little use of subcontracted outside work. Clients suddenly were surprised to see a disbursement billing for word processing and objections were raised quickly. Here, again, objections could have been reduced if lawyers had taken the time to explain to clients how that billing would be handled and that, in fact, the overall costs to the client were being reduced through the use of word processing.

Determination of Costs

It is true that most lawyers really do not know the cost of producing the legal services that they sell. Hourly rates, today, basically are billing rates based on competitive positions. The process of annually reviewing hourly rates generally involves securing information on what other lawyers are charging rather than how the cost of operating the firm has increased. Determining the total cost of producing legal services is a difficult and complex process. Costing cash payments made by the accounting department for the purchase of space, goods, supplies and equipment is not difficult. It is, however, very difficult to cost account the annual recruiting effort, the training of associates, marketing time and other operating costs that are, in fact, based on the time that the lawyers spend rather than on actual dollar payments. In order to perform an analysis of the actual costs of operating an organization of lawyers requires detailed and accurate time recordings of all nonbillable time. Some of this nonbillable time, i.e., lunch, social activities and the like, simply may not be part of the specific overhead required by operating the firm. These kinds of time records may be regarded simply as lost time that is not recoupable in billings to clients. Time spent in marketing, research and development, training, systems introduction, etc., are, however, components of general business overhead. Just as a company producing furniture would include the cost of its advertising and marketing as part of the cost of producing the item for sale and hence for pricing it, lawyers would have to perform a careful cost analysis of these kinds of time records in order to determine the accurate costs of producing an hour of legal services. With rare exceptions, the information necessary for this kind of cost analysis simply is nonexistent.

Using time records as a basis for determining the cost of production of legal services originally was and still is a valid reason for time-record keeping. It is not the "be all and end all," however, in setting a fee. Traditionally, the canons of professional ethics have listed criteria that are to be used in the mental process of setting a fee for a client. These have included the difficulty of the matter, the time proscriptions that the client has placed on the lawyer, the fact that by taking a certain piece of work the lawyer may be proscribed from taking other conflicting work and similar nonquantifiable judgments. Because members of the legal profession are selling services that presumably have a value to the client, as opposed to selling a product that the client can touch, feel and use, the process of value billing as opposed to hourly time billing, becomes one in which the lawyer must educate the client from the beginning. Many lawyers find the process of discussing fees distasteful and, as a result, do not take the time to discuss the fee process with the client at the very inception of the case except to explain that the client will be billed on a time basis at x dollars per hour. Value billing takes judgment, time, salesmanship and empathy with the client's ability and willingness to pay for value received.

Determination of Value

When a lawyer estimates a dollar-fee range based on value of services rather than purely on hourly rates, the lawyer must call on skill and experience. First, the lawyer must have a relatively accurate idea of what the base cost of the service will be — how many hours will be required and what fee is necessary to cover these hours. The next step is to move from the base-cost figure to a value-based fee estimate — this is the most difficult judgmental period. Sometimes a lawyer will enjoy the luxury of a few days to determine a value-billing judgment, but often a fee quote is asked for during a brief telephone call. To be able to weigh all the factors that influence a value-based fee estimate takes most lawyers years of trial, error and, hopefully, success.

No two matters and no two clients are exactly alike. Base cost must be modified mentally by such factors as the specific fact situation under consideration; the importance of the matter to the client and his or her business; the consequences to the client of not resolving the matter to his or her benefit; the personality of the client; the number of persons involved; the ability of the client to pay; the effect that handling the matter will have on the firm's resources, reputation and other clients; and a myriad of similar issues. Consideration of all of these issues, some pluses and some minuses, will result in a figure based on the value to the client and to the firm.

After an appropriate fee decision has been made, salesmanship often comes into play. What may appear to be an appropriate and justified fee to the lawyer may not appear so at first to the potential client. At this point that lawyer should back up the quoted fee by articulating some of the considerations that went into the decision-making process. What will reaching a satisfactory result mean to the client? What other problems can a solution prevent? What resources will the firm be required to use on the matter? What skills will be required and who will provide them? All these represent the *selling* of the fee to the client, and in most cases such salesmanship is required.

Reaching the point where a fair value-based fee can be quoted in a majority of instances takes practice and experience. It is much easier to quote hourly rates when asked about a fee, but as rate resistance has grown, the need for value billing also has grown. This technique must be learned if firms are to have a competitive edge and a profitable future. Most attorneys are not willing or are incapable of undertaking this process. Lawyers would, however, find that they ultimately save themselves many hours of work and reduce their accounts receivable markedly if they would expend this time.

The Risk Factor

Another factor that has entered into the billing equation in recent years (because of the rapid increase in malpractice suits against lawyers) is the degree of risk that the lawyer undertakes when he or she agrees to perform certain work for clients. Increased malpractice insurance rates are rapidly calling this problem to our attention. In addition, the damage caused by successful malpractice suits over and above the actual dollar value must be considered. A lawyer who undertakes work on a specific area of practice and who ultimately is sued successfully for malpractice may stand to lose all future work in that area of his or her livelihood. This is part of the risk undertaken with the work engagement.

One of the questions often asked concerns the influence of market acceptance on hourly rates. Market pressure simply is a reflection of the value of certain services as perceived by the client mentally and through his or her pocketbook. There may be a figure that the client feels exceeds the value of any services given, or there may be a figure that, in fact, the client simply cannot pay. Here, again, the problem of making judgmental decisions arises. The process of discussing the way in which the fee will be charged at the initial meeting with the client again is a prime factor. If "time billing at hourly rates" is the only explanation of the fee-calculation method, the client is making a decision based on the ability of his or her pocketbook to pay a given hourly rate but not on the value of the services in the short or long run. The lawyer should raise the question of the value of services and allow the client to make a determination as to whether or not he or she wishes to receive those services. A great deal of future grief may be avoided by such an initial discussion.

Technological Impact

A sidelight to this issue is the impact of technology on value billing. As attorneys themselves begin to use equipment, the phenomenon of reduced time required for work product (as experienced with word processing) will present itself again. In theory, the use of technology will allow the attorney to perform a service in less time. This will adversely affect billings, if services are billed solely on a time basis. It is, therefore, conceivable that wider attorney use of technology will serve as a catalyst in forcing law firms to address the value-billing question. In order to make proper judgments for piece-rate value billing, firms will need financial reporting systems that report the impact of technology on billable hours. Clearly, a reporting system that maintains comparative historical data on a matter-by-matter basis will be required to effectively track and determine the true, non-time value of a particular service. This type of analysis already is being conducted by in-house counsel at large insurance carriers to track the effectiveness and profitability of individual firms and cases. These systems have given rise to recent flat-fee arrangements between carriers and outside counsel for ordinary matters. It will be several years before law firms and clients can determine the fair value of such rate arrangements.

CHAPTER 3

William C. Cobb, *a principal of WCCI, Inc. Consultants, deals with sophisticated law firms on a national basis. He was a successful law-firm administrator before becoming a consultant. His approach to billing is more in the classical economics sense. Make yourself think in his terminology. Take time to understand thoroughly the Value Curve illustrated in Figure 1 and ponder its significance in your own practice setting. Then superimpose the competitive position profile shown in Figure 2. When you fully understand Cobb's theoretical explanations, consider your competitive position and the way you price legal tasks and products. This material goes beyond alternate billing methods to sophisticated pricing strategy in the legal marketplace.*

The Value Curve and the Folly of Billing-Rate Pricing

by William C. Cobb

The client, the buyer of your services, perceives relative value in the legal services offered to him by law firms and others. Although lawyers have taught most clients to accept the number of units (hours) produced as the basis for valuing legal services, clients are becoming much more sophisticated. This discussion will explain why billing-rate pricing is not endearing law firms to their client base.

Before starting, take an example familiar to most lawyers. How many times has one of the partners asked, "I know you put in six hundred hours on the recruiting program as chairman, but what did I get for it?" Even lawyers have a cost-versus-benefit orientation to people who provide them with services. Why then must the client endure the arrogance of lawyers who continue to quote fees based on "normal hourly billing rates multiplied by hours worked"?

Sophisticated clients do not tie benefits to hours; they tie benefits to the impact on their business. Some services are lifesaving. Other services are mundane, commodity services that must be performed in the course of getting the client's product produced and sold. In such situations, value has no real relationship to the hours involved.

In this discussion, *lines of legal service* is a term used to define what lawyers provide. The client buys a line of service, not a narrow specialty. A client buys services that solve business problems. Those services contain components that go beyond pure tax, securities or litigation. An insolvency strategy in negotiating the restructuring loans on a group of properties involves the specialties of tax, securities, environment, potential litigation and so on. The client is buying a line of service called "restructuring the financial package."

The Value Curve

The Value Curve shows relative value of services versus the volume of the work available to a law firm. The higher the available volume, the more price sensitive is the service. The curve can be likened to a product-life curve. The more time a product is in the market, the more the product is produced and the more price competition occurs for the product. For example, look at the desktop computer. Prices started in the range of $3,000 to $4,000 and have come down, with the production of clones and the increased number of producers in the market, to as low as $500 to $1,000. Legal services do not escape the laws of economics.

The lawyer must look at the types of legal services that he or she delivers relative to the competition in the market in which he or she competes. An objective assessment will show that clients, services provided and specific tasks performed (or legal products produced) fall at different points on this curve.

Several implications come from this assessment of the firm's approach to delivering and pricing legal services.

1. Not all work should be done with the average leverage of partners to associates to paraprofessionals. The mix will be different depending on the client, the type of matter or the task involved. Services in the commodity range need higher leverage to lower the weighted average billing rate. Services provided in the experience range can be accomplished with less leverage.

Figure 1

Value Curve
and Competitive Position Profile

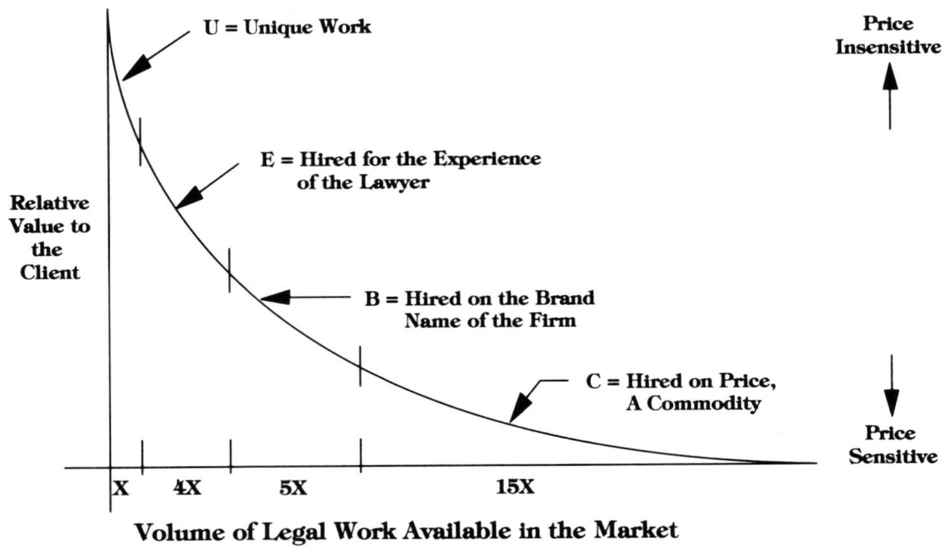

The vertical axis of Figure 1 shows the relative value of the service. The horizontal axis shows the relative volume of work available in the market. The solid curve denotes the value of services. Note that very little volume "X" can be classified as truly unique and very price insensitive. Also note the wide range of values that is associated with the unique work. Experience-based service, where the client "hires the lawyer, not the law firm," is "4X" by volume. Brand-name work, where the client hires the law firm because of an institutional reputation, is "5X" by volume. Commodity work, where clients perceive that practically any law firm could provide the same services, is "15X" by volume. The author has found, through the assessment of the mix of legal services, that these volume ratios hold true for most law firms.

2. Billing rates in a firm are developed in a budget based on the leverage of partners to other billing entities and based on the overhead that the firm has to carry in practice support, facilities and technology. Those rates are adjusted by what the market will bear for a particular lawyer's time. The reality is that most lawyers of similar tenure, regardless of expertise and experience, carry the same billing rate. The budgeting process assumes, therefore, that all work will be performed at or better than the average leverage. Because each matter and task has a different value to each client, use of the average leverage of the firm, and thus the average billing rate, becomes inappropriate. For example, when a partner is working alone on a particular matter, he or she should have a higher effective billing rate if the services provided are up the curve from Point 1 on Figure 2. Working alone on services that are at Point 1 would require a write-down of the effective billing rate to the weighted average rate for the firm. There also are implications on the work that partners continue to do that should be done by lower-rate people (e.g., paraprofessionals). If the client perceives the value of the service to be in a commodity area and yet pays a partner's rate for doing work that a paraprofessional could do, the firm eventually will lose the client to a less-expensive and more-efficient law firm.
3. Services provided by the firm in the commodity area (see Point 2 in Figure 2) will be overpriced because the law firm cannot increase the leverage enough to get the delivery cost (again refer to the accumulated hours and value on the billing memorandum) low enough to meet the value perceived by the client. The firm must become

Figure 2

Value Curve
and Competitive Position Profile
Adding the Cost of Delivery

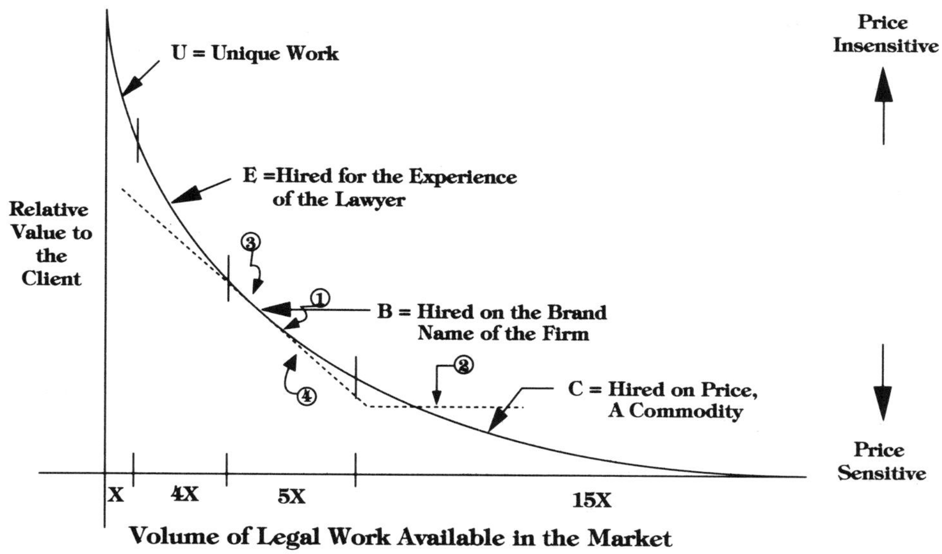

The billing-rate line (the dotted line) now has been superimposed on the value curve. The line represents the billing rates in the firm. Unfortunately, because of lawyer emphasis on hourly production, the values reflected on the billing memo do not reflect the value of the services rendered. When thinking in the context of hours worked equal value for a specific legal task or service, the fee is reflected on the billing memo anywhere above or below the value line. See Point 2 in Figure 2. The number 1 in the circle on Figure 2 represents the weighted average billing rate of the firm with the leverage of the firm. The implication is that all work is at that point on the value curve (e.g., homogeneous). That is a false assumption and shows the folly of pricing based on weighted average billing rates in a matter.

more efficient. It must create form files and the substantive systems to reduce the number of hours that it takes to produce the legal product. If the firm cannot make the investment in reducing the hours needed to produce the legal product, then the decision must be made to get out of that area of service or recognize it for the loss it causes to the firm. Increased efficiency in producing such commodity services offers three benefits:

(a) It reduces the cost of legal services for the client and places cost and benefits back in line. Better client relationships result.

(b) It provides opportunities to increase realization on the hours of personnel working on the matter. Realization (the percentage of the billing rate achieved at collection) can move up toward 100 percent and, if the legal product has a value not related to time, move above 100 percent.

(c) It frees up legal resources to work on more valuable matters for the clients.

Unfortunately, the assumption by lawyers that an hour of work has a value related to their billing rate has: (1) pushed inefficiencies (to produce more hours, just re-create the wheel), (2) created hoarding of work and poor delegation, (3) inhibited the creation of more efficient ways of producing legal product and (4) inhibited good project management to make more efficient uses of lawyers and paraprofessionals.

Competitive Positioning with the Value Curve

The Value Curve can be used to develop a competitive-position profile for the firm. Competitive position, relative to other firms and practitioners in the market, will be based on how the client perceives the worth of the lawyer's relationship relative to alternative providers. Relative value to the client is a function of uniqueness of the service, importance to the client, price sensitivity and the apparent quality of the service provided. Quality of service, from a client's perspective, is a function of such things as knowledge of the client's business, turnaround time, capability of the lawyer and responsiveness to the client's needs. Given the client's perception of where the services received from the law firm are placed on the value scale (the vertical axis), the law firm should be able to develop a delivery strategy to fit client perception.

Once the law firm recognizes the proper location of the service on the curve, it can begin to deal with how to deliver and price the service to fit the client needs.

Another way to look at the service is through tasks broken down within a matter. Each task performed on a matter is assigned a different value. Current thinking is that the billing rate of a lawyer or paraprofessional meets the need of valuing. The curve shows that the billing rates only work within a limited range on the curve (Points 3 to 4 in Figure 2). The best way to show the relationship of services or tasks to the curve is by example:

1. The unique capability:
   (a) If a lawyer can call the governor to set up a meeting for the client on a critical administrative matter, that thirty-minute telephone call is worth far more than the one-half hour multiplied by the partner's stated billing rate.
   (b) A unique, capital-creating legal product that may result in millions of dollars in new capital for a company may be worth far more than the fees at standard rates shown on the billing memoranda.
2. The experience of the lawyer:
   (a) The time that a lawyer spends in the courtroom as an expert witness may be worth more than the same time spent by the lawyer in supervising others in the firm meeting the clients' day-to-day legal needs.
   (b) The brief produced the first time was worth $15,000 to the client. A similar situation for a second client also required a brief on the same points of law. The generation of the second brief took less time because of the accumulated knowledge from the first brief. The billing memorandum for the second matter shows $8,000 in fees. Is the second brief only worth $8,000 or is it worth $15,000? The client perception of value should determine the answer, not the fee reflected in the billing memorandum.
   (c) The knowledge of a client's business and the ability to operate as a business adviser, as well as a technician, is worth more per hour than simply responding to needs for documentation of the transactions.
   (d) Using the experience of a key lawyer to set the scope of work and planning the project for the most efficient use of firm resources on behalf of the client may be worth as much as performing as a working lawyer in the project.
   (e) Caveat: Most lawyers do not want alternatives to hourly billing because they involve risks. The risk to the lawyer is that he or she may not consider all the possibilities or that the client will not perceive the value as the lawyer perceives value. Unfortunately, not taking risks places

the lawyer and the firm in graver jeopardy:

(i) The lawyer must take the risk of getting out of the office to understand the client's value system.

(ii) Quoting an average or range of hourly billing rates does not differentiate the firm from competing firms, as almost all firms do that.

(iii) The client does not get the opportunity of making the judgment on cost and benefit of the lawyer's services until it is time to pay the bill. He or she may not pay the bill, thus causing the firm to throw away productive hours.

3. Brand-name work:
   (a) Loan documentation can be performed on a fixed fee. If the experienced law firm fixes a fee that is acceptable to the client and within the performance capabilities of the firm:
      (i) The client can become more competitive in the marketplace by knowing its documentation fees on the front end. The bank can give assurances to the potential customer and improve the bank's marketing position.
      (ii) The firm is encouraged to find more efficient ways of producing the documentation to produce a fee in excess of the amount shown on the billing memorandum.
   (b) The large, sophisticated developer who produces a higher volume of interim financing on large projects will remain loyal to the firm that produces the work efficiently and effectively, thus ensuring a continued flow of work where standard billing rates (or more) can be maintained.
   (c) The focus on value moves the partners to their highest and best use, thus ensuring that work is delegated to the least cost producer and efficient delivery of legal services is promoted.
4. The commodity work:
   (a) Tasks that should be performed through leveraging associates and paraprofessionals supported by substantive systems should be identified. The firm will write off fewer hours and write down less time.
   (b) Simple forms will come into use with the generation of legal products. A creditor's claim, if priced by the product value, could generate significant premiums on a large volume of production if the firm created efficient ways of producing the document.

SUMMARY

The Value Curve still exists in the buyer's perception even though many have succumbed to the lawyer's hourly approach. Because the only way of controlling cost is to count units, the clients ask for printouts of the time sheets. Billing by the hour (on most services) reinforces certain perceptions of lawyers.

1. All legal work is assumed to be the same in value. The client makes cost-benefit deci-

sions each day and knows some work is much more critical than other work.

2. A lawyer is perceived as a poor delegator, spending hours on a problem.

Even in a law firm, lawyers would like to know what results will come from allocating time to a task—what are the benefits to me and to my draw?

The Value Curve can create a picture of relative competitive position. With that knowledge, the firm has a better understanding of the needs of its clients and can respond more effectively.

The Value Curve refocuses the partners on the client and on client service. After all, if it were not for the clients, there would be no lawyers.

CHAPTER 4

Jay G. Foonberg, *a lawyer from Beverly Hills, California, has spoken on law-practice management topics in every state and in many foreign countries. Additionally, he has authored books on the practical aspects of law practice. His past predictions, which to many seemed far-out, often have come true. Competitive law practice, according to Foonberg, is a reality for many practitioners. Here, Foonberg's target is the fixed fee, a fee that can be fairly set by using accurate cost accounting. Foonberg, the lawyer, is also Foonberg, the CPA, Foonberg, the innovator and crusader, and lastly Foonberg, the pragmatist. It usually pays to listen when Foonberg speaks.*

The Short, Happy Life of Hourly Fee Billings

by Jay G. Foonberg

It is my prediction that hourly rates for legal work will be replaced by fixed-fee prices. Hourly rates simply are an important evolutionary development in the legal profession and will wither and fall away in favor of the fixed fee for specific defined services.

As I shall demonstrate in this article, the evolution toward fixed fees will be based on six factors:

1. Hourly time records allow every person in a firm to record their time as part of departmental overhead or allocable to specific types of cases and/or clients.

2. Metering devices allow technical support (word processors, library costs, equipment, research costs) to be allocable to departmental overhead or to a specific type of use or client.

3. Specialty practice allows firms to accumulate and analyze costs of production based on a large number of cases handled by experienced people who do not have to waste resources reinventing forms and procedures.

4. The people who pay for legal services will demand a fixed fee whenever possible. Lawyers unable to quote fixed fees will lose clients to those who can.

5. By using affordable computers all the costs of producing specific types of services can be determined. A profit element will be added to the costs to arrive at the fixed fee.

6. Competition from a growing number of lawyers and law firms will force firms to analyze efficiency if they lose an unacceptable number of clients based on fees that were too high.

Hourly Billing—In the Beginning

Hourly billing as originally developed was intended as a method to fairly charge clients for services. It was a great step forward from "by guess and by gosh" or "Kentucky windage" fee setting. It was a departure from the classic "How big is the client?", "How big is the case?", "How big is the lawyer?" method of fee setting.

Hourly billing was and still is an extremely crude method of charging clients based only on time devoted to a case. Total desired revenue was divided by total hours available to come up with an hourly rate for the lawyer's service. Lawyers often kept time records by recording time on time slips, then periodically collating the slips into little piles of paper. The slips were then totaled by time and multiplied by the hourly rate to come up with a bill for the client. Hourly billing was a great step forward because lawyers became disciplined to keep time records and to think about fair fees and measurable definable units of product (i.e., time, rather than number of pages or number of dollars). The major defect of charging based only on lawyer hours is that it ignores the other costs of rendering professional services.

Thus, a lawyer could spend four hours of time in a setting where little or no paperwork or library resources would be required (negotiating a settlement or a price or a tax case or a court appearance in a minor criminal case) or the same lawyer could spend four hours in an interview for drafting a forty-page trust will or where a small amount or no paperwork was involved. A lawyer could spend four hours producing a pleading, such as a motion for a restraining order, and library facilities were required.

In all these cases, the client is asked to pay the same fee based on hourly billing, i.e., four hours of lawyer time, even though this method is patently unfair to the clients. One client is paying for the costs of a library and the availability of word-processing equipment and of support personnel where none is required for the matter and another client is asked to pay little or nothing for the huge library and word-processing facilities necessary to process the client's work. One lawyer might normally require personal assistance from a secretary, a paralegal and a word processor, while another lawyer of similar age and experience and compensation might require only occasional use of word processing and/or share a secretary.

Lawyers are vaguely aware that they have to charge for overhead. This often is done by various magical incantations, such as add two to four times the amount of the lawyer's compensation to cover overhead; or, conversely, the lawyer should get one-fourth to one-third of the hourly rate as lawyer compensation; or divide total expenses on the income tax return by the total number of hours to get the hourly amount for overhead.

While the application of these incantations does produce some degree of fairness to the law firm as an entity and all clients as a group, it still is unfair when applied to particular clients or when applied to particular types of legal work. Individual clients still are being overcharged or undercharged when the firm's resources are required.

Metering Devices

Computers have made it possible to accumulate the law firm's costs and to allocate these costs with a reasonable degree of accuracy and fairness based on the lawyer, on the type of work, on the type of case or on a combination of factors. Costs can be accumulated and allocated from meters placed on the word-processing equipment, the telephone and the postage equipment. Special library needs for specific types of law or lawyers can be identified and properly distributed. Every person in the firm easily can keep a time record to record when they work on an individual case. It is no more difficult for the intelligent, educated people in a law firm to keep a record of what they do on a particular legal matter than it is for Air Force mechanics in the motor pool, technicians in the radar-repair unit or mechanics on the flight line to record the work that they do on a particular piece of equipment. Computers then can allocate the accumulated costs to the particular client or type of law or lawyers.

Specialty Practices

In my opinion, general practice (or full-service legal work) is much more fun, more interesting and more professionally satisfying than specialty practice. Unfortunately, general practice is much-less efficient than specialty practice. General practice forces the lawyer and the firm to continually redesign and reinvent the wheel to solve a client's legal problems. Specialty practice allows a firm to develop a large number of standard forms and procedures that can be used over and over again with minor modification from case to case. The specialty-practice lawyer should accurately know just what total firm resources will be required in a particular type of case. The specialty-practice lawyer has the advantage of hindsight in knowing what is required based on a large number of prior similar matters. The specialty-practice lawyer should have no difficulty in most cases when quoting a fixed fee before the work is completed. The fee will be based on the costs accumulated by the computers from a large number of similar matters. A few surprises may occur upwards and a few surprises downwards, but an average fixed fee should be obtainable and usable. There will always be a novel or special case with no precedent where an hourly rate or a combination of fixed prices and hourly rates must be used.

Fixed Fees on Demand?

The public's increasingly consumeristic approach to legal services eventually may demand fixed fees from lawyers. Traditionally, clients have been effort oriented rather than result oriented. When clients know how hard the lawyer has worked, they were more willing to pay a larger fee. Clients really have no way to judge the quality of legal services per se. They have no way of evaluating whether a lawyer's silence in court reflects lack of preparation or a brilliant legal strategy. They don't know if a lease or will is well written or poorly written. It is my opinion, and the opinion of many other lawyers, that clients are becoming more result oriented. They are more willing than ever before to sue a lawyer when they don't like the result, no matter how hard the lawyer has worked. They often are encouraged to do so by other lawyers who are result oriented. This is not restricted to individuals. Banks and insurance companies and brokerage firms also are quicker than ever before to sue lawyers when they are unhappy with results. Part of the consumeristic trend is to shop before choosing a lawyer. Price may not be a significant factor in deciding on a lawyer, but the inability to quote a fixed fee may convince a client to use a lawyer who can do so. Inability to quote a fee may indicate to the client a lack of experience in the legal area involved.

Clients ask for fixed fees on cases whenever possible so that businesses can budget for it and individuals can determine the affordability of the legal service. The desire of law firms to fulfill client needs for fixed fees will be a practice builder.

I personally invented and pioneered the concept of a legal specialty of collection litigation for banks using noncontingency fees. I built up a multimillion dollar practice over a period of ten years by demonstrating to banks that they were overpaying, using contingency fees, and that lawyers would work harder and do the work sooner if they were paid monthly rather than at the end of the case. Money has a time value to banks and the rapidity of collection of funds is an important factor in determining the cost effectiveness of collection efforts. Accordingly, good banks want their collection work handled with an approach of "priority," not "filler" to be done during slow periods.

Using Affordable Computers to Compute Costs

I installed in-house computers to accurately accumulate time and costs and soon was able to quote fixed fees for most (not all) of the types of services routinely required in bank collection work. There were two prices for complaints. One was a standard complaint price and the other a nonstandard complaint price, but both prices were fixed. I had two prices for a judgment-debtor examination, but both were fixed. A motion for summary judgment or responding to a demand for a bill of particulars or defendant depositions or third-party examinations, an abstract of judgment and many other services all had fixed prices known in advance to the client who could use the service and know what it would cost. The prices were determined after using the computers to collect cost data considering the cost of firm resources required, including amortization of equipment costs and amortization of research costs as well as nonlawyer personnel costs requiring a particular service. I budgeted into the price a reasonable profit and then charged fixed prices. A small percentage of cases occurred where, because of unforeseen problems, the fixed fee resulted in a loss to me, but with other cases I received an extremely high profit. The fixed fee benefited me by giving a good monthly cash flow with a reasonable profit and benefited the client by providing predictable, knowable costs and by recovering funds sooner. Fixed and predictable costs are a major factor in the growth of the specialty practice.

I have been keeping and using hourly time records since 1957. Although lawyers generally did not begin keeping time records until the late 1960s and early 1970s and didn't begin using computers until the middle 1970s, I have been keeping time records for more than thirty years: first, in the 1950s, as a tax auditor; then in the 1960s, as a CPA; then in the 1950s and 1960s, in the U.S. Air Force Reserve, and since 1960 as a law student and as a lawyer. In the 1960s, I became familiar with computers such as RAMAC (a second-generation computer with tubes instead of transistors) to process time records.

As a tax auditor for the state of California, I was required to keep hourly time records so that the state could determine the cost and profitability of conducting audits by types of taxpayers and types of industries. Because the state was given limited audit resources, it wanted to concentrate those audit resources in those industries where they would obtain the most revenue per hour of auditor time and where it appeared audits could educate taxpayers as to what they were doing wrong.

Conversely, the state did not want to impose audit burdens on classes of taxpayers who were paying the right amount of tax or where audits would not educate the taxpayers as to their errors. The state of California also wanted to be sure that the auditors were not wasting time conducting extensive audits where audits were neither educational to the taxpayer nor revenue raising to the state. (It should be noted that the auditors were measured by "change per hour" so that a dollar of refund for overpayment resulted in the same measurement of the auditor as a dollar of assessment.)

Thus, I learned in my first job after graduating from the University of California at Los Angeles with a degree in accounting that time records used for financial-analysis records can be important management tools. The management tool helped the provider of the services (the state of California), the person who rendered the service (the auditor), the people for whom the services were performed (the taxpayers being audited) and the public as a whole (the state of California). The use of information from auditor time records compared to the tax income allowed the state to identify those taxpayers who individually or by industry were either overpaying or underpaying taxes. These taxpayers then became the subjects of audits to correct deficiencies in tax procedures. The taxpayers benefited because those who were paying the proper amount of tax (again by individual or industry) were not audited (except for random audits to prevent anyone from feeling that they were exempt from audit). The auditor benefited because his or her ability to identify and correct tax problems could be measured easily. Society as a whole benefited because the people of the state could feel that an attempt was being made to ensure that state resources were not being wasted and that those taxpayers who were errant were being educated to correct their errors.

As a practicing CPA in the 1950s and 1960s, I kept time records for basically the same reasons that lawyers now keep time records, i.e., to crudely attempt to measure approximate costs of producing services by client or type of services and to crudely attempt to fairly charge the client for those services. I noticed, however, that when I worked in the tax department, clients often wanted a fee schedule based on other than hourly rates. The business clients felt that hourly rates rewarded the inefficient and penalized the efficient and we accommodated them by charging in some cases by the type of return or the number of pages of schedules in the return or the type and number of schedules in the return rather than by the hour. We had sufficient experience regarding costs to do so.

I first began using computers for time records in the 1950s when I was in the U.S. Air Force. I was in supply and we were concerned both with reliability and cost effectiveness of three categories of equipment: aircraft, ground radar and vehicles. We kept time records as well as part-consumption records for all repair work required to put inoperable equipment back into service. Much of my unit's work was for the Strategic Air Command (SAC) and we were able to use their primitive (by today's standards) computers to collate and process the data. We used second-generation computers, such as RAMAC, which still were using tubes instead of transistors. The Air Force is justifiably proud of the fact that by using computer-generated data from the time records for the repair of the equipment of that period, namely the B52 Bombers, that these bombers still are flying as a mainstay of the Air Force after twenty-five years of flying service.

SUMMARY

Fixed fees for specific services is not new to the legal profession. Courts have long used fixed-fee schedules for specific services. I own a book printed in 1668 setting forth the fee schedule for the courts, the sheriff and the lawyer in the courts of the Star Chamber, Chancery and Common Pleas. The legal profession's dissatisfaction with these fixed-fee schedules stems from the fact that the amounts of the fees often are out of touch with current economics. Courts should be educated, not criticized, for using fixed-fee schedules.

By using modern computer technology, we can concentrate our attention on what is important, i.e., a reasonable fixed fee for the work required rather than quibbling over hourly rates and whether the letter should have been prepared by a lawyer, a paralegal, a secretary or a clerk. Fixed fees ultimately will reward efficient producers of quality work and punish inefficient producers or those who put too much work into a service. The public will benefit and will be encouraged to use more, not less, legal services, when they know in advance what these services will cost. Hourly rates may become an idea whose time is gone.

CHAPTER 5

Just as the Task Force was gearing up, the November 23, 1987 issue of The National Law Journal included a supplement on billing. We are reprinting it here with their permission.

Alberta I. Cook *is on the editorial staff of The National Law Journal.* **Kenneth Roberts** *is general counsel of Exxon Company U.S.A. in Houston.* **Mark A. Dombroff** *is a partner at the Washington, D.C., office of New York's Hughes Hubbard and Reed.*

Hourly Billing: A Thing of the Past?

by Alberta I. Cook

Hourly rates, for decades the mainstay of law firms' fee structures, continue to be gradually supplanted by more creative ways of putting a price tag on a case.

Task-based, or value billing—a system in which lawyer and client negotiate an agreed-upon fee for a case—is meeting broader acceptance by many firms and corporate in-house counsel.

Premium billing—adding a surcharge to an amount determined by a firm's hourly rate when a good result is obtained, or charging a higher-than-usual rate for complex cases—is used less widely, but has worked for lawyers handling high-priced deals such as mergers and acquisitions.

Many firms have devised their own combinations using hourly rates as only one factor in a complex equation. "The majority of law firms are still billing on a time basis, but they are all anxiously trying to get away from direct hourly (billing)," says Jon E. Klemens, a partner in the Ardmore, Pa., management consulting firm of Altman & Weil, Inc.

(Despite the advent of new billing systems, hourly rates continue to rise. Ninety-two of the 167 firms included in this year's survey of large-firm billing practices have maximum hourly billing rates of $250 or more. And thirty-one of them are charging more than $300 per hour.)

Clients Voice Objections

The impetus behind the change in billing practices often comes from the client in some cases, say consultants, clients actually are avoiding firms that bill on an hourly basis. And they object to the ever-increasing salaries of partners and associates, says Peter A. Giuliani of the Rowayton, Conn., office of Cobb Consulting Group.

Perhaps clients simply feel that under the hourly system they're not getting their money's worth, Giuliani indicates. "There are physically so many hours a lawyer can work," he says. "The combination of client resistance—having to pay so much for new lawyers and the fact that you can't get that many hours out of a lot of lawyers—requires you to think differently."

But law-firm economics may have as much to do with changing billing practices as has client dissatisfaction. The inherent inefficiency in hourly billing systems causes firms to lose thousands of dollars each year.

"Most attorneys hate to review and send out bills—it's time-consuming and in many situations there's a time lag from the time [the bill] is ready to go and when it's sent," notes Klemens.

Proponents of the newer billing systems say that hourly rates do not always reflect how firms really work.

Value Billing

Edward P. Leibensperger is a strong advocate of value, or task-oriented, billing. The corporate lawyer from Boston's Nutter, McClennen & Fish (and chairman of the Subcommittee on Billing of the American Bar Association's Litigation Section) says the system eliminates the "nitpicking about hours or disbursement" and helps firms and clients "reach a good result."

And New York's Cleary, Gottlieb, Steen & Hamilton has abandoned the hourly "taxi meter approach" for the most part—except when required,

Reprinted with permission from *The National Law Journal*.

such as in bankruptcy cases," says J. Speed Carroll, the firm's managing partner. "The entire circumstances of a project" determine what the firm will charge, he adds.

"If we provide routine advice about setting up and conducting a shareholders' meeting of a corporation, it takes five hours and everything happens in good order in the meeting," a certain fee would apply, he says. However, "if we spend five hours analyzing a tax problem and save a company $50 million, the value of those five hours to the client is very different."

Another variation on the task-oriented theme has been tried at CBS in New York, where lawyers have asked some outside counsel to set a fee range, or "mini-max" approach to cases—"but we haven't pushed it," notes Associate General Counsel Ronald E. Guttman.

Though CBS lawyers have not used a budget approach, they often negotiate a rate with outside counsel, basing it on the type of work needed. To keep costs down, Guttman says, he also on occasion has sought the supervisory services of a partner in a private firm, but assigned the legal legwork to CBS in-house legal staff.

Premium Billing

Manatt, Phelps, Rothenberg & Phillips in Los Angeles uses premium billing—though hourly rates, contingency fees, budgets and percentage deals all continue to play a role.

Premium billing works best in complex cases, such as a hostile takeover, says managing partner Alan I. Rothenberg. "If the firm turns outside work down and works around the clock for weeks on end, there's a price for that."

"The hardest thing about litigation is controlling some things that happen," Rothenberg says. "As long as the client understands that it cannot be ironclad," a case budget can work, he notes. Still, that approach is more adaptable to cases in which the phases are "measurable," such as a merger and acquisition or a public offering.

While not turning their backs on the hourly rate, some firms and corporate counsel have tried to set budgets for the specific type of legal work to be done.

Charles Hansen, senior vice president and general counsel at Emerson Electric Co. in St. Louis, says, "This insistence on detailed monthly bills as the basis for a control system is foolish. The buyer sees four of a Los Angeles lawyer's hours [billed] at $150 an hour. That's $600. It doesn't tell you anything if you're in Little Rock. It lulls the buyer into a false sense of security—you may be paying $75,000 for a $50,000 case."

Emerson Electric had an estimated 500 to 600 product-liability cases annually when Hansen created the company's litigation "cost control matrix." Using it, Hansen now requires outside counsel to submit a budget for the several phases of a product-liability case.

"Based on our evaluation of the job, we either pay or we don't pay it," Hansen says.

But if an unforeseen expense arises during litigation that goes over budget, says Hansen, "we're flexible." If the outside firm exceeds the budget, however, the corporation places the overage funds in a "suspense" account.

The matrix is not for the "blockbuster" $15 million cases, which are less predictable, Hansen says. But for the vast majority of the caseload, it has worked very well. Already this year, he says, the firm has saved $1 million in legal expenses over last year.

"Most firms come in with numbers we can live with," and most of the outside counsel to Emerson Electric have accepted it, says Hansen.

Hourly Billing—The Core

Still, hourly rates are not completely passé.

"No matter how you devise the bill structure, a core element of it has got to be a timekeeping system," says Carl D. Liggio, general counsel to the Arthur Young & Co. accounting firm in New York.

Adds Paul H. Dawes of San Francisco's Thelen, Marrin, Johnson & Bridges, who cochairs the ABA Litigation Section's Committee on Corporate Counsel, "There is a recognition that budgeting [a case] is a good idea, but it goes only so far.

Hourly rates are still key to determining how Milwaukee's Quarles & Brady sets its fees," says managing partner Arthur H. Laun, Jr.

"We almost uniformly require detailed billing on an hourly basis," says Laun. However, some clients with limited budgets ask the firm to take a case for a flat fee. When the budget is reached, he says, the client can review it and decide how to proceed.

And Dawes notes that today "there are more instances where a special arrangement is made. For example, outside lawyers will take on a matter at a reduced rate on the understanding that they need to improve their learning curve in the area. In return, they will get some business."

New York's Skadden, Arps, Slate, Meagher & Flom also adheres to the hourly line—but with a twist. "Time will certainly continue to be a factor, but it's still just one factor," says Peter P. Mullen, the firm's executive partner. The same goes for Houston's Vinson & Elkins, says managing partner J. Evans Attwell.

"We have not reached nirvana and we don't claim to do so," says Attwell. "But we make sure [the fees are] entirely satisfactory to the client and fair to the firm. The key to that is communication."

CLIENT INFLUENCE

In general, though, any changes in law-firm billing will have to reflect clients' needs, and growing sophistication.

"Clients are questioning [bills and costs] more and requiring more detailed bills," says consultant Linda R. Glowacki, a Dallas-based vice president of Somerville, N.J.'s Hildebrandt Inc. "More clients now are shopping around for services. Law firms can't necessarily get all the legal work from one client."

One client that shops around is Chicago-based United Air Lines Inc. "We ask law firms for an opinion on the cost of doing a particular piece of work—such as a motion to dismiss," says Stephen P. Sawyer, assistant general counsel.

The key to managing the billing system of a law firm seems to be flexibility, adds Glowacki. After a firm systematizes its practice, it takes lawyers fewer hours to produce a product—and the client gets a better deal. Today, Glowacki says, "the billing practices lawyers are seeking should not only help the client save money, but help them make money."

The Hourly Fee System Is a "Devilish Creature"

by Kenneth Roberts

In April of 1986, New York's Cravath, Swaine & Moore surprised the legal world when it announced an increase in starting salaries of $13,000—from $52,000 to $65,000. Other Wall Street firms immediately followed the Cravath lead; some adopted even higher starting salaries. This year, Cravath has upped its starting salaries again, to $71,000. (*National Law Journal,* October 26, 1988.) And today, the going rate for starting salaries in New York is around $70,000.

Most Wall Street firms also have announced similar increases in associate salaries across the board.

Law firms in other cities have responded by increasing their starting and associate salaries, but with more restraint than have firms in New York.

The latest increases have been explained as an attempt to compete with investment bankers for the brightest stars in each graduating class. The cause of these increases, however, is not particularly significant or interesting. The fascinating aspect of this situation is how law firms, in the face of runaway charges for legal services, can continue to provide seemingly limitless increases in pay for trainees.

Considerable logic supports the proposition that these inflated salaries for law apprentices are the direct result of the conversion of law firms to hourly economics.

The hourly fee system is a devilish creature that rewards inefficiency and penalizes productivity. This article will begin with a look at the impact of hourly fees on the escalation of starting salaries.

In earlier years, lawyers sold their services for fees based on a variety of factors permitted by the American Bar Association's Code of Professional Responsibility, with complexity of the matter, results obtained and other factors being as important as time spent on a case. Lawyers always kept an eye on what other lawyers charged for similar services and on what the client would consider reasonable.

Lawyers also always had strong motivation to minimize overhead costs in order to maximize profits. The cost of young apprentices was—like the cost of librarians, clerks, secretaries and rent—an overhead expense to be minimized to the extent possible. In those days, law apprentices were compensated much as medical apprentices are today. They were paid subsistence wages, and early years with law firms were considered simply an extension of law-school training.

Partners: Legal-Services Brokers

In more recent years, partners in law firms have become to a very large extent brokers of legal services. Of course, partners still sell their own services, but a major portion of the partners' profit comes from the sale of the services—at a substantial markup—of the law firm's associates. Of course, the higher the associate/partner ratio, the greater the significance of the partner's role as a broker. The law firms have learned that they not only can sell the services of more senior associates, but they also can sell the services of the young apprentices.

This discovery by law firms—which appears to be a fallout of the hourly fee system—has revolutionized compensation of the law apprentices just as the hourly fee system itself has revolutionized law-firm economics. Today, salaries of apprentices no longer are overhead costs to be minimized in order to maximize the profits but instead are a charge to be passed on to clients, with a profit tacked on top. There is no

Reprinted with permission from ***The National Law Journal***.

incentive for the law firm to minimize these costs. Eventually, of course, competition or consumer resistance might change this situation, but there has been no indication to date that either of these has had any significant impact.

The use of the hourly fee system to convert training costs from an overhead expense to a major profit center is only one of the strange aspects of the hourly fee system that dominates the charges of most law firms.

As mentioned earlier, under the hourly fee system, the greater rewards go to the most inefficient, and rewards decrease with productivity improvement.

In a business corporation, there is an economic driving force to improve efficiency and productivity—a financial incentive to eliminate unnecessary work. Under the hourly fee system law firms have a financial incentive for inefficiency. They can profit from unneeded work.

Common Inefficiencies

Some of the more common inefficiencies practiced by many law firms are:

- Too many lawyers assigned to a project;
- Too many lawyers attending conferences, depositions and hearings;
- Too much turnover of associates assigned to a project;
- Excessive discovery;
- Time devoted to issues prematurely and to marginal problems;
- Failure to take advantage of research on the shelf;
- Preparation of long formal opinions when a short, informal memo would meet the client's needs;
- Excessive intraoffice consultation; and
- Pressure on associates to generate billable hours.

These practices (the last one on the list is perhaps the most insidious of all) greatly inflate legal fees and offend clients.

Note that none of these things even marginally improves the quality of the work.

Firms tend to believe that they are efficient and avoid unneeded work. Many firms probably believe in good faith that they have policies to control these problems.

However, competitive businesses continually find more and more ways to produce better products and services at lower costs. Improvements never believed possible are developed. But as long as a firm has a financial incentive to be inefficient, the firm will be inefficient.

Other Cost Contributors

Of course, the hourly fee system is not the sole contributor to excessive costs of legal services. There are many other factors, including abuse of discovery and other procedural rules, increased complexity of cases, increase of the stakes in damage suits, inconsistency in the quality of the judiciary, the tendency of some courts to attempt to solve all problems of society (in law school we learned that the law does not provide a remedy for every wrong but some courts seem to have forgotten this) and other factors.

Nevertheless, the hourly fee system must accept its share of the blame. It is ironic that this system was forced upon many law firms by insurance companies and other clients.

The system, however, is now so deeply ingrained in the economics of most law firms that they cannot be expected to change voluntarily. It is doubtful that law firms could, at this date, revive the fee system of earlier years even if they wanted to.

Does all of this mean that partners in law firms today are overcompensated? Perhaps some are. Many people believe lawyers take more out of society than they contribute. However, that is not the point here. If inefficiencies were eliminated, partners could continue with the same level of compensation, but the cost to the client would be reduced.

Let's look at a very simple example. Suppose that the cost of maintaining a young associate at the firm is $50 per hour and the firm charges $100 for the services of that associate. If one hour of work were eliminated, the partner could increase his charges by $50 and still be compensated at the same level while the client would pay $50 less. While this is a somewhat simplistic example of a very complex matter, the fact is that this criticism of the hourly fee system is not necessarily a criticism of the earnings of law firm partners. Clients who frequently are preoccupied with the rates for partners, however, would have to adjust their thinking to make the example work.

Clients Combat High Costs

What is the solution? Clients today are attempting to combat the high cost of legal services in various ways. They engage in price shopping among firms, attempt to negotiate lower hourly rates, require somewhat precise budgeting of work to be performed, identify and police the hours for which they are billed and use many other techniques.

All of these things, however, are simply attempts to patch up a system that is inherently defective, Several things are beginning to occur that involve more fundamental changes and that will over the long term, have a major impact on law-firm compensation systems.

First is a trend of many businesses to perform more and more legal work in-house. Companies are finding that this can be done at considerable cost savings for a variety of reasons.

Second, many clients are starting to seek out smaller, more efficient firms. The greatest long-term threat to the big law firms may come from small firms whose partners' income is derived primarily from their own services rather than from brokering the legal services of associates. Eventually, competition in the form of these smaller, more-efficient firms could force major changes in the structure and operation of the legal industry. This process is slow, however, and poses no short-term threat to the big law firms.

Third, more and more clients will begin to insist on experimenting with alternative fee arrangements in an attempt to find new fee systems. Neither law firms nor clients are likely to want to attempt to revive the fee systems of earlier years. Clients are beginning to show a keen interest in developing some new systems that reward productivity and penalize inefficiency.

One example might be a cost-plus arrangement. The firm would be reimbursed for the actual cost of associates and paralegals. For example, if an associate billed sixty hours in a week, twenty of which were for a particular client, that client would reimburse the firm for one-third of the associate's salary for that week. Partners would be paid half of their normal billing rate. The firm's profit would come from a lump sum fee agreed on in advance with perhaps some adjustment based on results or other factors.

Other possibilities include such things as a cap on the total fee for a particular matter, increased hourly fees to partners but no fee at all for associate or paralegal time, reduced fees for overtime work (i.e., hours worked in excess of some number in a day or week), blended rates, a defendant's contingency fee or a lump-sum fee agreed on in advance and based on the estimated settlement value of a case.

Many practical problems make these and other similar approaches very difficult to implement. There is no easy solution to the problem of providing economic incentives for firms to minimize costs. Nevertheless, the ability of clients and law firms to devise some innovative fee arrangements represents the best hope for short-term improvements in the cost of legal services.

Helping Clients Understand the Billing Process

by Mark A. Dombroff

One of the most difficult, as well as the most important, tasks confronting any lawyer is the billing process. Whether it occurs on a monthly, quarterly or some other basis, there usually will come a time when a lawyer has to sit down and put together a bill for the client. The ability to do so in a manner structured to provide maximum usable information to the client is something that all lawyers should possess. The inability to do so inevitably will result in less than an ideal relationship between lawyer and client. From a lawyer's perspective, this result is obviously undesirable.

Perhaps even more important is the fact that the nature of the relationship between an attorney and a client is one founded on trust. As a result, anything that engenders tension in that relationship must be guarded against. Without proper attention, the billing process can engender such tension.

Explaining the Billing Process

Having said this, the focus of attention becomes those things an attorney can do in order to ensure that the billing process is one understood by the client and, in addition, that it is structured in such a way as to further enhance the attorney/client relationship rather than damage it. The following items present a number of ideas and techniques that will help accomplish these goals:

- In the letter of retention to the client acknowledging the assignment or representation, advise the client of the billing schedule and tell the client to let you know whether some other schedule is desired—e.g., quarterly instead of monthly.
- Tell the client which people in the firm will be working on the matter(s)—partners, associates, paralegals, law clerks, etc.
- Tell the client either what the hourly rate of each person working on the matter is or what the average hourly rate will be for the matter. If this latter number is used, a projection will have to be made of the number of hours that will be spent by each person on the client's matters, from which a single average hourly rate can be determined. My own experience is that this number is ascertainable with a fair degree of certainty based on overall experience.
- Consider offering the client the option of a "blended" rate instead of separate hourly rates. Essentially, this amounts to a single hourly rate for every hour put in on a matter without regard to who puts it in. Thus, one hour spent by a partner who has a normal hourly rate of $200 will be billed at, for example, $150, as will the hours spent by the associate, who normally bills at $160, and the paralegal, for whom the firm bills at $65. In effect, this is somewhat like the "average" hourly rate approach, but the "blended" hourly rate is established up front.
- To keep the bills down, suggest to the client that its personnel department perform certain tasks under your supervision. This may include document collection and production, drafting answers to discovery, etc. Even if the client declines, as many will, he

Reprinted with permission from *The National Law Journal*.

or she inevitably will appreciate being given the option.

- Advise the client that you will not be billing if additional lawyers, usually associates, work on the client's matter for training purposes, or if you supervise or monitor a younger lawyer where the purpose of your involvement is to train the younger lawyer.
- Tell the client up front what kind of description of work you normally provide in your bills—e.g., narrative, printouts—and give the client the option of indicating that he or she prefers a different format. Many clients will accept your format. However, in today's environment of rising legal costs, clients are far more attuned to billing procedures. As a result, many will require detailed printouts. It is important to know this early, so you can make sufficiently detailed entries on your time sheets to avoid having to reconstruct your activities and those of others when you are preparing the bills.
- Be prepared to provide to the client an estimate of the number of hours to be put in on his or her matters. Regardless of whether the client asks for it, do a projection for your own guidance and use it as a check against the time actually spent.
- Closely monitor the work being put in by yourself and others on the client's matters. Weekly or monthly meetings with other lawyers may be desirable to protect against duplication, nonproductive work and "runaway" bills.
- Be prepared to write off time that was not well spent or time that was duplicative or otherwise not justified.
- Carefully monitor the disbursements that are charged to the client and ensure that all disbursements have been charged properly. You may not want to bill secretarial or other overtime to any client unless that overtime is directly attributable to an emergency project, such as a court filing, etc. When overtime accrues simply because there aren't enough hours in the day to get the work done or not enough secretaries, without some other agreement with the client, the firm should consider not charging the client.
- Ascertain what the client will or will not pay for travel expenses, e.g., first class versus coach. Generally, a good policy is never to charge the client for anything other than coach fare unless the client otherwise indicates that first-class travel is authorized.

Properly handled, the billing process can enhance the attorney/client relationship. Giving proper attention to the process early enough will result not only in more satisfied clients, but in clients who realize that their dollars spent on legal fees are being well spent.

CHAPTER 6

Richard P. Delaney, *of the legal department of Exxon Company U.S.A., sent the Task Force a prepublication copy of the article by Kenneth Roberts that was included in the previous chapter. In response to our inquiries, Delaney summarized his own thoughts in the letter that follows.*

A Letter from the Corporate Counsel

by Richard P. Delaney

Re: Special Task Force On Value Billing

Richard C. Reed, Esquire
Reed McClure Moceri Thonn & Moriarty
3600 Columbia Center
Seattle, Washington 98104-7081

Dear Mr. Reed:

As promised, here are my thoughts about alternatives to billing on an hourly basis. As in-house counsel for a major corporation, I approach this topic from a client's perspective. As such, I am motivated by concerns over the value received by the client for fees incurred, and less interested in the relationship of the fees charged to the firm's costs.

This topic does not arise in a static professional environment. Our profession has undergone profound changes in the past twenty-five years. The number of American lawyers in 1987 is approximately $2^1/_2$ times that of 1960. Not only has the absolute lawyer number increased, but the organizational profiles of those lawyers has changed significantly. Average firm size has continued to increase, while the number of sole practitioners continues to drop. The lawyer profile also has changed, with the average age decreasing and the number of minorities increasing.

During this same period, the body of statutory law and government regulation has expanded almost on a geometric basis. This information and regulation explosion compels both increasing specialization by the practitioner and continuing legal education in order to achieve basic minimal competence in these new areas of law. An additional significant change is the growth of corporate in-house legal staffs and the resultant shift of law work from outside firms.

The status of our profession also has changed. It has lost its prior immunity from regulation, and now is in many ways treated like other businesses which encourage economic competition among members. Public perception of the profession's integrity has been shattered, with lawyers too often being at center stage when public scandals from Watergate to insider trading unfold. Too often the recognition that an attorney achieves, both within and outside the Bar, is measured by his or her economic status rather than his or her professional ability and accomplishments. This economic criterion of success has appeared increasingly as the guiding objective and the standard evaluation for both individual as well as firm law practices. The dominance of the hourly billing system has produced a system wherein the number of hours billed has become the controlling measurement of worth and productivity. For the young lawyer expected to produce a high quota of billable hours, time spent in professional development, educational but unproductive in terms of billable hours, and in other items like pro bono or civic and charitable endeavors has become increasingly hard to manage, while leaving any time for the quality of life outside the law practice. In all candor, not only are high entry-level salaries seen as a major factor in this system, but also the increasingly larger partnership incomes that have resulted from the ability to increase the leverage and profitability of associates.

What do these philosophical ramblings have to do with the question of alternate fee billing? I suggest that the current questioning of the hourly fee, while heightened by perceivable escalating costs, really is caused by the changes in both the profession and client base.

Charging on an hourly rate is basically a cost-plus arrangement. Having determined your costs—no matter how defined—you add a profit percentage, create an hourly billing rate and bill clients accordingly. As costs increase, you simply increase that billing rate enough to keep your profit margin constant. This cost-plus fee system is under increasing resistance from today's more-sophisticated law-service purchasers, especially corporations. Corporate law managers who recruit both summer associates and new graduates are able to judge the skill level and efficiency of new associates and apply this measure when analyzing fee bills.

The current hourly fee system does nothing to reward efficiency in the delivery of law services. In fact, the system may be counterproductive to any efficiency efforts—for the more hours generated result in higher profits to the firm.

Human experience demonstrates that there must be a valid relationship between any cost of service and the value produced. For example, if I contract with a housepainter to paint my home for a fixed fee, the painter has an incentive to complete the job quickly, for if he can do so, he will collect his full payment (fee) and be able to handle additional work. These same economic considerations may drive the painter to cut corners if he has underestimated the job length. On an hourly basis, his incentive is to go slower because he will be fully paid for his time. The hourly rate by itself, however, does not ensure that the quality of the paint job will be any better.

It is important for the sake of the profession that we analyze and try to change this escalating cost-price treadmill. This is not to deny that many law firms and lawyers work hard to control costs and improve efficiency in what is a changing legal environment. The current hourly rate-fee structure as it now exists creates, and in effect rewards inefficiencies, and may result in higher charges than would otherwise occur. I believe that more could be done to improve efficiency and thus control costs, if the incentives to increase costs were replaced by incentives to control costs. I recognize that associate salary compensation is a cost to be recovered in the hourly rate structure, and the costs of computerization and office efficiency must be passed along in some manner to clients. While there is no denying the need to obtain first-quality associates and to, of necessity, pay the competitive going rate in order to obtain and retain them, there must be an end at some point to the spiral that simply raises the hourly rate charge to clients to cover the increased salaries paid to associates. The incentive to inefficiency that results from the increasing pressure on associates to generate billable hours is obvious.

There probably is no right answer as to how to create the right efficiency incentives while maintaining the dedication of the people working and the quality of the work product produced. Just as in my painter analogy, too great an emphasis on cost control and efficiency may result in work product of lesser quality.

Over the past year, Exxon has been discussing with various outside firms proposals to develop a fee structure that strives to: (1) provide stronger incentives for the prompt disposition of cases in the most cost-effective manner where we are a defendant; and (2) create a modified hourly rate-fee arrangement that is fair to both parties while minimizing any possible adverse effects. One method used is a "split fee" concept composed of a base fee that is below the firm's ordinary rates, usually with a fee cap, and an incentive fee where the firm shares in the savings generated by a prompt and successful disposition of the case. Many law firms look on this as an opportunity to be as creative in handling their own economic business as they are in handling the legal problems of the client.

No doubt you will receive different viewpoints from other interested parties. These concepts lead themselves to a candid and open discussion.

Sincerely,
Richard P. Delaney

CHAPTER 7

***Leonard L. Loeb**, a Milwaukee, Wisconsin, attorney, raises the question as to whether the general prohibition against contingent fees in divorce litigation should be reexamined. This is illustrative of the broader issue of whether existing ethical, regulatory or court-directed policies that constrain billing tendencies should be altered to recognize current mores, social attitudes and economic realities. An argument could be made that current ethical rules are primarily for the protection of the client and that any reexamination or policy change also should involve a consideration as to what is fair and reasonable for the attorney. The reader should compare Rule 1.5, Model Rules of Professional Conduct (described later in Chapter 17) with the Model Code of Professional Responsibility, which is cited by Loeb.*

Hourly Charges in Divorce Cases Are Archaic

by Leonard L. Loeb

When determining what is a fair fee for services rendered in a divorce case, unique problems are presented that are caused by the strong moral and ethical policies associated with divorce by our society. As a result of these convictions, a majority of courts adhere to the general rule that "a fee contract contingent on procuring a divorce, or contingent in amount on the amount of alimony, support or property settlement to be obtained, is against public policy and void."[1]

A second rule that overlaps the first is required by the Model Code of Professional Responsibility DR 2-106(A) (1980): "A lawyer shall not enter into an agreement for, charge or collect an illegal or clearly excessive fee." These two rules in the past always have been considered separate and distinct; the former rule, however, should be reconsidered in light of the changing public policy caused by the adoption of no-fault divorce.

Public-Policy Reasoning

The first step in our analysis is to understand the public policy on which the first general rule is based. In *Burns v. Stewart*, 188 N.W.2d 760 (Minn. 1971), the court presents the underlying public-policy reasons for the rule:

1. If an attorney's compensation is dependent on the procurement of a divorce, the attorney may be encouraged not to seek reconciliation of the parties.
2. There is a possibility that the fee generated by such arrangements may prove unduly burdensome or oppressive to the parties.
3. The size of the contingent fee frustrates and defeats the court's efforts to make suitable provisions for the wife.

A majority of courts fail to address these policy concerns in light of the facts of each case, but rather most courts automatically rule such contracts are void. Because a few attorneys may violate these public concerns, the courts assure that these attorneys do not by denying such contracts in *all* divorce actions. This reasoning is faulty for several reasons: (1) A person may have no other means of obtaining competent counsel other than by using a contingent fee; (2) the policy considerations may not be violated, yet the contract still will be held void, and (3) a court can control the size of attorneys' fees by applying DR 2-106(A). Declaring all such contracts void regardless of the unique circumstances of each case results in overprotecting the public at its own expense.

The Model Code of Professional Responsibility EC 2-20 (1980) states the reasons for allowing contingent fees:

1. They often, and in a variety of circumstances, provide the only practical means by which one having a claim against another can economically afford, finance and obtain the services of a competent lawyer to prosecute the claim.
2. The successful prosecution of the claim produces a res out of which the fee can be paid.

Automatically declaring all such contracts in divorce actions as void may be denying a party his or her sole chance of obtaining competent counsel. This goes against the very purpose for which the

Reprinted with permission from the *American Journal of Family Law*.

rule was established, i.e., to protect the public against improper counsel.

The Minnesota Supreme Court addressed this problem in *Burns v. Stewart*, 188 N.W.2d 760 (Minn. 1971). The court initially restated the general rule as stated in *Baskerville v. Baskerville*, 75 N.W.2d 762, 768 (Minn. 1956): "a contract for the payment of a fee to an attorney contingent upon his procuring a divorce for his client or contingent upon the amount of alimony and property awarded to the wife is void as against public policy." The court in *Baskerville* increased the severity of the rule of expressly overruling previous decisions insofar as it allows recovery under quantum meruit to attorneys whose clients sign a contingent fee contract pursuant to divorce actions.

In *Burns*, the court appears to have taken exception to this absolute rule. The court stated there was "no reason which would preclude the wife from bringing an action, independent of an action for divorce, for her equitable share of personal property obtained through their joint efforts during coverture."[2] The husband in that action deserted the wife and absconded all the securities and liquid assets of the marriage, leaving the wife without any means of support. She could not afford to pay the extensive legal and investigative services required in order to secure a return of her share of the assets. The court, therefore, ruled it was not against public policy for her to divide her action into two separate actions, one for divorce and one for property settlement, where the latter action was based on a contingent-fee agreement.

California also follows the general rule that a contingent-fee contract between an attorney and a client looking to the institution of divorce is void and against public policy. In *Krieger v. Bulpitt*, 251 P.2d 673, 675 (Cal. 1953), however, the court expressly rejects the enforcement of this rule to the extreme that such contracts always are and automatically void:

> **There should not be a dogmatic condemnation of every contingent-fee contract in a divorce action regardless of distinguishable circumstances. Rather, the validity of such contract should be determined in the light of the factual background of the particular case and considerations of public policy appropriate thereto.[3]**

Both Minnesota and California therefore have adopted the policy that legal contracts will not automatically be declared void as against public policy without the court first considering the independent facts of each case and then determining what the public policy should be according to those facts.

Test of Reasonableness Requirement

Regardless of whether the courts allow a contingent-fee contract in divorce actions, *all* fees must meet the test of reasonableness required by DR 2-106(A). The court's ability and basis of review of the reasonableness of fees is generally accepted and well stated in *Herro, McAndrews & Porter v. Gerhardt*, 214 N.W.2d 401 (Wis. 1974):

> **It is established that courts have the inherent power to determine the reasonableness of attorneys' fees and to refuse to enforce any contract that calls for clearly excessive or unreasonable fees.**

The standard by which courts measure the reasonableness of a fee is set forth in DR 2-106(B):

> **A fee is clearly excessive when, after a review of the facts, a lawyer of ordinary prudence would be left with a definite and firm conviction that the fee is in excess of a reasonable fee.**

In applying this standard, it becomes apparent that the scope of the court's authority is very broad. The court can determine that a fee is excessive and therefore invoke sanctions against the attorney involved,[4] or the court can determine that the fee awarded was inadequate and thereby award a higher fee.[5]

No uniform set of rules exists by which a reasonable attorney's fee may be computed; numerous factors, however, have been set forth by the courts that are to be considered by the attorney in determining a fee. In *Herro*,[6] the Supreme Court of Wisconsin presents the following factors to be considered:

1. The amount and character of the services rendered;
2. The labor;
3. The time;
4. The trouble involved;
5. The character and importance of the litigation;

6. The amount of money or value of the property affected;
7. The professional skill and experience called for;
8. The standing of the attorney in his profession;
9. The general ability of the client to pay; and
10. The pecuniary benefit derived from the services.

All of the above factors should be considered, but the attorney's discretion still controls what factors will receive greater weight and what will receive less.

In *Goldman v. Eisinger*, 425 A.2d 1356 (Md. 1981), the court analyzed two factors that the court considered controlled the fee that was to be charged. The first was whether the services rendered were reasonably necessary to benefit the clients. Although the attorney acted in good faith, the court determined that the extensive services rendered were not reasonably necessary. The court realized that there was no correlation between hours expended and results obtained. In fact, very often the hours expended depend on the skill and experience of the attorney involved. The court thereby refused to encourage the policy of expending time on a case simply for the sake of justifying the fee.

The second factor considered by the court in *Goldman* was the results obtained from the services rendered. Results obtained are stated in DR 2-106(B) (4) as an appropriate factor to consider in setting a fee. In *Goldman*, no question existed in the judge's mind that the attorney did spend the amount of time on the case that he claimed, but the court ruled that "the services of the attorney should in some way be beneficial to the estate, either by enlargement or the protection of it."[7] The court reasoned that an attorney cannot simply bill according to the hours expended without any consideration as to whether those efforts produced any tangible results for the client.

RESULT FACTOR

In the more recent case of *Head v. Head*, 505 A.2d 868 (Md. App. 1986), the court addressed the issues of including a result factor and the subsequent reasonableness of an attorney's fee. In *Head*, the wife appealed the lower court's award of attorney's fees to the husband in the amount of $120,000, which included a result-obtained factor of $75,000. The wife argued that the trial court erred in allowing an award of which two-thirds represented a result-obtained amount that altered the agreement so that it became a contingent fee. The appeals court first had to consider whether including a result factor caused the fee to become contingent and therefore void in a divorce action; then, if the court found that the result factor properly could be considered, the court had to determine what was a reasonable result factor.

In addressing the first issue, the court initially states the definition of a contingent fee:

> **An arrangement between attorney and client whereby attorney agrees to represent client with compensation to be a percentage of the amount recovered; e.g., 25 percent if case is settled, 30 percent if case goes to trial.**[8]

The court found that "the fee was not directly related by percentage or formula to the amount recovered or protected."[9] As a result, determination of results obtained could not be considered as changing the agreement into a contingent fee.

Having determined that a result factor was considered properly, the court then had to review the reasonableness of the fee. The trial court awarded a fee of $120,000 based on the testimony of a witness presented by the husband as an expert in domestic-relations fees. The witness presented three alternative methods for computation of a fee. In the first analysis, he concluded that $75,000 would be an appropriate fee on a quantum meruit basis, to which he added a result factor of $50,000 for a total fee of $125,000. His second analysis computed the time spent (stipulated to be 227 hours and rounded to 200) at a $200 hourly rate, to which he added a result bonus of $85,000 based on the tremendous financial exposure of the husband, for a total fee again of $125,000. His last analysis started with the $40,000 hourly figure, to which he added a result factor of $80,000, which was computed by doubling the hourly figure, for a total fee of $120,000.

In holding that the result fee was unreasonable, the appeals court disregarded the testimony of the expert witness because he could not justify the final amount awarded. The result factors the witness presented ranged from $50,000 to $85,000; the witness, however, failed to offer any explanation to support three different result factors determined from the same result.

Prior to this decision, little guidance was available to determine a reasonable result fee. The *Head* case does provide some guidance for the court ruled that a result fee more than one and one-half times the hourly figure was unreasonable because "it no longer serves as a bonus, but instead becomes the primary source of funds for counsel."[10] The court goes on to state that "in a fixed fee or quantum meruit case, a result fee should not be disproportionate to the base fee."[11] The result obtained may, therefore, be considered as *a* factor, but "its prominence in the total fee must bear a reasonable relationship to the time and labor required."[12] Although the court does provide some guidance, it reemphasizes that "counsel should have the responsibility of setting his or her own fee."[13]

Unit-Billing System

The unit-billing system provides additional guidance to attorneys in determining a fair fee. This system assigns weighted units based on the time, labor and skill required for each procedure in the divorce action. For example, the time, labor and skill required to draft pleadings should be less than the time, labor and skill required in preparing for and negotiating a settlement; a greater number of units, therefore, should be assigned to the latter. At the conclusion of the action, a dollar value is assigned to each unit after a careful consideration of all the factors previously discussed and listed in *Herro*, especially the results obtained. If minimal results are obtained, a low dollar value should be assigned to each unit. If maximum results are obtained, the reverse should be true, subject to the test of reasonableness. The resulting fee will be based on the unique facts presented by each case and, therefore, will be a more reasonable fee for both lawyer and client than charging strictly by the hour. The unit-billing system thereby benefits both the attorney and the client by encouraging efficiency, expeditiousness and, above all, superior results.

Conclusion

The adoption of no-fault divorce, coupled with the adoption of equitable distribution by an increasing number of states, substantially has increased the number and complexity of divorce actions. The application of absolute rules, such as requiring attorneys to bill on a straight hourly fee, no longer is practical.

The use of the unit-billing system soon may replace the hourly billing system because of its two distinct advantages. The unit-billing system allows the attorney to consider the traditional factors, such as the time and labor expended by the attorney. It also allows the additional advantage of considering factors that vary from case to case, such as the skill of the attorney and the results obtained for the client. It rewards efficiency and discourages "running a meter." The ultimate result of the unit system is the fairest fee for services rendered for both the client and the attorney.

ENDNOTES

1. 7 AM. JUR. 2d, Attorneys At Law Sec. 257 (1980).
2. *Burns v. Stewart*, 188 N.W.2d 765 (Minn. 1971).
3. *Krieger v. Bulpitt*, 251 P.2d 673, 675 (Cal. 1953).
4. *See Attorney Grievance Commission v. Kerperman*, 438 A.2d 501 (Md. 1981).
5. *See Foster v. Foster*, 364 A.2d 65 (Md. 1976).
6. *Herro, McAndrews & Porter v. Gerhardt*, 214 N.W.2d 404 (Wis. 1974).
7. *Goldman v. Eisinger*, 425 A.2d 1360 (Md. 1981).
8. *Head v. Head*, 505 A.2d 874 (Md. App. 1986) (citing Black's Law Dictionary 553 (5th Ed. 1979).
9. *Id.* at 875.
10. *Id.* at 877.
11. *Id.*
12. *Id.*
13. *Id.* at 878.

CHAPTER 8

John G. Iezzi, *formerly general manager of the law firm of McGuire, Woods, Battle and Boothe, Richmond, Virginia, has written and spoken widely on economics and management topics. The increased utilization of technology in law practices, while bringing many benefits, has caused changes in the role of the lawyer, necessitated increased capital outlays, created confusion as to how to charge, caused reexamination and debate as to what constitutes overhead and, as Iezzi states, affected the bottom line regarding profitability. We suggest that the challenge is to find ways by which the utilization of technology can produce benefits for both the client and the lawyer. Iezzi now is a Senior Manager in the Law Firm Services Consulting Group of Price Waterhouse.*

Automating Lawyers: Does It Help the Bottom Line?

by John G. Iezzi

Law firms across the country continue to wrestle with the lawyer-automation issue. The main point of debate focuses on the two now most widely used words in the profession, *productivity* and *efficiency*. In my opinion, no one has been able to determine adequately a way to translate these two words into what should be the essence of the whole debate: increasing firm income.

Productivity is "yielding or furnishing results, benefits or profits." Efficiciency is "productivity without waste." If you put these two definitions together, it appears that the proponents of *increased lawyer automation are out to yield profits* by producing a product in the least-expensive way possible. To me, this means that automating the lawyers will create a situation where the work product for a client can be produced more quickly at less cost than with the present system.

This concept certainly is an appropriate profit-enhancing mechanism in an organization that produces a product at a relatively fixed selling price. By producing without waste, costs can be reduced effectively and the profit margin therefore increased. Unfortunately lawyers sell a service that, rather than having a fixed price, instead has a floating price that again unfortunately, is determined in most cases by the amount of time necessary to produce the product. If we just reduce the time, thereby reducing the selling price, do we gain substantially? In other words, are we getting more efficient and productive, but at the same time losing money?

Hourly Billing Versus Value Billing

The question of billing by the hour, which has been bred into most lawyers and clients, ought to be *replaced by a more-subjective and value-based billing system*. Another alternative, of course, simply is to raise hourly rates to compensate for the reduction in the amount of time now required. Both these potential solutions appear to be unacceptable to our clients. Therefore, we continue to pass the automation savings on to our clients through a reduced selling price without increasing firm profits.

How a firm or how the legal profession in general can make a 180-degree turn and adopt a value-based billing system after so many years of billing by the almighty hourly rate is a question that must be addressed before the lawyer-automation issue can be resolved. It is my feeling that for this new phenomenon to take place, the following must occur:

- *All lawyers in the firm must be sensitized to the value-billing concept.* This means that all bills must be individually reviewed by the billing attorney in concert with all the lawyers and legal assistants participating in the matter. A review must be undertaken to ascertain the extent to which production of the work product was enhanced through the use of automation techniques. These techniques include the use of sophisticated word-processing capabilities, exotic spreadsheet applications, retrieval of previously produced work products on a similar legal problem or computerized legal research—all of which reduces lawyer time.
- When the firm prepares to enter into the lawyer-automation mainstream, *it must examine the effect on its "back-office" personnel* who are required to provide systems

Reprinted with permission from the *Law Office Management Administration Report.*

support, maintenance and training for those who now will perform work previously done by others.

- *The awareness of clients must be enhanced by candid discussions* with the lawyer to acquaint them with the significance of automation in the production of their legal services. The preparation of a detailed bill, which the computer establishment has thrust on the profession, must be replaced with *a more narrative and subjective statement of services* that still provides the client with sufficient detail. At the same time, however, the lawyer should be permitted to attach premiums to the work to the extent that automated techniques have been used.
- The firm must examine not only whether it can utilize technology, but also *whether it should be performed by lesser-paid specialists instead of lawyers.* In other words, does it make sense for lawyers to prepare spreadsheets, perform typing tasks or do their own automated legal research?

TECHNOLOGY: BENEFITS VERSUS DRAWBACKS

Automation equipment and software often are purchased without a careful examination of the profitability question, with the result that firms have increased overhead without correspondingly increasing gross income.

Many recent analyses concerning the decrease in lawyer hours have been voiced across the country. A number of the larger firms that still maintain a sweatshop mentality (and that get all the press) will tell you that their hours basically have not changed over the past several years. The facts are, however, that a majority of firms, the ones you do not hear about, have experienced a reduction of hours. In many cases, this has come about through technological advances that encourage faster production.

In its September issue, *Law Office Management & Administration Report* quoted a lawyer on the question of value billing with his clients. He stated, "They recognize that technology has a role in productivity and you are just doing the same thing that they are to improve speed and service." I am not so sure that our clients, who again are working on a product that has a fixed selling price, are *able to relate the technology benefits to their lawyer in the same way that they relate such benefits to themselves.* What they are doing instead, I believe, is saying to their lawyers that hourly rates have become too high and that to compensate for these higher rates, the lawyers must perform services with a faster turnaround. The client is satisfied with this result because legal bills for the same services now are lower.

Lawyers who cannot raise a rate already deemed unacceptable, however, bear the cost of the technology, pass the savings on to clients and then must, through increased marketing efforts, *find more clients to take up the slack in hours saved through automation.*

My point is not to downgrade the use of technology, which certainly has a definite and important place in the legal profession. The problem is that *we have not been able to find a way to translate computerization into bottom-line dollars.*

Most firms spend many hours solving critical internal issues—partner compensation, mergers, escalating associates' salaries and marketing. I do not believe that they have spent the same amount of time in examining whether the profitability of automation, which they assume somehow will happen magically, is, in fact, occurring.

In addition, computer and software manufacturers constantly are changing their products and services. Automation decisions made today without proper review can become obsolete tomorrow. Software purchased for $99 through some computer magazine, if not examined in light of the overall automation objectives of the firm, may do nothing more than *create unanticipated compatibility problems with existing equipment.* Strategic Automation Planning (SAP) now must be accorded the same priority that other strategic-planning efforts have, to produce a result that is in the best economic interest of the firm.

Webster defines automation as the "automatically controlled operation of an apparatus, process or system by mechanical or electronic devices that takes the place of human organs of observation, effort and decision." I am not certain whether legal services can be provided without "human organs of observation, effort and decision." If they can, then somehow we must charge for the computer effort on the same relative basis that we charge for the human effort.

CHAPTER 9

Roger Fisher, *Williston Professor of Law at Harvard University, in the March-April, 1985 issue of* The Harvard Business Review, *dealt not so specifically with billing methods, but more generally with the attitudinal approach by outside counsel toward litigation. The author raises the critical question of whether existing billing methods stand in the way of a commonsense, client-oriented approach to legal representation.*

He Who Pays the Piper

by Roger Fisher

March 1, 1985

Mr. C. Ewen Cort
Litigation Department
Marshall, Holmes, Lincoln & Stone
Wall Street
New York, New York 10005

Dear Chuck:

As we get started on the new fiscal year, I thought we might jointly review the relationship between our company and your firm to see if it could be improved. I am sure that at times we have not been as helpful to you as we might have been. And on some occasions, particularly when we receive your monthly statements, I wonder if we are making the best use of the great talent found in your firm.

This is going to be a long letter, spelling out some of my concerns and advancing a few ideas for our joint consideration. Don't get worried: We are not planning to switch our major litigation business to some other firm (although negotiation theory suggests that we always should have our best alternative in mind). What I propose to do is to identify some symptoms, diagnose possible explanations and advance some general approaches and specific remedies that we may want to think about together.

After you have had a chance to read this letter and to discuss it with some of your partners, I suggest that a few of us—perhaps two or three from your firm and two or three from my company—schedule half a day or more when we can talk about how we might work more effectively together. I am sure that jointly we can come up with better ideas than those I have produced alone.

What Concerns Us

One issue, of course, is the amount of money that we have devoted to paying legal fees, particularly for matters in pending or anticipated litigation. If you will review the total sum that we have paid your firm over the past several years for litigation, I am sure you will agree it is large. Some would call it staggering.

A second concern is the amount of our corporate executives' time that lawsuits consume. Interviews by lawyers, interrogatories, depositions, searches through the files for relevant documents and attempts to recall just what was said when—all these take valuable time away from business. And it is not just a question of time. Litigation also entails stress, worry and energy, all of which divert our attention from creative pursuits. Being in a fight is upsetting. Our emotions get caught up in a lawsuit. Preparing for deposition or cross-examination has a high human cost even if, as so often happens, the case is settled before trial.

From the point of view of the parties to a lawsuit, the costs are in vain; almost every litigated case is a mistake. If we and our adversary in a given lawsuit were smart enough (or well enough advised), we could settle the case together, even before it is filed, for roughly the same amount as the final judgment. We could avoid the agony and save the legal fees. And in many cases, if we had worked side by side with the other party, we could have agreed on a creative solution that served our interests far better than any judgment a court might order.

Sometimes, to be sure, we are interested in establishing a good precedent or avoiding a bad one. Experience suggests, however, that it is hard enough just to win a case, let alone do so in a way

Reprinted with permission of the ***Harvard Business Review***.

that will establish a desirable legal precedent. And a bad precedent is more likely to be set by a judicial opinion than by a unique settlement. Moreover, one large public judgment against us is far more likely to stir up additional litigation than a half-dozen quiet settlements.

My concerns come down to this: The costs of litigation are high; too many cases are litigated; and those that are settled tend to be settled late, less than optimally and only after large amounts of time and money have been spent on depositions, document discovery, motions and other pretrial measures. Why? What are some possible reasons for unduly expensive and time-consuming trials and late settlements?

Why We Don't Settle Our Cases

Employing foresight and wisdom, we and our litigation adversaries ought to settle most of our disputes at an early stage. Why don't we? Let me advance a number of hypotheses.

Litigious Working Assumptions

American business people suffer from a lawyer's perception of what constitutes the *normal* way to deal with a dispute. Lawsuits often are filed and answered without anyone even talking with the people on the other side. If we ask your firm's advice about a dispute that might end up in court, our query goes directly to the litigation department. As much as I approve of the efforts now being made in behalf of mediation, minitrials and other forms of "alternative dispute resolution," I don't like that name. It reinforces the assumption that the normal way to deal with differences is to take them to court and that to talk with the other side about settling a case is a new and unusual alternative to what lawyers regularly do.

Other assumptions, widely held by lawyers, tend to aggravate the pressure toward litigation. If I am correct, members of the litigation bar usually operate on the premise that it is a sign of weakness to be the first party to propose settlement talks. "If we suggest settlement," the thinking goes, "they will think we must have a poor case; their expectations will go up."

I also have heard lawyers say, "We can't talk settlement until discovery is completed." Others insist that until the case is fully prepared for trial and until they know what judge is going to sit on the case, it is too early to contemplate settling. Even then, some are reluctant to favor settlement because "you just can't tell what a judge or jury will do." While such uncertainties may deter lawyers, we in business make decisions every day under conditions even more uncertain.

Another obstacle to settlement is the lawyer's rule that the most likely time to settle a case is just before trial "on the courthouse steps." With that norm in mind, lawyers tend to postpone all settlement discussion until the last minute.

You probably can provide us with an even more accurate and persuasive set of working hypotheses for why lawyers tend to prevent or postpone settlement.

Clients' Distorted Judgment

A number of factors tend to make both this corporation and your firm litigation prone. Let me first look at those that may cause us to litigate more often than is in our own best interest.

Emotions. In any dispute, a partisan becomes emotionally involved. We are likely to get angry. Our egos are on the line. We want to be vindicated. We do not want to be "taken." We do not want to be seen as backing down.

Passing the Buck. To the corporate officer involved in a dispute, a recommendation to settle may suggest that he or she has made a mistake. (In one case that I know of, the "mistake" cost more than $180 million. No corporate official wants to admit errors like that.) From the corporate officer's point of view, it looks better to refer the case to the lawyers, to outside counsel. If the case is lost, it is the fault of the lawyers or of the judge or jury. And besides, the judgment will not be entered for years, by which time the corporate officer may well be in a different job.

Not only do officers feel the pressure to pass the buck but, in a large case, the board of directors itself also feels it. If the board approved a pricing policy or an action causing environmental pollution, members may prefer to pass that issue on to the courts—even at great corporate expense—rather than settle a case from which others could infer that their judgment had been mistaken.

Conflicts of Interest. In some instances there may be a clear conflict of interest between an officer and the corporation. The corporation pays the legal fees; if vindicated in court, the officer "wins." Suppose an officer is clearly responsible for a very profitable but controversial decision that is a central issue in a major dispute headed for court. Objectively, the company may have only a 30 percent chance of winning the case. At the same time, it has an opportunity to settle on terms that are fair and will avoid a large downside risk for the corporation. From the officer's point of view, it makes little difference whether the corporation pays a substantial amount now or a much larger amount later; both are bad and reflect poorly on the officer's judgment. But because a lawsuit just might, conceivably, vindicate the officer's judgment, it may be far better for the officer to have the corporation litigate. In any event, postponing the bad day, if bad it must be, is more attractive than paying up now.

Time Is Money. Perhaps the most important disincentive, especially when large amounts are at stake and when interest rates are high, is the value of money over time. A corporate defendant may know that, eventually, it will have to pay, say, $100 million. Because most claims do not accumulate prejudgment interest, every year's postponement of the evil day saves the interest on $100 million. Settling a big case in which we are the defendant may hurt this quarter's bottom line. Generally, whatever the amount involved in either a settlement or a court decision, financial managers would prefer to put off bad news. Other things being equal, a large negative-line item will, if possible, always be put off to the next fiscal period.

Partisan Bias. Whether any of the factors I have mentioned operate on a conscious or an unconscious level, a corporate officer is likely to take an unduly optimistic view of any controversy in which he or she is involved. Simply looking at a situation as a partisan tends to distort one's judgment. A professor has tested this notion by giving students identical facts about a hypothetical company that is for sale—balance sheets, cash flow, inventory and so forth. One-half the students act as potential buyers of the company and the other half as sellers. After they have prepared for negotiation, but before negotiations have begun, the professor asks each student to write out privately his or her best estimate of the price that an impartial arbitrator would set. Of the more than 1,000 students who have engaged in this exercise, sellers routinely name a substantially higher figure than do buyers. Simply looking at the same information from a different point of view causes people to collect and emphasize the data that best support their interests.

I am sure that the longer we consider our side of a controversy, the more biased our judgment becomes. Certainly, we look at our side of a dispute more often than we do our opponent's side. It is only natural that we talk ourselves into believing even more strongly in the justice of our cause. Such corporate overconfidence may help explain why so often we urge you to pursue litigation.

LAWYERS' DISTORTED JUDGMENT

Admitting that we clients may be more prone to litigate than we should be, it seems to me that you lawyers are subject to many, if not more, of the same weaknesses.

Emotions. Certainly some trial lawyers practice litigation because they love the contest. They find pleasure in representing a client with the full zeal that the legal canons of ethics call for. They like to engage in battle and they like to win. *Their* egos, too, are on the line. For some lawyers, negotiating the settlement of a case being prepared for trial has about as much appeal as negotiating the settlement of a football game or a prizefight would have for the athletes. (For others, I am sure, a good settlement can feed the ego as much as any trial.)

Passing the Buck. You lawyers are human, too. You surely must have a tendency to avoid taking responsibility for recommending either that the large claims sought in a court battle be settled for lesser amounts or that substantial sums be paid out in settlement of a claim that you are contending is worthless. (One lawyer told me that he felt a little silly having his client accept his recommendation for a settlement in one of the aluminum cases and then seeing co-defendants, who did not settle, win their cases and get off scot-free.) If you win a case, it is a great victory for you. If you lose, you did your best; you can blame the defeat on the court or on the conduct of the corporation.

Conflicts of Interest. Even when a firm's long-term interest in providing high-quality service at minimum cost might favor settling a case, the incentives for individual lawyers may pull in another direction. You expect your young associates to turn in a large number of billable hours. Indeed, in many firms today the more billable hours young lawyers turn in, the better their chances of making partner. Rarely, I daresay, are they thanked for being cost-conscious, for limiting the amount of time they spend on a case and for going home early in the evening.

On the other hand, should those lawyers ever fail to find an obscure but relevant precedent—a needle in a haystack discovered by opposing counsel—they would run the risk of incurring serious criticism. Under these circumstances, young lawyers must feel pressure to keep the meter running.

Financial Disincentives. From the point of view of your firm as a whole, the financial incentives to litigate a case or to settle at the last moment, rather than earlier, must be enormous. Just look again at the aggregate amount of the legal fees that your litigation department has earned working on our cases. Most of that high-priced time was spent on discovery, motions, trial preparation, trials and appeals, not on negotiating settlements. You have high overhead costs and high salaries for your young lawyers, all of which you must pay before you partners can receive the large incomes that you have come to expect. A big case is to a law firm as a good milking cow is to a dairy farmer: a reliable source of steady income. I don't mean to be critical; I'm just stating facts.

Is this also true for lead trial counsel like yourself? One or two major law firms, I understand, divide annual profits equally among all partners. Most, I believe, apportion the firm's net income among the partners in ways that reflect time spent, new clients brought in and revenue generated by the cases the partners have brought in or on which they worked. For example, would your personal income, and that of some of your colleagues in the litigation department, have been lower over the past couple of years if more of our company's cases had been settled at an early date? If so, is there any chance that personal financial consequences subconsciously affect your judgment about which cases we ought to settle and which we ought to litigate?

What is true for you, of course, may also be true to an even greater extent for opposing counsel. A solo practitioner may have only one big case—one milking cow. The possibility of settlement may loom as a major disaster. Another lawyer may be on a contingent fee and have time available. The possibility of a whopping fee, no matter how remote, may be far more attractive than a quick settlement in the client's interest.

I have heard of lawyers with a contingent-fee contract preventing a settlement the client wanted. A manufacturing company offered to settle a claim for defective products by providing the next year's supply of parts free. The lawyer was not the least bit interested in receiving one-third of such parts as his fee.

Partisan Bias. At the start of a case, outside counsel perhaps are more pessimistic than optimistic. Because they try to avoid raising their client's expectations, they look at a case from the adversary's point of view. But the longer you lawyers work on one side of a case, the more likely you are to become convinced that that side ought to prevail.

Part of your effectiveness as an advocate depends on your first persuading yourself that your arguments are sound. Lawyers sometimes fail to persuade courts of their case's merits, but they rarely fail to persuade themselves. Even when they are far from certain that they will win, they tend, I believe, to overestimate the odds. A 50-50 case becomes a probable victory; a 20 percent chance of winning becomes a 50-50 case. Rather than help offset the client's bias, a lawyer's judgment may instead reinforce it.

Again, what is true for you also will be true for lawyers on the other side.

ROLE OF COUNSEL

These factors, which tend to operate against settlement and in favor of litigation, suggest that perhaps we should reexamine the role in which our current client-lawyer relationship places you. Too often, I fear, we both see your job as that of skilled advocates and guns for hire—soldiers we retain to do battle against our adversaries. As a corporate plaintiff, we see ourselves seeking justice from those who have violated our rights. As a corporate defendant, we see ourselves resisting outrageous suits stirred up by unscrupulous lawyers hoping for large contingent fees.

In either case, we see you as our knight in shining armor, ready (for a fee) to fight to the end in vindication of our cause. In the tradition of the military hero, off you go to fight the good fight, to overcome every obstacle and to persevere to the end, whether it be bitter or sweet.

But maybe we need less of a brave Sir Galahad and more of a wise Merlin—someone to cool our partisan tempers and to remind us of the corporate interest in settling cases quickly, efficiently and fairly. Maybe we have the wrong image of what we want you to do. In the end, most of our cases get settled rather than determined by the judgment of a court. If this is true, then perhaps, for starters, you should change the name of your part of the firm from the "litigation department" to the "settlement department" or the "negotiation department." Might such a change in nomenclature help us see your role in a different light?

LITTLE WORK ON SETTLEMENT

It's fair to say, I believe, that although most lawsuits get settled, your time still is largely devoted to the alternative means of resolving differences, namely litigation. Our judgment on whether to settle or litigate may suffer from the disproportionate amount of time that you spend on the litigation option. Together we spend a great deal of time trying to prove the worst case about our adversary's past conduct but little time trying to structure a future arrangement that would be to our mutual advantage.

You develop a litigation strategy but no settlement strategy. You think at length about the best questions to ask during cross-examination, but you rarely devise the best questions to ask in negotiating a settlement. You have a clear idea of the most we should ask for in damages, but you have little notion of the least we should accept in settlement. You formulate clear arguments for why, when we are the defendant, we owe nothing, but you arrive at no clear figure for the maximum amount we should be prepared to pay in settlement.

We corporate clients probably are even worse when it comes to thinking about settlement. Once we have given a case to outside counsel, we are likely to see it as "their problem."

CAN WE CHANGE OUR PRACTICE?

These diagnoses point to some remedies that we should explore.

FOSTER A NEW WORKING ASSUMPTION

Could we introduce into your way of doing business and ours the premise that it is in the interest of all parties to settle every case promptly and fairly? Litigation should be a last resort. It is better than dueling but much more expensive. As soon as you could prepare yourselves to do so, you might initiate settlement talks with the other side—not because your case is weak, but because your client has given you standing instructions to that effect.

Nor should you postpone settlement talks until you have gathered all possible evidence and removed all possible uncertainties. Even with the best of discovery, litigation always is uncertain. Gathering data may well not be worth either the cost or the time. Furthermore, uncertainty may promote settlement. Depending on the parties' aversion to risk, a modest and quick payment to resolve a dispute in which neither side has invested much may be an ideal outcome for both. Like an insurance premium, it may be a small price to pay to avoid uncertainty. And when we are the plaintiff, particularly when we are business people whose time probably is best spent in other ways, a bird in the hand may be worth quite a few in the bush.

Presumably, if we clients make our wishes clear, you lawyers can pursue our interests in settlement with all the zeal that you now devote to litigation. What general guidance could we propose, what working assumptions might be most useful, to switch outside counsel's pattern of behavior away from litigation and toward the prompt settlement of disputes?

AN ADVOCATE FOR SETTLEMENT?

To improve the quality of judicial decisions, you lawyers rely on the adversary process. You have convinced yourselves—and most of us—that it is difficult for a judge to decide wisely without hearing both sides. No lawyer is expected to argue the case for both sides. The chance of the judge's reaching a sound decision is enhanced by having different people present the cases for different courses of action.

Because we end up litigating more often than we should, I fear that as a client I am making poor decisions. Perhaps I, like a judge, would benefit from the adversary process. Perhaps we, as a corporation, would reach wiser decisions if we had one lawyer develop the case for litigation and a different lawyer press on us the case for settlement. Wouldn't that be a logical application of the adversary process to which you are so deeply committed?

There seems no feasible way to avoid emotional involvement, partisan bias and the natural desire to pass the buck. If we have to live with these risks, shouldn't we create a countervailing force that will give us the opposing case clearly and persuasively? If a judge needs advocates to produce a good decision, perhaps we, too, would benefit from having an advocate for settlement to oppose those counsel who advise us to litigate.

OVERCOMING THE FINANCIAL DISINCENTIVE

I would welcome your suggestions for how we might overcome the financial disincentive to settle.

I know of at least one law firm that will quote a fixed fee for handling a case all the way through litigation or until a settlement satisfactory to the client has been produced. If the law firm is of high quality and has a wide base of experience on which to quote the fixed fee, I can see great advantages in this approach. The law firm has an incentive to use its time efficiently and, if possible, to produce a quick settlement satisfactory to the client. (To be sure, because the firm has little incentive to obtain a settlement better than the minimum the client is willing to accept, a client in such a situation has to be on guard.)

Some corporate clients, I realize, do fix a monthly or annual ceiling with a law firm. Although this practice avoids the worst aspects of runaway costs, it does not change the incentives.

More regular means of keeping expenditures under control also might be useful. We should be able to devise a better method than putting a case out for competitive bids. Perhaps we should explore the possibility of having your firm make fairly detailed estimates of monthly costs, followed by monthly reports of actual expenditures. Some corporate clients are now asking their law firms for detailed figures on overhead to satisfy themselves that the high hourly rates they pay in fact go to reward talent, not to reimburse the firm for lavish expenditures.

What techniques does your firm use to keep your lawyers cost-conscious? Is there some way that you could divide profits that would reward lawyers not for bringing in bigger fees but for more accurately estimating the costs and the eventual outcome of each case?

How about awarding a contingent bonus for any lawyer in the office who is able to settle a case to the client's satisfaction against the recommendation of the litigation department? (Such a bonus could come from funds that otherwise would be divided among partners in the litigation department.) Alternatively, maybe we should pay your firm some kind of contingent fee for developing a settlement proposal and convincing both sides that the settlement is preferable to litigation.

Can you think of some way to reduce the pressure on associates in your firm to maximize the billable hours they devote to a big case? It is easier to compare the number of hours that two associates have worked in a year than to compare the quality of their work on different cases for different partners. There must be a risk—in other firms if not in yours—that you will reward associates for spending more time rather than less in accomplishing a given task. I am sure you can tell your best young lawyers from your worst, but on the margin, how do you avoid rewarding inefficiency?

We may want to get some expert consultant in to advise us on how we might best line up the personal financial incentives with the interests the lawyers' work is intended to serve. Perhaps we should look more seriously at other incentives, such as prestige or publicity for settling cases, extra vacation time, a bigger office, more assistants or whatever. Your thinking about this will, I am sure, be helpful.

A TWO-TRACK APPROACH

It probably is impossible—as well as undesirable—for lawyers to abandon the role of knight in shining armor. But how about creating a second and parallel role for lawyers: the problem solver, the mediator, the conciliator? In our effort to reap the benefits of the adversary process, I propose that for every major case we have one lawyer pursue litigation and another (who might well be a member of your litigation department) explore and develop, at the earliest possible date, the best settlement option obtainable. This "advocate for settlement" would be expected to impress upon us the reasons for accepting a settlement (or making an offer) and would provide a counterweight to the litigator's partisan bias by pointing out weaknesses in our litigation position.

Just as lawyers are capable of arguing either side of a given case, obviously many are fully capable of litigating a case and negotiating a settlement of it. But this does not mean that they should try to do both at the same time. The psychological orientation of a general engaged in battle is quite different from that of a diplomat engaged in peace negotiations. While a soldier should have little concern for suffering on the other side, a negotiator should emphatically appreciate an adversary's interests. The soldier-lawyer looks back at the causes of the dispute and seeks to demonstrate and vindicate the wrongs committed; the diplomat-lawyer looks forward to the opportunities for reconciling differences.

You may respond to this suggestion by pointing out that having two teams work on the same case would tend to increase rather than reduce legal fees. For the time being at least, I am prepared to take that gamble. My specialist in settlement might well be one of those doing research on the case and helping others prepare it for litigation. I do not propose erecting a Chinese wall between litigators and settlers. But I do think we would be well served if your firm had specialists in negotiation and settlement—perhaps people with experience as mediators and business negotiators—who were devoting their energies to trying to settle our disputes quickly, wisely and amicably.

This two-track approach should benefit both the litigator and the settler. The litigator would be under no pressure to pull his punches for fear that an unduly adversarial approach might damage the chances of settlement. And the harder the litigator pursued that option, the more it would strengthen the hand of the lawyer working toward settlement. It would be a classic Mutt-and-Jeff—good cop, bad cop—approach, but with no deception of any kind.

Of course, both lawyers would not have to be in the same firm. I have thought that if we retain your firm to handle litigation, we might develop within the office of our in-house counsel some experts in settlement.

Another alternative, which some companies have adopted and which I would like to consider, would be to hire an outside expert in settlement to work in parallel with your firm's work on the litigation front. There are negotiation experts who might be hired either to mediate (if the other side were interested) or simply to generate a settlement of interest to both sides. Such an expert might have full authority to negotiate on the understanding that no settlement would be binding until the corporation had approved. Before giving such approval we would, of course, expect to hear from litigation counsel.

AN ORGANIZED SETTLEMENT PROGRAM

Whether or not we develop or bring in a settlement specialist, your firm probably could do more on a regular basis to reduce the risk of our litigating cases when it would be in our interest to settle them. As a basis for our discussion of specific actions we might ask you to undertake, let me throw out the following ideas:

Develop a Settlement Strategy. Once we have someone in charge of settlement, that person should carefully identify our interests, assess our opponent's interests and make an informed guess of the other side's currently perceived choice. What do they think that we are asking them to do? How do they perceive the consequences of their saying yes and of their saying no to what they believe we are asking them to do? (Presumably, they currently are saying no.) How would a choice have to look for them to say yes? How might we change their choice so that a settlement option we would accept also might look acceptable to them?

Such a strategy might well involve lowering the adversary's expectations of the outcome of litigation. The strategy also might involve putting a new proposal on the table, one that meets the adversary's most important interests and lets them look victorious or at least allows them to avoid feeling taken. A settlement strategy should include a program and schedule that clearly indicate who is going to do what.

Estimate the Value of Litigating. The more I think about it, the more inexcusable it is that we have not asked you to generate and keep current your firm's best dollar estimate of the outcome of litigation. Of course, it is impossible to be precise, and any figure you might provide would have a fair degree of uncertainty. But you can let us know how wide the range of uncertainty is and how differently various lawyers working on the case estimate the chances of success. I recognize that not all cases are money cases, but many are. All involve financial considerations.

Let me be specific. For every potential money-judgment case of ours that you are handling, I would like to know the maximum dollar figure you believe we should be willing to pay to settle the case or the least we should be willing to accept in settlement. I am not asking your lawyers to make the business judgment that we should make. Rather, I am asking you to guess as best you can who will win how much and how probable the different outcomes are, and to let me know how uncertain you are about those outcomes.

I would like to receive this figure in writing quarterly (to reflect any changes in assessment) for every case in litigation. We are paying a small fortune for you to pursue litigation. Is there any reason why we should not ask for your best judgment concerning the likely outcomes of our cases?

I also would like you to include in such reports an estimate of legal fees and disbursements for pursuing the case through the various stages of litigation, as well as an estimate of how long those various stages are likely to take. These estimates would not be your routine assurance that your statements are based on standard hourly charges and that it is impossible to predict how many hours will be required. Rather, they would include budget figures by months over the course of the expected litigation. My well-founded belief is that although anticipating costs is difficult, you will get steadily better at it—but only if you make budgets and try to live within them.

In making business decisions under conditions of uncertainty, we often use a decision-tree analysis. We estimate when critical events may happen and the odds of one outcome or another happening at that time. We then continue along each branch, repeating the process as we expect different contingencies to occur. I am sure that you do this informally as you consider whether we have a "good" or "excellent" chance of success and what the magnitude of potential judgments might be. The quality of your estimates might improve if you and your colleagues (at first independently) went through the anticipated future of one of our cases assuming that at no point would it be settled.

Let me suggest how that might be done. The first critical point might be when the court considered motions for summary judgment. You would make your best present guess of the chances of the motion's being granted for the plaintiff (say, 10 percent), granted for the defendant (say, 30 percent) or denied for both (in this case, 60 percent). Each possibility then would be pursued. If the plaintiff obtained summary judgment, would the defendant appeal? If so, how long before a decision would be reached? What do we think would be the chances for affirmation or reversal?

Continue similarly for the other two branches of our tree. If the judge denied both motions for summary judgment, how long would it be before we went to trial? What are some realistic outcomes of such a trial? Perhaps there would be a 10 percent chance that the plaintiff would "win big" (maybe $2 million); a 20 percent chance that the plaintiff might win a judgment of about $80,000; and a 70 percent chance that he would lose. We then can go on to another stage, considering the possibility of appeals and the probable outcome of such appeals.

As you estimate the future course of the litigation, you might concurrently estimate what the legal fees and costs would be to go through the different stages. With a little arithmetic (including discounting to find the present value of any future judgments) you could produce the figures that represent the present value of the case for the plaintiff and for the defendant. There is no magic. The calculation simply says that if these assumptions are right, then from a financial point of view, the plaintiff might be well be advised to accept X dollars instead of litigating and that the defendants might be better off paying Y dollars now rather than taking their chances on litigation.

By going through such a process we're all required to think clearly. By having several lawyers make separate estimates, we'd get both a better idea of the range of uncertainty and, presumably, a better final estimate of the value of the case. Such a calculation might take a couple of hours of each lawyer's time. One lawyer could interview the others working on a case, prepare the different decision trees and then have the lawyers spend an hour or so together discussing their differences and producing a firm estimate.

Can you think of a better way to help us get a handle on just how much we should be willing to pay or accept in settlement?

Develop a Specific Settlement Option. Once we have done our homework and have talked with the other side, we should be ready to develop a settlement proposal. Of course, there would be tactical questions of when and how to present the proposal to the other side, but at all times we ourselves should know the realistic terms on which we would be prepared to settle the case. To say "it is too early" is no answer. No matter how early it is, once we have had a chance to prepare, there always are some terms on which we should be willing to settle.

Keep a Settlement Log. We should keep a running log of the settlement process, including your quarterly advice to us on the value of the case, offers made and received, a summary of discussions with the other side, considerations given to formulating and revising settlement offers and so forth.

An Autopsy of All Cases. One big step in the advancement of medicine was the autopsy. Until then, doctors buried their mistakes. I would suggest that if we are to become better at deciding when to litigate and when to settle, and on what terms, we need to learn from experience. We do not know how good we are at estimating the value of a case in litigation and we are unlikely to get better unless we note when we did well and when we did poorly.

I suggest that following the settlement of any case and following final judgment of any case not settled, we review the history of our settlement efforts to see what we did well and what we might have handled better. The purpose, of course, would not be to assign blame but to learn for the future.

Well, this letter should give us plenty to talk about. After you and a few of your partners have had a chance to read it and think about it, please give me a ring and let's set a time for a brainstorming session, first to generate ideas and then to evaluate them.

Perhaps there are other things we could do to improve the working relationship between our two institutions. A couple of law firms I know have invited officers of some of their corporate clients to participate in training sessions on negotiation and settlement being held for lawyers in the firm. The joint exploration of expectations and assumptions proved illuminating. Joint simulation exercises helped to generate a common language for ongoing dialogue and gave each a better and very real understanding of the other's concerns.

Some of us here have discussed the idea of inviting one or two lawyers from your firm to spend six months or a year working here at the corporation and perhaps having a lawyer from our general counsel's office spend six months or so working within your firm. Maybe we should meet for lunch regularly a few times a year, not to discuss any particular case but to consider such ideas as well as other things we might do that would improve our effectiveness in working together.

If for some reason you are not interested in talking about such things, please do let me know—and we can talk about that.

As ever,
Roger Fisher

CHAPTER 10

Jeffrey L. Tolman, *of Roof, Tolman and Kirk, practices in the small but scenic town of Poulsbo, Washington. He approaches law practice innovatively and with zest and humor. This chapter includes three of his offerings. The first, "Learning from How Others Bill," was prepared for the Task Force. The second, "Billing by the Hour Should Be Banned," is reprinted from* The Washington State Bar News, *July 1987. We couldn't resist the third, a proposed tear-off billing sheet drafted, as Tolman says "half in jest," which lists areas in which his firm practices, but reflects client attitudes that might affect a fee. "The particular categories are less-than serious, the concept is not."*

Learning from How Others Bill

by Jeffrey L. Tolman

The consensus among my partners and me is that sending out a fair and reasonable bill is the second most difficult aspect of practicing law. (Collecting the bill is first.) There seem to be six common billing methods in the law:

1. **Billing by the hour.** An hourly rate is set and all work on the file is billed on a tenth-of-an-hour basis, including telephone calls, correspondence, reviewing materials and consultations with clients. This is the most common billing method among lawyers.
2. **Flat rate.** A fee is agreed on between the attorney and the client, no matter how much or how little time the lawyer spends on the case.
3. **Equity.** This method encompasses billing at the end of the matter, based on the criteria set forth in the Code of Professional Responsibility. Such factors can include the time and labor required; the novelty and difficulty of the questions involved; the skill requisite to perform properly the legal service; the likelihood that the acceptance of the particular employment will preclude any other employment by the lawyer; the fee customarily charged in the locality for similar legal services; the amount involved and the result obtained; the time limitations imposed by the client or by the circumstances; the nature and length of the professional relationship with the client; the experience, reputation and ability of the lawyer or lawyers performing the services; and whether the fee is fixed or contingent. The goal of this holistic approach to billing is to have an equally satisfied client and attorney at the end of the matter.
4. **Cost-plus billing.** This method includes computing a fee based on the lawyer's overhead plus a reasonable profit. Harris Morgan, one of the gurus of legal economics, for years has urged attorneys to charge three times their cost of each item in the office. Harris' method would fall under this "cost-plus" billing method.
5. **Punitive billing.** Punitive billing simply is a bill in an amount that punishes a client who has fallen into the same legal problem after being previously advised on how to avoid such pitfalls. This method is not based on time or equity, but rather is a method to punish the client for his inability to follow instructions and keep himself out of his present bind.
6. **The de Sade billing method.** Put simply, this method involves billing a client until he or she screams. Although not a commonly accepted billing method, this is one that every lawyer has seen our less-reputable colleagues use from time to time.

Every month my partners and I agonize over the bills to be sent out, weighing the time spent on the file, the result obtained and other applicable factors. Over time we have realized that other professions do not agonize as lawyers do over bills. They simply send a bill and expect to be paid. Perhaps, I have always theorized, our self-inflicted pain is the result of a less-than-perfect billing method.

So what can we learn about billing from other businesses? A lot, I think.

Billing by Event

From physicians, for example, we can learn the advantages of billing by event. Rather than computing

---

Reprinted with permission from the *Washington State Bar News*.

how many tenths of an hour we spent consulting with a client, we easily could divide our office time into categories like physicians do: Brief, Intermediate, Extensive and (for those folks whose narratives almost never end) Exhaustive. We then could bill per category instead of by time. Though I have no concrete proof, I suspect that physicians discovered long ago that billing by event is more palatable to patients (and hid the hourly rate being charged a great deal better) than per-hour billing.

Time Method

From body shops and car repair shops we could establish the estimated time for particular charges—not a fee schedule as has been abolished by the Supreme Court decision, but rather, an estimate of time that would be charged for particular acts such as interrogatories. It is reassuring to me as a customer when I take my car in to have it tuned, the brake drums turned and my windshield replaced, that my repairman can look in a book and let me know what the charges are likely to be, based on the time the book says the activity should take. Both of us win. I know I won't have to pay extra for an extraordinarily slow mechanic. The mechanic realizes that if he is more efficient than the book anticipates, he will make some extra money. One of the most common complaints clients have about lawyers is that the time spent on legal work seems to mount up incredibly fast. It would be very helpful if at the beginning of a civil matter a lawyer could pull out a book that would show the estimated time for specific acts and tell his client:

> **"Mrs. Smith. In this dissolution action I anticipate drafting the following pleadings:**
> **Summons, Petition for Dissolution of Marriage, Motion and Affidavit for Temporary Restraining Order and Order to Show, Order to Show Cause, Temporary Agreed Order or Order to Show Cause, Interrogatories, Findings of Fact and Conclusions of Law, Settlement Agreement and Decree of Dissolution of Marriage. Our Book-of-Anticipated-Time indicates that these tasks should take me X amount of hours. In addition, I more likely than not will take the defendant's testimony by deposition. That will be based on the actual amount of time that the deposition takes. Telephone calls and correspondence will be on an hourly rate, billed at a minimum of .2 of an hour per item. Court hearings and preparation will be based on the actual amount of time, plus, for many court hearings, preparation time of approximately one to three hours."**

This would give the client an idea of what time will be expended on the items that probably will occur in the matter and sets the guidelines for billing other items that may come up. From my experience, mechanics and body shops may receive complaints about the quality of the work done, but they seldom receive complaints about the time spent on the work. Lawyers are just the opposite. The most common complaint is not the quality of the work done, but, rather, the time spent on the work. Were we to adopt the time method used by body shops and repair shops, we could bill effectively and at the same time cut down on client complaints.

Tear-Off Billing

Finally, we could learn another valuable lesson from physicians that would save a great deal of time: the tear-off billing statement.

The other day I saw my physician for a minor ailment. At the end of the examination he pulled out a billing sheet, checked two boxes and handed the document to me. I took my bill to his receptionist, who filled in the charges for each of the checked boxes and told me how much I owed. The billing process was quick, easy and efficient. No filling out time sheets, then having them fed into a computer to be printed, revised, re-printed and sent out, like we do in our office.

> **"Why don't we do that?" I asked my partners at our next office meeting.**
>
> **"Because our practice has too many variables: office consultations, research, contacts with clients, court appearances. It would be impossible to put on paper our services and all of the potential problem-causers involved in a case," one of my partners responded.**
>
> **"Baloney," I retorted. And I mean that. A tear-off billing statement could be drafted to cover most of the areas of practice for particular firms and fees for each line-item easily could be set. Doctors have been doing it for years. If nothing else, a tear-off bill would be simpler and processing the bill would be less costly. Obviously, tear-off billing is quicker than most law-office billing systems. Most importantly, it is efficient. Maybe that's why attorneys haven't put it to use yet.**

Billing is one of the most complicated parts of being an attorney and business person. By billing by the item and using a checklist that includes many variables, as physicians do, we can make reasonable money while at the same time cutting down some areas of common client complaints. By using a book to give a client an idea about the acts anticipated in their litigation and the best estimate of the time each act will take, we provide the client with some estimate of the legal fees that he or she can anticipate. It is certainly not a perfect system, but it's better than the system used by most attorneys today: the straight per-hour system. Almost anything is.

Billing by the Hour Should Be Banned

by Jeffrey L. Tolman

The public believes that attorneys take simple situations and complicate them beyond recognition. In one area, at least, lawyers have done the reverse. They have taken a complex process—billing—and simplified it to the point where only one factor—time—is considered.

Billing solely by the hour is a symptom of our failing and falling professionalism. Instead of negotiating an agreeable fee with our clients, as true professionals would, we attorneys have become servants to time.

The inherent problems in billing by the hour make the practice unfair and undesirable.

1. Billing by the hour puts the client's and the attorney's interests in direct conflict. The client wants his or her matter resolved as quickly, smoothly and as inexpensively as possible. The lawyer, on the other hand, gets paid more the longer the matter carries on.

2. No relationship exists between the task and the bill for that task. A telephone call or letter that produces no effect is nonetheless billed out at the amount of time it took or at a minimum charge (often .2 of an hour). For unproductive tasks, the client receives no benefit; the attorney does.

3. The client has no input into how the attorney's time is spent on the file. Certainly, no client would encourage his or her attorney to spend time "reviewing the file," for example. Each of us know attorneys who bill a file to death. Allowing the person who benefits from dotting the i's and crossing the t's to bill at will, regardless of the impact, is like throwing Br'er Rabbit into the briar patch.

Attorneys may feel that it is inappropriate for me to question the ethics (or time records) of my fellow professionals. Perhaps a few questions will clarify my concern and bring this issue home for more of us.

Would you be agitated if you received a bill from your physician for $40 for reviewing your records?

Would you without complaining pay $15 per letter for your physician to correspond with all of your former health-care providers to ensure that your physician has your complete health information?

How would you feel about paying for all the time it took the physician to review these records to make sure that he or she was up to date on your health history?

Most attorneys would be furious, I think.

A Modest Proposal

What do I propose? Washington attorneys are governed by the eight criteria of RPC 1.5 in setting a fee. The criteria to be considered are:

1. The time and labor required, the novelty and difficulty of the questions involved and the skill requisite to perform the legal service properly;

2. The likelihood, as apparent to the client, that the acceptance of the particular employment will preclude other employment by the lawyer;

Reprinted with permission from the ***Washington Star Bar News***.

3. The fee customarily charged in the locality for similar legal services;

4. The amount involved and the result obtained;

5. The time limitations imposed by the client or by the circumstances;

6. The nature and length of the professional relationship with the client;

7. The experience, reputation and ability of the lawyer or lawyers performing the services; and

8. Whether the fee is fixed or contingent.

In only one criterion is "time" mentioned. Yet the criteria, when taken together, describe and prescribe a fee that, based on all of the facts, is fair to both the client and attorney.

BILLING PROFESSIONALISM

To have a fair fee should be the basic goal of billing, whether the final bill reflects a fee of $10 per hour or $250 per hour. Fairness, although a simple concept, is diluted by the obsession by lawyers and judges with "time spent" and "the hourly rate." It is simple to bill by the hour and it certainly makes sense, at first blush. The simplicity of the process does not compensate for its inherent inequities, though.

Professionals should be willing to negotiate fees with clients based on the criteria of RPC 1.5. Our professional stature is eroded by the inherent unfairness of billing on time alone and this unfairness is not unnoticed by the public. Clients and attorneys should look at *all* the criteria of RPC 1.5 before setting a fee, not just at the time expended. Our profession will gain credibility and, to some extent, get back in the good graces of the public if we look at fairness first and time expended later.

Billing solely by the hour should be banned.

10 Jeffrey L. Tolman

TEAR-OFF BILLING SHEET—BY JEFFREY L. TOLMAN

Firm Name __________
Address __________
Phone number __________

1 - Attorney #1
2 - Attorney #2
3 - Attorney #3
4 - Attorney #4
5 - Paralegal #1

- -

Client Information:
Date of Service
Service Provider # __________
Name __________
Address __________
Phone (w) __________ (h) __________
SSN __________
Employer __________
Fee Agreement __________
Terms of Payment __________
Present Balance

DOMESTIC RELATIONS	
Dissolution	
Mental Cruelty	
Physical Abuse	
Adultery	
Bestiality	
Other Perversion	
Hates Spouse	
Hates Kids	
Hates Life	
Lots of $ to pay attys.	
No $ to pay attys.	
Wants to fight about everything	
Will follow advice	
Won't follow advice	
Legal separation	
Premarital agreement	

PROBATE	
Testate	
Intestate	
CPA Settlement	
706 Filing	
Fighting heirs	
Guardianship	

ESTATE PLANNING	
Simple Will	
Simple Client	
Trust Will	
Non-Trusting Client	
Complex Will	
Complex Client	
Community property agreement	
Power of Attorney	
Directive to Physician	
Trust Agreement	

REAL ESTATE	
Review documents	
Draft documents	
Explain documents	
Re-explain documents	
Litigate documents	
Try to understand documents	
View property	
Try to get property as attorney's fee	

CIVIL LITIGATION	
Plaintiff	
Defendant	
Self	
Friend	
Law Partner	
Other:	

PRO BONO

CRIMINAL DEFENSE	
Misdemeanor	
Felony	
Traffic	
Juvenile	
Real stupid act	
A person who has preached that defendants should have no rights	

INJURY/DEATH	
Plaintiff	
Defense	
Minor injuries	
Moderate injuries	
Permanent injuries	
Death	
Probable malingerer	
Convincing witness	
Absolutely incredible	

BANKRUPTCY	
Debtor	
Creditor	
Self	
Law partner	

SURCHARGES	
Unbearable Whiner	
Nitpicker	
Says "it's the principle"	
Calls continually	
Has an attorney-relative	
Has an atttorney-friend	
Wanted to be an attorney	
Knows bar assn's #	
Achieved great result	
Other:	

OFFICE VISIT		OUT-OF -OFFICE	
Minimum		Call at home	
Brief		Talking about the case with spouse	
Limited		Talking about the case with kids	
Intermediate		Talking about the case with strangers	
Extended		Thinking about the case at home	
Unbearable		Dreaming about the case	
Never-ending		Worrying about being sued for malpractice	

PLEADINGS			
Notice of Appearance		Summons	
Answer		Complaint/petition	
Counter-claim		Motion	
Affirmative defenses		Final documents	
Interrogatories		Brief	
Temporary orders		Other:	

COURT APPEARANCES			
Arraignment		Bench trial	
Chamber conference		Jury trial	
Pre-trial conference		Arbitration	
Settlement conference		Coffee with court staff	
Motion		Discuss case with other attorney	
Show-cause hearing		File/record documents	
Finalize dissolution		Sentencing	
Ex parte hearing		Making a ridiculous argument at client's insistence	
Appeal			
Change of plea		Other:	

OTHER SERVICES			
Correspondence		Review documents	
Telephone call to client		Draft documents	
Telephone call to opposing counsel		Lunch with opposing counsel	
Telephone call to court		Having a beer with opposing counsel	
Telephone call to others:		Thinking about the case	
Research		Other:	

Total Amount Due: $

Comments:

CHAPTER 11

In this reprint from the March/April 1985 issue of Legal Economics, *the author emphasizes three major criteria that should be used in setting legal fees: Responsibility, Expertise, Productivity—("The REP factor"), arguing that to value a lawyer's services based primarily on hours spent ignores the true worth of those services and rewards incompetence. In today's environment where lawyer malpractice claims and high errors and omissions insurance premiums add to the profit squeeze, responsibility, accountability and prospective liability should be recognized as important factors in setting fees.* Reed *leaves unanswered how the REP factor can be quantified in setting fees.*

Responsibility, Expertise, Productivity: The True Measure of Value of a Lawyer's Services

by Richard C. Reed

To value a lawyer's services to a client based primarily on hours spent ignores the true worth of the lawyer's services and rewards incompetence. It is unfair to both client and lawyer to do so.

To value a lawyer's services to his or her firm primarily based on production or the total of hours spent likewise fails to recognize properly what should be the criteria for true value to the firm for the lawyer's contribution.

The measure of a lawyer's value, both to the client and to the firm, should include three key ingredients: (1) Responsibility, (2) Expertise and (3) Productivity, all of which should be weighted equally and used both while setting fees to be charged clients and in awarding compensation by the firm to the lawyer.

AS TO CLIENTS . . .

RESPONSIBILITY

The first of the ultimate criteria, is the state or quality of being responsible. It carries with it the duty of accountability and connotes reliability and faithfulness.

In acting for the client, the attorney accepts the obligation to act solely in the best interests of the client and to be accountable in all respects to the client for actions taken or advice given. In choosing a lawyer, the client selects that person who will be answerable for the consequences of duties assumed. Therefore, in the client-lawyer relationship, there is the inherent obligation of the lawyer to be able to respond or answer to the client, intellectually, legally, financially and morally-ethically. The client places his trust; the lawyer must be trustworthy. The greater the trust or responsibility placed by the client, the higher the degree of accountability, answerability or liability of the lawyer.

As compensation to the lawyer for the agreement of the lawyer to be responsible, the client agrees to pay a fee. The greater the responsibility (or accountability), the higher the fee that should be charged. The lawyer who forecloses a note and deed of trust for $10,000 may perform essentially the same acts as the lawyer who forecloses a note and deed of trust for $10 million, but the degree of responsibility for doing the job competently in these two examples differs vastly, the higher responsibility justifying a greater fee.

Matters undertaken for a client differ also in degree of complexity, predictability of result, and effect on the client in terms of exposure to loss. Each of these elements relates also to the quantum of responsibility that the lawyer assumes. Not only does the amount of responsibility assumed differ from case-to-case or from client-to-client, but also there are varying needs for expertise on the part of the lawyer.

EXPERTISE

Classically, an "expert" is "one who has been taught by use, practice or experience, a person who is

Reprinted with permission from ***Legal Economics***. ABA.

clever, skillful, adept, adroit and proficient." To be adept is to be masterly proficient. To be proficient is to be well-advanced in a branch of learning or knowledge. Not all lawyers are born with or possess the same levels of expertise. Nor is it necessary for lawyers to have the same degree of expertise, for some client matters can be handled with a lower acceptable range of expertise by those who are the less expert. Impliedly, in the client-lawyer relationship is the obligation of the lawyer to accept employment only in those matters where the lawyer possesses that level of expertise necessary for proper representation. As in any endeavor where the personal skills of another are purchased by the payment of money, truly outstanding or unique skills or expertise should command the highest price and be of the greatest value.

This is true whether we speak of a basketball player, a brain surgeon, an actor, a corporate manager, an artist or a lawyer. Mediocre talents are entitled to average compensation, but the truly expert can and should command the highest fees.

In lawyering, expertise relates essentially to the possession of a high level of substantive knowledge in that area of the law in which the lawyer practices and in which the client requests services. Expertise may be broad or very narrow or specialized. Possession of expertise by a lawyer ideally should be paired up exactly with the needs of the client in a specific engagement.

The world's most expert litigator may commit legal malpractice if he or she undertakes to draw a will; the most renowned tax lawyer may fail mightily in products liability litigation.

This imposes the need for the prospective client to seek out expertise in the area in which his or her problem lies, and the concomitant obligation for the lawyer to accept employment only in his field of expertise and at the appropriate level of expertise.

As stated earlier, in the legal profession expertise involves substantive competence, the possession of that measure of knowledge or skill required to fulfill the needs of the client in any specific representation.

Linked with responsibility, expertise suggests the undertaking by the lawyer to act faithfully for a client in an area of law in which the lawyer has the proper level of legal proficiency.

PRODUCTIVITY

The third measure for value of a lawyer's services, linked to responsibility and expertise, is *productivity*. To be productive, from the client's viewpoint, the lawyer must possess those traits and abilities that produce or furnish favorable results, profits or benefits to the client.

While the facts of a given matter may preclude favorable results in some cases, the client desires and is entitled to expect from the lawyer prompt, considerate, skillful and caring efforts on the part of a lawyer in furthering the client's cause, or in minimizing the adverse effects upon the client. Lawyers are not required to guarantee results, but lawyers should guarantee the appropriate level of effort and attempt to bring about a favorable outcome.

Productivity involves the performance competence of the lawyer by the delivery of benefits to the client. Initially, the lawyer in entering into the employment agreement with a client agrees to be responsible to the client and agrees to possess the required level of expertise or substantive knowledge. Superimposed on these two undertakings is the third essential element for the setting of fees: the ability of the lawyer to perform or produce, to translate knowledge, expertise and skill into a product that meets the ultimate needs of the client. The process of transforming the acceptance of a trust (responsibility) and a level of performance of a professional skill (expertise) into a beneficial performance is what productivity is all about. "Productivity" implies effort, timely performance, efficiency, communication, cost effectiveness, concern for the client, and in the ultimate analysis an end product or result that is of value to the client.

The fee that a client pays should fairly reflect all three, *Responsibility, Expertise* and *Productivity*.

AS TO COMPENSATION OF THE LAWYER

The ways in which law firms compensate the lawyers of the firm are diverse. Many of the systems employed are based on seniority, fees produced, clients originated or controlled, profitability and chargeable hours billed, with heavy emphasis on the latter. But in thinking through what should be the basis for compensation decisions, a strong case can be made that the same three criteria, *Responsibility, Expertise* and *Productivity*, should be utilized. In considering the value of an individual lawyer to the firm and in determining how a lawyer should be compensated, there are subattributes of these three dominant elements.

RESPONSIBILITY

In varying degrees, lawyers within the firm display responsibility in the sense of accountability, reliability and faithfulness. The most valuable lawyers display responsibility in the following ways:

1. *Responsibility* to originate and maintain client relationships;

2. *Responsibility* to the firm in contributing to management and to the ultimate entrepreneurial and professional success of the firm;

3. *Accountability* to the clients of the firm and to the firm itself with an unwavering high level of dependability;

4. *Reliability* in the consistent high-level professional performance of assigned duties; and

5. *Faithfulness* by a conscientious concern for the firm and its constituent members and the clients on whom the existence of the firm depends, overriding on occasion personal self-interest.

EXPERTISE

The attainment of knowledge and professional skills and the ability to translate these qualities into a product that is of benefit to clients is the heart of the practice of law. Again, there are subattributes on which distinctions should be made in determining compensation:

1. *Intellectual capacity*, the sheer ability to excel in problem solving and to perceive a course of action that permits a favorable outcome;

2. *Knowledge*, the accumulation of relevant information through formalized education; research; experience—including the ability to find an answer by skillful use of information sources, particularly in areas of practice that are in high demand and which are not uniformly possessed by other members of the profession—with particular emphasis on the uniqueness of the possessed knowledge;

3. *Communication skills*, both oral and written, which articulate possessed knowledge and the products of intellectual capacity;

4. *Managerial skills*, evidenced by the adroit handling of client matters, internal operation of the firm, and the effective organization and motivation of people who are working together in the performance of common tasks; and

5. *Training skills*, the ability to impart knowledge and to teach others in the requisite professional skills needed for the ongoing success of the firm entity.

PRODUCTIVITY

The ultimate exercise of responsibility and the maximization of expertise must be translated into an end product that is useful to the client. Definitionwise, productivity is that level of competence in performance that combines all of the essentials of law practice. A catalog of subattributes includes:

1. *Effort*, the input of genius plus the sustained hours of productive time necessary to meet goals of both clients and firm. More than hours worked or energies expended, effort connotes that effective and efficient use of time spent to accomplish a favorable result.

2. *Timely performance*, the effective culmination of effort within the preestablished or required time limitations. It is more than an avoidance of procrastination and implies a planned utilization and scheduling of effort to meet deadlines, whether self-imposed, required by clients or required by court or statutory time limitations.

3. *Delegation*, the functional approach to the accomplishment of a task whereby the subparts of a given task are performed by the most competent yet most cost-effective level of skill to the end that each performer acts at an acceptable level of competence and at the lowest cost to the client or to the firm. Delegation is accomplished through the adept use of systems, technology and people.

4. *Economic benefit*, accrued from the selection of areas of practice that are most highly in demand and that most effectively utilize sought-after professional knowledge and skills. It is axiomatic that some fields of practice, some specialties and some types of clients lead to a higher level of remuneration or profitability than others. If the practice of law has as one of its objectives to make a profit, the practitioner who by selectivity or skill engages in a highly demanded, lucrative field of practice benefits the firm economically to a greater degree. That individual lawyer should be compensated commensurately.

5. *Delivery skills*, the composite of all the requisite personal and professional skills needed to organize the total practice to meet the needs of the client in a timely, cost-efficient, profitable manner. This subattribute is more than the sum total of the subattributes of responsibility, expertise and productivity previously enumerated. It is the ability to plan, organize, supervise and perform all professional tasks necessary to benefit both clients and the firm.

THE REP FACTOR

The criteria of *Responsibility, Expertise* and *Productivity* in combination reflect ultimate values that establish worth to the client and to the firm—the REP factor. In the context of setting fees, the responsible and reliable use of expert and skilled knowledge to furnish results, profits and benefits lies at the heart of professional practice. Without any one of these three qualities, the client has justification for feeling short-changed.

The REP factor encompasses most of the criteria for compensation now found in formula and nonformula systems of compensation, but changes the emphasis by recognizing qualities in greater measure that reflect true value to the firm.

Under the general category of *responsibility*, with subattributes of client relationships, contribution to management, accountability or reliability, high-level performance and faithfulness, are included traditional criteria such as origination and maintenance of clients; internal management and entrepreneurial success; consistent performance; seniority; stability and dependability; competence and reliability; team effort; statesmanship and interpersonal relationships.

Recognition of *expertise* as a primary criterion encompasses substantive skills and knowledge; the ability to communicate verbally and in written form; efficiency in practice; and the ability to impart knowledge and skills in training others.

Productivity includes hours worked but emphasizes quality hours more than quantity. Also encompassed is the notion of punctuality, efficiency through delegation, profitability (which would include type of work as well as collection of accounts receivable), and finally, but most importantly, excellence in delivery skills, which is the ability to produce a product that is useful to the client—that is, competence in performance.

Charging on an hourly basis and compensating the lawyer primarily on chargeable hours billed produce inequities that can be avoided by use of the REP factor. The increased utilization of technology, systems and paralegal talents makes time spent an unreliable index of value. Ten hours of manual briefing may be accomplished in one hour of skillful computerized research, yet the product may be the same or better by the use of the computer. Twenty hours of lawyer time in setting up a system may produce a product useful to the client in a fraction of the time it would take to produce a custom document. Fifty hours of lawyer time spent training others may produce cost-effective results to the firm and, ultimately, to the client. Hours spent should be recorded to determine the cost of production, but not for purposes of billing.

The REP factor recognizes intangible contributions that are invaluable though hard to quantify. Once the validity of the REP factor has been accepted, ingenious minds can perhaps devise means of quantification both for purposes of billing clients and for compensating lawyers to reflect fairly *Responsibility, Expertise* and *Productivity.*

CHAPTER 12

Jesse D. Miller *is a partner in the Los Angeles office of Philadelphia's Pepper, Hamilton and Sheetz. This article, reprinted from the March 14, 1988, issue of* The National Law Journal *stresses the need for both in-house and outside counsel to work out a billing system that permits appropriate incentives to the outside firm through adequate profitability, while providing the best possible legal result at a fair and reasonable cost. It deals with perceived inefficiencies inherent in hourly billing. From there, Miller considers billing alternatives and the ultimate issue of exposure to risks.*

Pros and Cons of Alternative Fee Structures—Beyond Hourly Fees

by Jesse D. Miller

The hourly fee system is much like the weather. Everyone talks about changing it, but no one really does anything about it.

It is in the interest of both in-house and outside counsel to work together in delivering the best and most cost-effective services to the client, while permitting appropriate incentives to the outside firm through adequate profitability.

Most corporate counsel are not simply trying to beat down the costs of legal services at the expense of outside counsel, and outside counsel are not attempting to profit out of proportion to the "value" produced for the client.

The objective of the outside firm is to render the highest-quality legal services to the client, for fees that enable the firm to maintain a profitability level commensurate with the value of the services rendered.

The objective of in-house attorneys is to obtain the best possible legal result for their client, the corporation, at a fair and reasonable cost.

Sentiment exists among many inside counsel that the hourly fee system does not achieve the fair-and-reasonable-cost objective.

Prevalent View

Evidence of the prevalence of this view is found in the increasing number of in-house legal staffs and their increased size.

Further evidence is found in the competition among law firms created by the tendency of corporate legal departments to send their work to a number of firms rather than to a single firm and to "shop around" for lawyers. The use of the term *shop around* is not intended to be pejorative but rather to state a legitimate tactic to achieve the objective of the general counsel.

It is important to note some commonly perceived inefficiencies of outside law firms to determine if alternative fee mechanisms deal with them better than the hourly fee system does.

A perception has developed that law firms don't work hard at keeping the hours lower, because under the hourly fee system a law firm gets paid more when more hours are devoted to a matter. Outside counsel can make some legitimate arguments that these perceptions are wrong.

Certainly, a law firm desires to have repeat business from its clients and therefore is strongly motivated to hold the charges down. And a number of the perceived inefficiencies can be justified in terms of proper preparation and the delivery of quality services.

Common Problems

Among the most common perceived inefficiencies are:

- Outside law firms overstaff cases and have two or more attorneys present at depositions or meetings with opposing counsel when only one attorney need attend.
- Outside law firms engage in excessive discovery under the theory that leaving no stone unturned is the best pretrial preparation. Critics would say that although in

Reprinted with permission from the *National Law Journal.*

some so-called you-bet-your-company types of cases this may be the appropriate handling of a case, most cases can be well-prepared without making certain that the last rock is turned over.

- Outside law firms engage in excessive research. Some say that issues are researched prematurely—and in many cases, unnecessarily. They also claim that outside firms do not resort often enough to research on recurring subjects they already have "on the shelf."
- Outside law firms engage in too many intraoffice conferences. Though some "strategy" sessions certainly are appropriate, the critics say that it is not really cost-effective to have frequent brainstorming conferences with several lawyers present.
- Outside counsel wait too long to enter into serious settlement discussions. Beating up the opposition may soften them up for settlement, but do the costs outweigh the benefits?
- Outside law firms experience frequent turnover of associates and bill the client for the training time of the replacements.
- Outside law firms pressure their associates—and sometimes their partners—to generate billable hours, promoting that practice as the best route to upward progression within the firm.
- Outside law firms bill the client for costs that should appropriately be included in the hourly rate, such as word processing and secretarial overtime.

Billing Alternatives

With the above list in mind, there are a number of alternatives to, or variations of, the hourly fee system.

Some of the theoretical alternatives involve—in varying degrees—the shifting or sharing of the risks of inefficiencies from those perceived to be inherent in the hourly fee system.

In other instances, the alternatives would be designed to reward outside counsel for good results while requiring them to take some risk of a lower fee if those results are not achieved.

It is important for outside counsel in particular to keep an open mind when examining these alternatives. Some may present opportunities to improve the firm's profitability. One criticism of the hourly fee system is that hourly rates continue to rise as expenses and salaries for younger lawyers escalate.

The upward pressure on rates has contributed to the buildup of in-house staffs and the quest for more cost-effective handling of cases.

Set a fixed fee per case: No "ups," no extras. Under this arrangement, inside and outside counsel agree on the total fee to be charged for a matter or for a series of cases. This is an example of the need for the outside firm to budget very accurately for litigation.

Fixed Fee

This alternative places the outside firm at risk and provides direct incentives for outside firms to eliminate perceived inefficiencies, with the exception of billing inappropriate costs.

Under the fixed-fee system, it probably still will be necessary for costs to be paid by the corporate client. Costs related directly to the handling of the client's case should present little problem.

Other costs, such as word processing, secretarial overtime and the like, which cannot always be directly allocated to a specific case, should be discussed in advance. Agreement should be reached as to how these items should be billed, if at all.

It is possible to include such costs within the fixed fee, but this would have a great impact on the risk taken by the outside firm and the amount of the agreed-upon payment per case to be made by the client.

Traditional thinking indicates it is a rare case that would tempt an outside firm to operate under this mechanism and run these risks. However, heretical as it may seem, there are some cases that lend themselves to this particular arrangement.

For example, if a company had a series of cases arising from the failure of a minicomputer it has stopped manufacturing and it was aware that these cases had a settlement value that varied from plaintiff to plaintiff, it would appear quite possible for inside and outside counsel to analyze each case and arrive at a settlement figure.

Exposure to Risks

Under this type of arrangement, as in all of the others suggested here, there must be a high level of co-operation and respect between in-house and outside counsel. For example, if a settlement offer were received that was greater than the agreed settlement value of the case, but was within a reasonable range, the outside firm would have to be confident that the in-house staff would not unreasonably withhold consent to the slightly higher settlement.

Many other individual cases could be handled efficiently on a fixed-fee basis as well. It would be risky; but if a law firm were willing to experiment, it might find that it would become extremely adept at budgeting and efficient in the handling of its cases.

Budget and pay fees for various stages of a case. Under this arrangement, the outside and inside counsel would agree on a budget for each of the various stages of a lawsuit.

Budget Evaluation

Evaluation points would be established for when the budget would be compared to the actual fees. For example, the first stage might be the period beginning with the receipt of the complaint and ending at the motion to dismiss or the answer stage.

Say that a budget of $5,000 has been set for this stage. In fact, the fees related to that stage of the suit end up being $4,000. The client would pay the $4,000 and place the $1,000 to the credit of the outside firm in a suspense account.

The next stage of the case might be the discovery stage, culminating in a motion for summary judgment. Assume that the fees for this stage of the case were budgeted at $25,000, but the actual fees turned out to be $35,000. The client would pay the $25,000 that was budgeted to the outside lawyers and would treat the $10,000 overrun as a negative balance in the suspense account on this particular case.

Because there was a $1,000 credit to the outside lawyers as a result of the first stage of the suit and a $10,000 negative charge because of the overrun on the discovery stage, there would be a $9,000 negative balance in the suspense account at this point.

Compare Accounts

This procedure would be followed through the next stage, which might be preparation for trial, and then another stage, which might be the conduct of the trial itself. When the matter is concluded, the client would look at the suspense account. If the outside attorneys had delivered the matter under budget, the amount standing to their credit could be paid to them and would result in the realization of more than the hourly fee charges.

If, however, the actual time devoted to the matter times the hourly rates exceeded the budget, some mechanism could be provided for evaluating whether, under all the circumstances, the overrun accounts—or some part thereof—could be paid to outside counsel.

Under this arrangement, in which the corporate client agrees to pay the budgeted amount, incentives for efficiencies are directed to the law firm. It would appear that this particular fee scenario should be applied to a great number of cases.

Bill at reduced hourly rates with a bonus for an agreed-upon good result. Under this arrangement, the outside law firm agrees to perform its services at a reduced rate, e.g., 50 percent of normal. Inside and outside counsel agree in advance as to the desired result in the case.

For example, if the suit claims damages of $1 million and the parties agree that there is a genuine exposure of $500,000, then in exchange for the lower hourly rate that is being charged, the defense counsel would participate in the difference between $500,000 and the amount at which the case is settled or for which judgment is entered, provided that amount is less than $500,000.

Percentage Varies

The percentage of the outside firm's participation could vary depending on the extent of the reduced payment made to dispose of the case. Thus, if there were a defense verdict and no money was paid, it may be that outside counsel should receive 50 percent of the difference; but if the amount paid by the client was $400,000, it may be that outside counsel should only share to the extent of 10 percent of the $100,000 difference.

Arriving at this arrangement is complicated primarily by the inherent difficulties in assessing the value of a plaintiff's claim and the degree of realism in that assessment on the part of both inside and outside counsel.

This arrangement, however, presents a variation that changes the incentives for efficiency to some extent, but certainly places a premium on obtaining a good result.

Set a pure defense contingency. This arrangement is simply a variation of the scenario of a reduced fee with a bonus for a good result. It presents the same basic considerations as described in the preceding alternative, but it is obviously more risky for the outside counsel and would require a greater percentage of participation in the reduced settlement or judgment paid by the corporate client.

Pure premium billing: Set the fee at the end of case. Of all the alternatives discussed, this one requires the greatest level of confidence in the fairness of the in-house legal department. The handling of a case for which the client pays no fees during the course of an action and does not specifically agree to pay any fee at all can give an outside lawyer an uneasy feeling, unless he or she is confident of being treated fairly at the end of the matter.

It would be a most unusual situation in which either party would be inclined to attempt this sort of arrangement, but some such situations may exist. The mechanism for setting the fee would have to be clearly specified. First, the person or body within the client's organization that would set the fee would have to be specified.

Outside attorneys should have an opportunity to present their position about the fairness of the fee. If the parties cannot agree on a reasonable fee, some mechanism such as binding arbitration might be appropriate. Because most lawyers do not wish to be their clients' adversaries, even in arbitration over fees, the use of this alternative will be limited.

Pay hourly for the defense of a complaint with a contingency arrangement for a cross-complaint. Under this arrangement, the regular hourly fees would apply to the defense of an action. In the course of analyzing the strength of the client's legal position with respect to the defense of the claim against it, however, it may be determined that the client has a good case and should cross-complain against the plaintiff.

Much of the legal defense work done frequently would be the same as—or closely related to—the legal position that would have to be established to prevail on the cross-complaint. This results in a serious question as to how the time should be apportioned for the purposes of billing the hourly rate against the complaint defense. The parties would have to come to some understanding about that.

Clearly, some portion of the legal work done in connection with the cross-complaint is allocable to the defendant's action against the plaintiff, such as establishing damages. Such difficulties are not insuperable.

When the corporate client is the plaintiff, charge normal hourly rates up to a point with a contingency thereafter. All of the previous scenarios relate primarily to situations in which the corporate client is a defendant. It is not uncommon today to see a substantial corporation suing another corporation. It is worthwhile to consider some basis for handling the plaintiff's case in those instances, on a basis other than normal hourly fees or as a pure contingency.

Combination Approach

One approach would be to charge the regular hourly rates for developing the complaint and commencing the action up to an agreed-upon fee limit. For example, it may be that the parties agree that regular hourly rates would be paid up to a maximum of $50,000. If the hourly fees exceed that figure, there are a number of alternatives available. One would be to have the corporate client pay 50 percent of the normal hourly rates on the next $50,000 of time expended, with the outside firm also receiving a 15 percent contingency if the matter were concluded within that period.

Thereafter, the outside attorneys would be paid no further percentage of an hourly rate but would go on a pure contingency of perhaps 25 percent or 30 percent. It would seem that such an arrangement would protect inside counsel from protracted litigation with huge fees as well as provide the outside counsel with some minimum amount of comfort in the payment of the early hourly charges with a possibility of a profitable contingency participation.

Other arrangements are merely variations on the hourly fee system. A number of billing methods are frequently mentioned as alternatives to the hourly fee system when, in truth, they are merely variations of that system.

A number of corporate clients today are seeking to obtain lower-than-normal hourly rates from law firms in exchange for the promise of handling a substantial volume of cases for that client.

It may be attractive for the outside law firm to offer the reduced rate to obtain the new business it would not otherwise get or to retain business that might otherwise be lost to another firm. Not only is this not a true alternative to the hourly fee system, it is simply a cost-cutting technique that may achieve the corporate client's objectives at the expense of the outside law firm's objectives. On the other hand, in some situations it may be mutually advantageous.

Charging a blended rate regardless of which attorney or legal assistant works on the matter is not new and has been used effectively by a number of very fine law firms. It is not, however, really an alternative to the hourly fee system but simply a different twist.

As long as the outside law firm can control the mix of the attorneys and the legal assistants who work on a given matter, it may be that a blended rate—which results in a rate substantially below that of the average partner within the firm—can nonetheless be profitable. To the extent the client insists on partner-intensive participation, the system either does not work or would require a higher blended rate.

Supervising the Work

Having outside counsel supervise the work, most of which is done by in-house attorneys, is in no way a variation of the hourly fee system. It is merely designed to reduce the number of hours that outside counsel will bill. It also provides that most of the work by way of interrogatories, depositions, research, etc., will be done by the in-house attorneys, who charge lower rates.

Although a number of companies seriously propose this arrangement, the degree of participation of the in-house counsel dwindles after some of the initial, routine stages of a lawsuit. However, this scenario poses some serious problems for the outside lawyer who does not have the same confidence in the in-house people, and who does not exercise the same supervision over them that he does with lawyers in his own firm. Outside counsel frequently feel they are being used almost as a mail drop and may also be concerned about the quality of the work.

This concern is not because of the competence of the in-house staff but because of the lack of direct supervision, difficulties in communication, and lack of familiarity with the particular skills of the in-house attorney handling a particular phase of the case.

Not very many outside law firms or inside counsel are actually using alternative billing systems. Surely, the hourly fee system will remain the method for handling most cases and will be an important element even in the use of an alternative billing system.

However, the increased competition among law firms, the increasing tendency to handle work in-house and the increasing demands on corporate counsel to reduce legal costs all contribute to a professional climate in which a firm that fails to consider such alternatives is burying its head in the sand.

There will be a reallocation of the legal work available from corporate America, and those firms willing to experiment and be innovative will participate in that reallocation more than those firms that are not. In addition, the use of alternative billing systems may cause some firms to become more efficient and reduce costs to their clients. This may simultaneously result in higher profits for the firm.

CHAPTER 13

Geoffrey Furlonger, *formerly a New York attorney now in London, England, displays the influence of his Oxford University background with this historical perspective of attorneys' fees as reprinted from* Law Office Economics and Management *(Summer 1986, Volume XXVII, No. 2, pp. 171–183). He takes a slightly different view of the advantages and disadvantages of time-based systems of billing, and suggests the benefits of a fixed fee approach. His comparisons with investment banking fee practices are thought-provoking. After reading this you will be better equipped to understand the attitudes of clients and society toward attorneys' fees.*

Time for Business-Lawyers to Stop Billing Time?

by Geoffrey Furlonger

Throughout history, ancient and modern, the nature of the reward that lawyers should receive for their services has been a matter of keen debate. This matter has troubled the consciences of lawyers and public alike. William Forsythe, an English barrister, wrote in an essay published in 1849:

> From the very earliest times, and in every country where advocacy has been known, it has been the custom to look upon the exertions of the advocate as given gratuitously, and the reward which the client bestows as purely honorary, in discharge not of legal obligation, but a mere debt of gratitude. There can be little doubt that this notion has been encouraged and kept up, from a jealous apprehension lest the profession should degenerate into a mean and mercenary calling. For there is one peculiarity which distinguishes it from all others, and that is the disfavor with which men regard a presumed readiness to espouse and support by argument either side of a question. This is a circumstance so repugnant to the ordinary sense of duty, and apparently so subversive of the distinction between right and wrong, that there has been always felt an unwillingness to admit that a man is entitled to barter the powers of his intellect for money indifferently in the cause of virtue and of vice.[1]

In the early stages of the Roman republic, legal services were rendered free of charge, the honor attached to successful advocacy being considered of itself to be sufficient reward. Later, however, as Roman law became more complex and the lawyer's craft more difficult, legal advocacy was used as a means of obtaining money. Such practices were nevertheless deemed scandalous, and the famous Cincian law was passed prohibiting the acceptance of pecuniary gifts. With the fall of the republic, however, lawyers again sought financial incentives for their craft. Even a decree of the senate by the Emperor Augustus, prohibiting counsel from accepting remuneration under the penalty of forfeiting four times their fee, was insufficient to prevent widespread abuse.[2] The problem was to some extent solved by the Emperor Claudius, who, after hearing arguments on the merits and disadvantages of the financial remuneration of lawyers, issued a decree permitting the acceptance of money up to a prescribed maximum fee.

Even under the Claudian decree, however, a client was under no legal obligation to reward his lawyer. Thus legal fees in ancient Rome constituted no more than large "tips." It is to the theory of gratuitous service that William Forsythe referred in 1849. The theory still persists in England, where barristers today, just as in Forsythe's time, are unable to sue for recovery of unpaid legal fees.

One suspects, from his "apprehension lest the profession should degenerate into a mean and mercenary calling," that Forsythe would be shocked at modern American fee practices. Not only are American lawyers entitled to fees as a matter of legal right, they are entitled, within limits, to obtain part of the client's recovery by means of contingent fees, which would be champertous under English common law.[3] Yet, with the expansion of lawyers' rights in connection with legal fees has come an accompanying awareness that if the lawyer is entitled to a fee as a matter of absolute right, then the fee should be reasonable and proper, lest indeed "the profession degenerate into a mean and mercenary calling."

Out of this desire to bring respectability to the process of charging legal fees has come the modern-day practice of presenting business clients with a full

Reprinted with permission from *Law Office Economics and Management*.

amount of the services provided. Furthermore, with the increasing sophistication and cost-consciousness of clients has come an increasing insistence from clients themselves that they receive such an account. It is the purpose of this article to reexamine the fee practices currently employed by business lawyers and to suggest that an alternative method of deducing an appropriate fee might be adopted.

The Disadvantages of Time-Based Systems of Billing

The most common method used by business lawyers when quoting a fee for their services is to charge according to the amount of time that they estimate lawyers and others have spent on the given client's file. This is commonly referred to as "billing time." Other incidental expenses for ancillary services such as copying and long-distance telephone charges also are generally included in the final bill, yet the bulk of the fee generally represents an attempt to estimate the time spent by individuals on the given client's case. On first inspection this appears to be a fair and logical method of deducing an appropriate fee. The Model Code of Professional Responsibility states that one of the factors to be considered in determining the reasonableness of a fee is the time and labor required.[4] A bill that reflects the time spent on a file thereby implies an attempt to calculate a reasonable fee. The inherent reasonableness of recording time, however, and billing accordingly, only will actually result in a fair and reasonable final bill if the record of lawyer's time is accurate.

Yet, even assuming that a bill accurately reflects lawyers' use of time, there are other defects in a time-based system of billing. One such defect is a lack of incentive for firms to quickly and effectively train young lawyers. Because young lawyers contribute to the income of the firm by spending time on files, it follows that it is more cost-effective to give them on-the-job training rather than make young lawyers spend time in a classroom. The result is that the typical young lawyer receives a random and haphazard education gaining detailed knowledge of certain areas of his or her chosen field, according to the particular files on which he happens to work, while remaining ignorant of other very important areas. It is not only the young lawyer who suffers; a client who pays for three hours of a young attorney's time for a task that might have been performed in two hours, if properly trained in a classroom, probably also has grounds for complaint. By contrast, investment banks and trading companies that derive a substantial portion of their income from fixed-fee arrangements have an incentive to ensure that their young executives achieve a high degree of competence at the earliest opportunity; for the shorter the amount of time it requires an individual to perform a task, the more tasks he or she may perform, and therefore the greater income he or she may earn for the firm. Thus, it is that the investment banking profession, not noted for its adoration of overhead, is prepared to make its new recruits spend months in classrooms before they get down to the business of deriving income for their firm.[5] In contrast, the greater the length of time spent by lawyers on a given file, the greater the income for the firm from that file,[6] with the consequence that a time-based billing system has the tendency to encourage both incompetence and inefficiency. Furthermore, such billing practices encourage both the quantitative and qualitative misallocation of legal skill, for a firm may sometimes increase its income by assigning more lawyers than necessary, with more experience than necessary, to tasks which might be accomplished by fewer individuals with less experience, but whose time is billed at a lower rate.

The prevalence of time-based billing arguably also contributes to the length of legal documents; while it isn't always true that the length of a document reflects the time spent on its preparation, for a long document merely may be a simple adoption of an existing model, there will exist a rough connection between the length and complexity of a document and the time spent in its development and therefore also the aggregate sum billed various clients over a period of time. Now, of course, to that school of legal thought that believes that "bigger is better" and that advocates that the length of a document reflects the care taken in ensuring that all eventualities, contingencies and relevant laws and regulations are considered, that believes the fact that some modern financial documents bear a strong resemblance to telephone directories does not pose a problem. However, to an opposing school of thought, admittedly in the minority in the United States, that believes that the forest (the purpose of a document) often is lost in the trees (superfluous detail) and that clarity often is lost in documents perhaps containing sentences of a page in length, the increasing length of legal documents is a matter of concern. Even accepting that lengthy legal documents are undesirable, however, it is perhaps too cynical to suggest that this is the consequence solely of the desire for pecuniary gain but rather, perhaps, the lawyer's natural desire to fully protect the client sometimes leads to overzealousness in the production of clauses of a document.

Whether or not the astonishing length of American legal documents constitutes an argument against time-based billing, a less contentious aspect of this method of determining a legal fee is the amount of administrative time, effort and expense associated with recording time and preparing a bill. Typically, each lawyer who works on a file must record the time attributable to a file using time sheets; this information then is transferred to a central recording system, often a computer, where telephone charges, copying charges and other incidental expenses that also have been laboriously attributed to the given file number are added to the bill. When the time comes to bill the client, a partner usually will review the accumulated charges in order to determine the appropriate sum to be demanded of the client. Thus a significant amount of time that otherwise might be spent on legal work is spent performing administrative tasks. Furthermore, significant expenditure is incurred in computer time and the employment of accounting personnel who must ensure that the various charges are correctly assigned to the right files.

Now as an alternative to time-based systems of billing, law firms might simply negotiate a fixed-fee prior to the provision of legal services. By way of contrast with time-based systems of billing, the only administrative tasks associated with fixed-fee arrangements are the preparation of a fee agreement and the collection of the prearranged fee on completion of the lawyers' work. So having considered the disadvantages of a time-based system of billing, it is perhaps now appropriate to more directly examine and consider the advantages of fixed-fee systems of billing.

Investment-Banking Fee Practices and the Advantages of a Fixed-Fee System of Billing

Investment banks generally provide a variety of financial services, including the management of mergers and acquisitions, project financing and the management, underwriting and sale of securities. The investment banks typically will arrange their fee so that they take a percentage of the capital sum involved in the given transaction. If, for example, the investment bank is arranging the financing of an industrial project, it typically will charge a certain percentage of the funds supplied. The percentage involved often will vary according to a sliding scale such that the greater the capital amount involved, the smaller the percentage charged. However, this does not mean that the actual fee diminishes and that generally the higher the face value of a financing, the greater will be the fee. Invariably, the investment bank's fee, expressed as a percentage of the capital value of a transaction, will be contingent on the successful completion (closing) of the transaction. Whether or not the investment bank receives any compensation for its services if a transaction fails to close will vary from deal to deal, but the fee involved almost certainly would be less than that associated with a successful closing. While investment banks do provide consulting services and the fee charged might be related to the time and effort expended, investment banks typically do not record the time spent by individuals on projects. Hence, investment banks may be fairly accurately described as using fixed-fee, as opposed to time-based, systems of billing.

The main advantage of fixed-fee systems of billing is that they do not incur any of the disadvantages associated with time-based systems of billing discussed previously. Yet there are other advantages, perhaps the greatest of which is that a client already will have sanctioned the fee that it is to be charged before any services are provided. This would serve both the best interests of the client and the legal profession. The client will have gained the advantage of having negotiated a fee with which it is presumably satisfied and it also will benefit by avoiding the uncertainty, surprise and disappointment associated with bills prepared ex post facto by the summation of multifarious sources of expense. While the law firm will gain the advantage of avoiding unseemly disputes over legal bills that appear unexpectedly high to the client, it will be able to avoid unnecessary anguish and to devote more time to legal matters.

It might nevertheless be argued that while time might be saved in avoiding fee disputes under a fixed-fee system of billing, an equal amount of administrative time would have to be spent negotiating the fee prior to the provision of legal services, thus cancelling out this advantage for the law firm. Yet even if this were true, the undertaking of the negotiation of an appropriate fee with the prospect of business to come probably would be a more pleasant process than the rancor associated with fee disputes under time-based systems of billing following the presentation of the bill. It probably is not a necessary consequence of the adoption of a fixed-fee system that much time would have to be spent negotiating fees, for a firm could presumably fix a fee according to the particular type of transaction involved, whereupon the client could decide whether or not the given firm's pricing was acceptable.

A further attraction of fixed-fee arrangements for firms that serve as legal counsel in transactions involving very large sums is that such firms probably could increase their income.[7] Investment banks enjoy very high income as a direct consequence of fixed-fee arrangements. While investment banks' fees in absolute terms are very large, they are small when compared to the sums involved in transactions in which investment banks typically are engaged, or rather, to adopt economists' jargon, the marginal utility to be derived by the client from the completion of the transaction just offsets its high cost. It is a well-established economic principle that a dollar to a rich man is worth less than it is to a poor man; an entity providing a service in connection with the transfer of a large sum of money is able to charge a higher absolute fee than would be the case with a lesser sum. Because investment banking transactions usually involve large sums, investment banks by observing this economic principle derive large incomes. Law firms, however, by using time-based systems of billing that inflexibly determine a final fee according to expenditure of time irrespective of the capital sum involved, forgo potential income. Yet, alterations in the billing practices of law firms that might entail an increase in their income inevitably raise questions concerning the legal ethics and the feasibility of the new system of billing. It is therefore appropriate to examine such aspects of fixed-fee systems of billing.

The Legal Ethics and Feasibility of Fixed-Fee Systems of Billing

In considering the legal ethics of fixed-fee systems of billing, one should first examine the Model Code of Professional Responsibility (the Code), for this represents the code of professional behavior to which members of most American bar associations must adhere. The Code directly considers lawyers' fees in only two contexts; one being the question of division of fees among lawyers,[8] the other having regard to illegal or excessive legal fees.[9] Only the latter has any relevance to the present discussion. It is suggested, although it has yet to be tested, that lawyers providing services in connection with major financial transactions could increase their income by the adoption of fixed-fee systems of billing. Might such fees become excessive? The Code states that "A fee is clearly excessive when, after a review of the facts, a lawyer of ordinary prudence would be left with a definite and firm conviction that the fee is in excess of a reasonable fee."[10] The Code lists factors to be considered as guides in determining the reasonableness of a fee.[11] Now, it would seem that all the factors listed could be taken into consideration by the client when it either negotiates a fee or reviews the law firm's standard fee for a certain type of transaction. For example, the Code lists "the fee customarily charged in the locality for similar legal services"[12] and "the experience, reputation and ability of the lawyer or lawyers performing the services"[13] as factors to be taken into consideration in determining the reasonableness of the fee. A client easily could discover all such information by inquiry in the local community, just as it could unearth relevant information to enable it to weigh all the other factors, save possibly one,[14] listed by the Code. Thus, a client given various information at its disposal, by negotiating or accepting a certain fee, tacitly acknowledges the reasonableness of the fee; and, given the abundance of lawyers in the United States, if a client is unable to negotiate what it considers to be a reasonable fee with one law firm, it presumably will negotiate a lower fee with another firm. By this reasoning, a fixed-fee system of billing that yields a predetermined negotiated fee has a better chance of yielding reasonable fees than time-billing systems that yield ex post facto surprises with which the client may or may not be content.

It is in fact with respect to the question of contingent fees that fixed-fee systems of billing pose a significant ethical dilemma. As already mentioned, investment banks' fees are very often linked to the successful completion of a transaction. While this may represent sensible business practice for the investment banking profession, it would create problems for the legal profession. The quicker a transaction is closed, the better the investment bank has performed its role, but the quicker a transaction is closed, the more likely it is that the law firm will have compromised its duty to ensure that all relevant legal issues have been addressed and that the client has been properly protected. If a law firm receives substantial remuneration on the closing of a transaction, but is not compensated if the transaction is not completed, there exists a clear incentive to ignore potentially troublesome issues, which, although they might hinder the process of agreement, are best addressed if both the best interests of the client and the law are to be respected. To give an example, a lawyer might wonder whether a certain aspect of a contract renders the contract illegal. The issue might require extensive legal research, yet the lawyer is under pressure to quickly review relevant documents and give his or her approval so that the opposing party to the transaction does not change its mind and withdraw from the deal. Given a contingent-fee arrangement, the lawyer is facing a clear conflict of interest. On the one hand, he or she desires his or her contingency fee, but on the other hand, by glossing over the question of illegality, the lawyer both renders a disservice to the client who might not in fact receive the rights under an ostensible contract for which it bargained and a disservice to the law, if laws or regulations have been ignored or given insufficient attention. For these reasons, one could predict that bar associations might not readily accept the introduction of contingent fees in the context of business transactions.

By employing a fixed-fee system of billing, however, where payment of a fee is not contingent on the successful completion of the given transaction, one is confronted by another obvious problem. Should a law firm receive a fee calculated on the presumption of, for example, six months' work and the successful completion of a transaction, if the transaction is abandoned two weeks after the signing of the fee agreement? Under such circumstances, the fee clearly would be excessive and the client would in any event probably refuse to pay. Thus, advocates of fixed-fee systems of billing are confronted with a dilemma. Either they opt for a contingent-fee agreement and possibly perpetrate a breach of legal ethics or else they opt for a non-contingency system and risk either windfall profits,[15] or the refusal of the client to pay the agreed bill. Given such a dilemma, the only solution would seem to be a partial retreat to a billing system that although essentially fixed-fee in nature, also involved some record of time and effort expended. For example, a firm might negotiate a fee agreement whereby the fee is fixed as a certain percentage of the capital sum involved, subject to the condition that if the transaction is not closed and the law firm has completed less than "x" hours of lawyer's time, a bill is to be calculated according to the time actually spent on the project. While such a hybrid fee system would preserve some of the evils of time-based systems of billing, it would dispense with others. If lawyers still were required to keep track of their time in case the given transaction closed prematurely, the factors tending to distort the accuracy of such timekeeping would still be present, as would the administrative expense of recording time. However, because in most cases transactions successfully move to fruition, it follows that the fixed-fee personna of the hybrid would move to the fore, and therefore factors leading to the poor training of young lawyers, inefficient allocation of legal personnel, excessive legal involvement and the unnecessary length of certain legal documents would be removed.

When considering the feasibility of fixed-fee systems of billing, an obvious problem is whether such systems would be acceptable to the client. It already has been noted that it is preferable from the client's point of view to be aware of legal costs before the actual provision of legal services, rather than receive an unpleasant surprise following the completion of the lawyer's task. Certainty has great value in the marketplace, for example, individuals are prepared to pay higher interest rates for fixed-rate mortgages on real property rather than opt for the lower rates initially associated with variable-rate mortgages. It has also been noted that in a free-market economy one of the advantages of fixed-fee systems of billing is that the client is relatively free to retain law firms that offer a fixed fee that is acceptable to the client. Yet one of the more interesting aspects of a transition from time-based systems of billing to fixed-fee systems is the possible reaction of clients in transactions involving very large sums of money. If law firms that regularly provide legal counsel in such transactions, which also might involve investment banks, were to mimic investment banking fee practices,[16] the question arises as to the possible reactions of the financial community to the transition. The answer to this question depends on several parameters, one of which is whether the majority of law firms typically involved in such transactions make the transition contemporaneously.[17] Another is whether law firms attempted to take advantage of those natural economic forces, of which investment banks take full advantage, and increased their fees. Yet, another unknown quality is the esteem with which clients view those firms typically involved in major financial transactions. If such firms were to adopt investment banking fee practices and other smaller firms did not, the possibility arises of client defection from the former to the latter. Yet, this would depend on the perceived quality of the legal services provided by the former and the extent to which fees increased, assuming that they increased at all.

While the purpose of this article has been to discuss and to some extent promote the idea of a transition to fixed-fee systems of billing, such an idea does not entirely represent a revolutionary concept. Indeed, most firms that presently employ time-based systems of billing typically tend, in practice, to modify time-billing in an ad hoc fashion such that the result resembles a fixed-fee system. For example, clients often request and are granted "caps" on bills. That is to say, they demand that the final bill not exceed a certain fixed sum. More frequently, partners in charge of the final bill will write off time, which is to say, they decide that a final bill is too great and reduce its size. By so doing, the lawyer actually is ignoring the data supplied through a time-based system of billing and is substituting a fixed fee. Whereupon, the obvious point to be made is that perhaps it would be better to have quoted the same sum as a legal fee ab initio and thus have avoided the problems necessarily associated with time-billing systems. Admittedly, it may be contended that without a proper record of the use of time, it is more difficult to quote a fee that equitably rewards the lawyer for his services. Yet, this assumes that the record of lawyers' time is accurate and thus we return to our point of departure in the discussion of the disadvantages of time-based systems of billing.

Time-based billing systems were adopted with the best of motives. It was felt that the client preferred to be given a full account of the lawyer's activities. Thus, time-billing was born, in part, of a desire to further the integrity of the legal profession. Yet if in practice, time-based systems present merely an appearance of reasonableness, a caricature of honesty and a facade of client-consciousness, we may fear that William Forsythe would be unimpressed. It therefore is surely best that wherever possible,[18] an alternative system of billing be adopted, which more truly honors those good intentions that first brought forth time-based billing practices.

ENDNOTES

1. William Forsythe, "Hortensius or The Advocate," a historical essay, ch. IX at 410.
2. *Id.* at 415.
3. *See* Aronson, Attorney-Client Fee Arrangements: Regulation and Review at 76, Federal Judicial Center (1980).
4. The Code of Professional Responsibility (the Code), DR 2-106 B.1.
5. For an article on Salomon Brothers and Investment Banking training programs *see* "The Boot Camp for top M.B.A.'s," *New York Times*, Sept. 9, 1985, § D., p. 1, col. 3, New Yorkers & Co. *See generally*, Marion L. Salzman and Deidre A. Sullivan, *Inside Management Training: The Career Guide to Training Programs for College Graduates*.
6. Of course, a firm's overall income may in the long term diminish, if it were to acquire a reputation for inefficiency.
7. This certainly was the opinion of the journalist in "Headnotes, War of the Tombstone" 1, *The Am Law* (March 1985). However, it is possible that the incomes of such firms might actually diminish, for clients might encourage competitive bidding among law firms. Much would probably depend on the clients' perception of the quality provided by the blue-chip law firms. If clients with large pockets perceive the blue-chip firms as providing a significantly better legal service, then they will continue to use these firms. The fact that other firms are less expensive is irrelevant—an individual seeking a Rolls-Royce will not be persuaded to purchase a Toyota on the grounds that the latter is less expensive. If this reasoning is correct, competitive bidding, if it emerges at all, would be between the blue-chip firms themselves. Yet it is difficult to imagine such firms engaging in "fee wars" in the same manner as airlines engage in "fare wars." Thus, it is the author's opinion that the income of blue-chip firms would increase, rather than diminish.
8. The Code, DR 2-107.
9. The Code, DR 2-106.
10. The Code, DR 2-106 B.
11. The Code, DR 2-106 B.
12. The Code, DR 2-106 B.3.
13. The Code, DR 2-106 B.7.
14. The Code lists as a factor in determining the reasonableness of a fee "The time and labor required, the novelty and difficulty of the questions involved and the skill required to perform the legal service properly." (DR 2-106 B.1.) The client would not necessarily be aware of these factors, and hence it may be suggested that time billing is preferable in that it more accurately gauges these factors. While this might be true of the layman client, however, very often the person responsible for selecting counsel for a corporation is "in-house" counsel who *would* have the necessary knowledge to assess such factors as the novelty and difficulty of the question involved and the skill required to perform the legal service properly.
15. The excessiveness of which might constitute another breach of legal ethics, in particular, a breach of DR 2-106 of the Code.
16. Within the constraints demanded by the ethical considerations discussed ante.
17. According to *International Financial Law Review*, December 1985, several major United States law firms have made the transition away from time-billing.
18. There certainly are some areas of legal practice where fixed-fee systems would not be practical, lengthy defensive litigation being an obvious example. Fixed-fee systems probably are best suited to business transactions where the closing date is reasonably certain.

CHAPTER 14

Robert S. Hochdorf *is a lawyer and consultant specializing in legal consulting for the CPA firm of Holland Shiper Vann, P.C., in Atlanta, Georgia. In the summer 1987 issue of* Legal Administrator, *he dealt with approaches for recouping automation investment. With the increased cost of technology and the decreased amount of lawyer time required to produce a legal product, hourly billing poses problems for profitability unless there is an effective billing method. He sets forth a method for determining technological overhead charges.*

Billing for Technological Overhead

by Robert S. Hochdorf

The traditional concept of overhead in a law firm includes all the components necessary to operate a firm to provide legal services to the client. Overhead includes office rent, salaries, benefits, cost of equipment and supplies and any other similar costs. Firms always have had to recoup these costs from their clients in one way or another, in addition to charging for the legal work performed. Usually, the costs were built into the hourly fee charged for the lawyer's services.

Recent Changes in the Meaning and Significance of Overhead

Today, perhaps more than ever before, the question of how to recoup the cost of overhead in a legal practice is being reexamined. The primary reason for this is the increased use of technology in law firms, creating a whole new class of overhead and involving very substantial costs.

It is not uncommon for a firm to spend more than $100,000 in one investment in technology. Word processing, time and billing and other data-processing functions, data-base management for litigation support and work product retrieval, docket control and conflict of interest checking all have become automated in the last five years.

Large expenditures for technology in law firms are a relatively new phenomenon. Only a few years ago the standard equipment for a secretary in a law office was an electric typewriter. Today, in many offices the same secretary has a word-processing terminal at her desk. The average cost to equip a legal secretary today is between $8,000 and $10,000, compared to less than $1,000 only a few years ago.

With firms spending larger amounts of money on technological overhead, the overhead factor in the cost equation of running a law firm has changed dramatically. At the same time, private law firms are finding increasing cost-consciousness on the part of clients, especially corporate clients who closely monitor the bills they receive from their outside counsel and constantly strive to keep the corporation's outside legal costs as low as possible.

How then are law firms to recoup their costs?

Separate or Combined System

Two basic approaches exist. One method is to bill the lawyers' and other timekeepers' time separately from charges for technology such as word processing and litigation support. The other method is to charge a flat hourly rate for each timekeeper that is set high enough to recoup all costs of the firm, including the timekeeper's time and all overhead associated with that timekeeper. (Of course, the hourly rate charged would not include the traditional disbursement charges for such items as travel, lodging, meals, long-distance telephone charges, etc.)

Advantages of Separate Billing

There are several advantages to billing separately a timekeeper's time and technological overhead costs. By providing an itemized bill that separates the charges for time and overhead, the client receives a clearer, more-understandable bill.

Such a system also may help to avoid increases

Reprinted with permission of the ***Association of Legal Administrators***.

in the hourly rates charged by lawyers and other timekeepers. (Frequently the reason for increases in hourly rates is the impact of the increased cost of technology on the firm.) The client sees that the fees of the firm are not being increased and that the increase in costs is because of the firm's investment in improved technology.

The firm also should point out that the investment in technology will make the lawyers in the firm more productive, allowing them to turn out their work more efficiently and at lower cost to the client. This means that ultimately the client receives the benefit of a contract completed, for example, in 75 percent of the time it normally would take to prepare the contract. Although the client pays for technology, the client also benefits by paying for less of the lawyer's time.

A final benefit in billing for overhead separately from time for legal work is that the firm sees exactly what the costs are of producing the legal work. Billing separately for time spent and technological overhead forces the firm to look more closely at what comprises the cost to the firm of producing the work and to bill accordingly.

Disadvantages of Separate Billing

There also are disadvantages to the system of billing separately. The major drawback is that clients will balk at the approach, believing that a lawyer's hourly rate ought to include all the overhead costs of providing the legal services rendered. If the firm has not billed separately for general or technological overhead costs in the past, a new charge on the client's statement may be seen as simply another way to charge more for the same services that the firm has been providing at a lower rate.

Another disadvantage of separate billing for technological overhead is that it may become more difficult to increase hourly fees. Whenever an increase in fees occurs, it is attributable solely to the fee charged for the work. There is no leeway to attribute the increase in fees to increases in the general costs of overhead.

Know Your Client's Position on the Matter

The type of client base that your firm has will have some impact on the policy that your firm adopts in charging for technological overhead. Ultimately, of course, the choice of what and how to bill the client is the province of the firm's management. An incorrect decision, however, may have a negative impact on the client base of the firm. Some clients are more likely than others to accept a separate charge for technology. It is, therefore, appropriate to gauge how clients feel about such matters and to make efforts to educate the client about the reasons for the charge.

Explain Your Normal Policy to the Client

It is essential that the client understand the policy that the firm will follow in billing for overhead. This is especially true if your firm decides to implement a new policy based on the increased impact of the cost of overhead because of technology and whenever the firm acquires a new client.

In either situation, the existing clients or the new client may not be accustomed to the idea of a separate charge for technological overhead. You are likely to realize greater success in implementing a policy of charging for technology if the reasons behind the charge are fully explained to the client.

Probably the most effective argument that a firm can make to its clients for charging separately for overhead, rather than including it in the hourly rate, is a usage argument.

The usage argument says that *different clients will require more or less use of technology.* If a client's work requires a considerable volume of documents, then it should logically bear more of the cost of the technology that supports more efficient creation of those documents than the client that generates few documents. If the firm charges a straight hourly rate for its lawyers that includes overhead for technology, there is no means to equitably distribute the overhead charges to those clients that make the biggest use of these capabilities.

Reach Agreement with the Client

You should anticipate that at least some of your clients will be unhappy or even unwilling to accept a policy of charging separately for overhead. In this event, you will need to reach an understanding with such clients as to how these costs will be recouped when work is done for them. It may be that after further discussions the client will come around to the firm's approach to the matter. If not, then some other arrangement will have to be made for a few clients. One approach may be to increase the hourly rate charged to that client.

Many corporate law departments say that they prefer that the hourly charge of outside counsel include all such overhead for technology and other professional staff-support services. In such a situation, an increase in the hourly fee charged will be required to recover the cost of technology as it affects work for that client.

Apply the Policy Consistently

Aside from the exceptions discussed above, the policy should be applied across the board to your clients. This will help to ensure broad acceptance of the change by the client base. Consistent application of the policy also will make it easier for the firm to track how well it is doing on recouping the cost of its investment in technology. The firm will be able to generate statistics on the amount of revenue technological overhead charges are bringing in, compared to the cost of the technology used.

Summary

With adequate information about the cost of technological overhead in the firm's practice, the firm can make an informed decision about how to recoup the costs involved. Based on the evaluation and the method decided on, the firm can more easily explain the approach to all of its clients. Even if all clients are not happy about the new policy, at least this approach will allow the firm to provide its clients with a complete explanation and justification.

As more firms invest in some degree of automation and develop procedures for charging out their investment, clients will become more accustomed to new billing approaches. (Many law firms now are charging clients for word-processing services and for litigation support.)

Ultimately, clients will evaluate their legal-service providers in terms of value received versus cost. The automated firm, however it handles overhead charges, is more likely to produce services that meet that test in a competitive manner.

How to Determine Technological Overhead Charges

UNDERSTAND WHAT YOUR OVERHEAD IS

As part of your evaluation of how to charge for overhead, you should consider exactly what your technological overhead is and what charges your firm will want to include. Aside from the cost of technology as it relates to word processing, there are other costs that your firm may want to evaluate.

One is the cost of data-base management tools that the firm may be using either for work-product retrieval or litigation management. Although your firm may be charging for automated litigation support in relation to large cases, if the firm decides to embark on a program or has one of using automation to support all of its litigation, it may be wise to consider a separate charge to each litigation client for automated support of the case.

If the firm has developed an automated work-product retrieval system, whenever that work-product retrieval data base is used for a client's work, some type of overhead charge should be applied to cover the cost of maintaining the work-product retrieval data base.

The cost of maintaining such a work-product data base may be quite significant for a large firm. Certainly, use of the work-product data base benefits the client by eliminating unnecessary research, thus saving the client lawyer research time. In such a situation, charging the client for use of the in-house work-product data base is analogous to passing through to the client the cost of using one of the commercial legal data bases such as Lexis or Westlaw.

DETERMINING CHARGES

Two points of view have been adopted by firms. One says that the price charged for technological overhead ought to be set high enough so that the firm doesn't just break even but actually makes money on the investment. The other philosophy says that charges for overhead ought to be aimed at a break-even charge to cover the cost of making the firm as efficient as possible to meet the clients' needs for legal services in the best possible way.

In the author's opinion, it is best not to attempt to make a profit center out of technological overhead charges. The better way to make the technology pay for itself is to reuse work more effectively, thus increasing the amount of work that can be billed because of technology advances. This involves adjustment in charging for services rendered to take advantage of the impact of technology by *charging on a per-job basis where appropriate*.

For example, if a particular type of contract can be prepared in half the time because of the use of a boilerplate in a word-processing system, then under the charge-per-job approach the firm still would charge the same—or almost the same—amount for preparing the contract, even though it can be prepared in half the time. The theory for doing this is that the value to the client of the contract still is the same. It is the real time originally used to research and prepare the contract that the client should be charged for. The value of the research into the law is the same to all clients who want an effective contract under applicable law.

(Practically speaking, the firm probably will charge less than before, but not half the previous rate. In other words, the client perceives a benefit to having the work done using automation, but the firm also retains part of the benefit, thus paying itself back for its technological investment.)

The cost-recovery methodology presented in Figures 1 and 2 depicts one method by which a firm could recover the costs of its technological overhead. Many other approaches could be devised to support technological overhead cost recovery.

As shown in Figure 1, for certain categories, such as conflict checks and litigation case support, a standard flat rate is charged. For other categories, an incremental charge is used, as for word processing and work-product retrieval searches.

Figure 2 indicates how the firm will recover all of its investment in technology over the same five-year period in which its investment is amortized, plus recovery for personnel directly associated with running the automated system. There is no attempt to make a profit center out of these charges.

Figure 1

ASSUMPTIONS:					
Initial cost of system	1,500,000		Growth rate	15%	
Financing rate	10.50%				
Number of months	60				
Monthly payment	32,241				
Related personnel costs	70,000	75,600	81,648	88,180	95,234
BILL PREPARATION:					
Average bills per month	625	720	830	950	1,090
Standard surcharge	10.00	10.00	10.00	10.00	10.00
LITIGATION SUPPORT:					
Litigation-support cases per month	10	12	13	15	17
Surcharge per month	40.00	40.00	40.00	40.00	40.00
Average queries per case	50	50	50	50	50
Query charge	5.00	5.00	5.00	5.00	5.00
CONFLICT CHECK:					
New clients per month	150	170	200	230	260
Conflict check charge	20.00	20.00	20.00	20.00	20.00
DOCKET CONTROL:					
Docket entries per month	500	580	670	770	890
Docket entry charge	5.00	5.00	5.00	5.00	5.00
WORK-PRODUCT RETRIEVAL:					
WPR searches per month	50	58	66	76	87
Search charge	10.00	10.00	10.00	10.00	10.00

Figure 2

	Year 1	Year 2	Year 3	Year 4	Year 5	Total
Monthly payment (P&I)	386,890	386,890	386,890	386,890	386,890	1,934,451
Personnel	70,000	75,600	81,648	88,180	95,234	410,662
Total costs	456,890	462,490	468,538	475,070	482,124	2,345,113
Recoveries						
Bill preparation	75,000	86,400	99,600	114,000	130,800	505,800
Word processing	120,000	158,700	206,310	273,758	367,291	1,126,059
Litigation support	34,800	40,020	46,023	52,926	60,865	234,635
Conflicts check	36,000	40,800	48,000	55,200	62,400	242,400
Docket control	30,000	34,800	40,200	46,200	53,400	204,600
Work-product retrieval	6,000	6,900	7,935	9,12	10,494	40,44
Total recoveries	301,800	367,620	448,068	551,209	685,250	2,353,948
Net cost (recovery)	**155,090**	**94,870**	**20,470**	**(76,139)**	**(203,126)**	**(8,835)**

CHAPTER 15

Robert J. Arndt, *Partner, Law Firm Services Group, Price Waterhouse, in two specially prepared articles points out changes that have occurred that justify a changed approach to items of overhead and suggests methods for selective charging for types of law work. In the second article, he describes "Economic Profitability Levers" that affect profitability and the economic realities in today's market. The Value Factors Matrix, based on ComplexityValue and Supply versus Demand, provides a methodology or tool for setting fees.*

The Argument for Separate Billing of Some Overhead Costs

by Robert J. Arndt

Many law firms traditionally have, and still do so today, applied the concept of using an all-inclusive billing rate, i.e., the lawyers' billing rate which is intended to recover the compensation and overhead costs of the lawyer and produce a reasonable profit.

There is a growing view, however, that some costs (previously considered as overhead) should be separated from the lawyer's hourly rate and charged only to those matters specifically benefiting from that cost.

This article discusses the concept of overhead, what is causing this change in thinking and how this change can be applied to a law firm.

What Is Overhead?

Overhead costs are those costs that cannot be charged directly or allocated to a specific product or service—thus they are "indirect" costs. This concept of overhead costs is an accounting concept that has withstood the test of time. An associated concept is that overhead costs can be appropriately allocated to a product or service based on direct labor hours or dollars, gross revenues or some other appropriate "driver." A further concept is that some costs, although direct, are too difficult to charge directly or are "insignificant" and, therefore, can be treated as indirect costs.

The basic definition of overhead costs remains the same, but in some industries the associated concepts of direct-hour allocation or other allocation method are being replaced by more appropriate concepts. This is because of the following:

- The direct-labor component of most products and services is declining and
- Indirect costs do not contribute to the end product in the same manner as labor hours or revenue dollars would suggest

Lack of recognition of these changes is what has caused apparent excessive amounts to be charged to the Department of Defense for hammers, coffeepots, toilet seats, etc. The Department of Defense and many commercial organizations have recognized these changes and are adopting new methods to account for overhead costs.

Now may be the time for the legal profession also to consider such changes.

What Is Being Changed?

Basically, two changes are taking place:

- A growing recognition that:
  - —Some "indirect" activities do not benefit all products or services;
  - —The benefit of some "indirect" activities varies by product or service in a manner different from traditional thinking (e.g., not by direct labor hours or dollars); and
  - —It is more appropriate to allocate indirect costs only to those products and services directly benefiting from that indirect cost.
- Development of several new methods to allocate indirect costs.

Applying These Changes to the Legal Profession

There are two parts to this issue:

- Recognizing changes;
- Deciding what to do.

RECOGNIZING CHANGES

A number of changes have occurred over the past several years and similar changes will continue (maybe some of these changes have only become apparent recently). These changes must be recognized by practicing lawyers, by the judicial system and by clients. For example:

- Document creation time does not vary directly with the lawyers' time.
- Use of computer technology and other support services do not benefit all matters similarly or in relation to the lawyers' time (e.g., document management, expert systems, long distance calls, etc.).
- Space needs often are different for different areas of law; e.g., complex litigation compared to simple tax matters.
- Malpractice insurance risks (and related costs) are different by practice area.
- Paralegal and other support-staff use does not vary directly with the lawyer's time, but generally varies substantially by area of law.
- Work-product data bases do not necessarily benefit matters in relation to a lawyer's time.
- A calendaring system does not equally benefit all matters.

This list probably could go on further, but the point to be made is that there are differences in how support services are used and that the desire to provide equity among clients indicates that some alternate cost-allocation mechanisms must be developed.

DECIDING WHAT TO DO

Here one needs to keep in mind that separate *billing* for support services may not be appropriate for all situations or for all clients. However, separate *charging* into work in progress for support-service use will:

- Give the billing lawyer the *choice* of whether the cost of support services should be separately billed and
- Assist in assessing the profitability of a particular client or service.

Uniform answers cannot be applied to all firms or all situations. Some techniques and approaches, however, can be considered:

- Add a multiplier to the charge for certain costs, such as copying, telephone and computer research, to recover some or all or any costs for monthly usage, equipment depreciation, space, maintenance or necessary support staff.
- Charge separately for support staff working directly on a matter, such as legal assistants, word processors, secretaries and messengers.
- Charge separately when computers or data bases are used specifically for document management or analytical purposes.
- Consider varying lawyers' rates by area of law to recognize differences in space needs and malpractice-insurance costs.
- Charge separately for the investment of lawyer time to create forms or other multiple-use documents.

A FINAL THOUGHT

Chief Justice Warren E. Burger has remarked that "a more productive judicial system is essential for justice." I, and I believe others, would add that a productive legal system is essential to the efficient and effective provision of legal services, and appropriate use of support services can contribute to enhanced productivity.

Many have commented that "all-inclusive" hourly rate billing is counterproductive to productivity, and others have said efficient and effective legal services require the use of modern tools and well-trained support staff.

A final and possibly more compelling thought is that an "all-inclusive" billing rate may not be equitable to all clients.

Separately charging of certain overhead costs should help deal with some of the above-mentioned issues.

Setting Billing Rates: A New (?) View

by Robert J. Arndt

Billing rates serve two basic purposes; they are to:

- Facilitate the billing process; and
- Assist in the assessing profitability.

This article deals with both, albeit from an economic standpoint, and therefore has a profit motivation. The article will cover:

- The economic profitability levers;
- Some economic realities;
- A new (?) view; and
- Some tools for applying the concepts.

THE ECONOMIC PROFITABILITY LEVERS

The acronym RULES is used to describe the economic profitability levers of a professional practice. It stands for:

- *R*ates
- *U*tilization
- *L*everage
- *E*xpenses
- *S*peed

Each of these impacts a firm's profitability and must be considered in connection with one another. For the moment, let's define each one.

- *R*ates means the hourly rate we recover for a lawyer's or other timekeeper's time.
- *U*tilization is the chargeable time of each timekeeper.
- *L*everage is the number of profit contributions per owner (sole practitioner, partner, shareholder).
- *E*xpenses are all the expenses of the firm.
- *S*peed relates to the elapsed time it takes to bill and to collect for the lawyer's time or other charges.

Interrelationships occur in areas such as:

- The same gross revenue can be generated by appropriate adjustments to rates and chargeable time, i.e., lower rates may make it easier to sell "hours" but "hours" more in demand many justify a higher rate.
- More leverage should mean more profit per owner (all else being equal).
- Some clients who are easy to obtain may be willing to pay only lower rates and/or may pay slower than others.
- Clients producing more revenues may require more support staff.
- Some areas of law may effect hourly rates, utilization and expenses differently.

SOME ECONOMIC REALITIES

When looking at economic realities, at least four factors should be considered:

- Supply and demand factors
- Value factors
- Cost factors
- Leverage factors

In any market, we all know there is a demand for services (or products) and there is a supply of these services (or products). We also know that the greater the demand, the greater the price that can be charged (if supply remains constant). Similarly, the lesser the supply, the greater the price that can be charged (if demand remains constant). And the converse is true in both cases.

These economic factors also apply to law firms. The problem is that law firms do not generally think in these terms. While there are some notable exceptions, many firms set firmwide billing rates (and billing policies and practices) based on:

- What their perception is of "competitive" rates and
- What the more vocal clients "insist" on.

Neither is appropriate when setting rates applicable to each matter because:

- Firms do not serve the same clients with identical services, thus supply-and-demand factors frequently are different among firms.
- Not all clients "insist" on the same rates or billing practices.

In addition:

- Some hours produce greater value for some clients than similar hours for the same or other clients.

A NEW (?) VIEW

Rule 1.5 of the American Bar Association's Code of Professional Ethics is not new, but greater emphasis on this rule may be new. In any event, firms should be able to profit and at the same time offer more equity to their clients by reassessing their billing rates and billing policies and practices by using this rule. It provides recognition to the above-mentioned concepts.

Basically, Rule 1.5 states:

> (a) A lawyer's fee should be reasonable. The factors to be considered in determining the reasonableness of a fee include the following:
> (1) the time and labor required, the novelty and difficulty of the questions involved and the skill requisite to perform the legal service properly;
> (2) the likelihood, if apparent to the client, that the acceptance of the particular employment will preclude other employment by the lawyer;
> (3) the fee customarily charged in the locality for similar legal services;
> (4) the amount involved and the results obtained;
> (5) the time limitations imposed by the client or circumstances;
> (6) the nature and length of the professional relationship with the client;
> (7) the experience, reputation and ability of the lawyer or lawyers performing the services; and
> (8) whether the fee is fixed or contingent.

The new view, therefore, is to *apply the old rules* and *get out of the hourly rate billing trap*.

APPLYING THESE CONCEPTS

What is needed are "tools" to assist a billing lawyer to get out of the hourly billing-rate trap. While some of these tools can be somewhat informal (such as a billing review process), firms should be able to benefit from using matrix techniques. This tool provides lawyers within a firm a common framework to assess differences in supply and demand, value, costs and leverage, as well as other factors, and to take these differences into account when determining billing rates or amounts to be used on individual matters.

Basically, a matrix looks like the following:

	High				Low
High	100	110	120	130	140
	90	100	110	120	130
	80	90	100%	110	120
	70	80	90	100	110
Low	60	70	80	90	100

The center of the matrix is the 100 percent value point or that point where the horizontal and vertical factors being considered (say complexity or value/supply and demand) are at their midpoint, e.g., a reasonable case result and a balanced supply versus demand.

Departure from the 100 percent point would then be made higher or lower, depending on value to the client, or right or left, depending on differences in supply-and-demand factors. Downward adjustments must, of course, be considered very carefully.

The percentages shown in each box need to be established for each firm and may need revision from time to time or for specific matters as circumstances change.

Use of this technique should, of course, be discussed up front with the client and may, in some states, be required to be clearly described in an engagement letter.

Let's look at a few examples of how this tool might work.

COMPLEXITY OR VALUE/SUPPLY VERSUS DEMAND DIFFERENCES

In a situation where an exceedingly good result was obtained in a lawsuit and the availability of experienced lawyers in the community dealing with the related issues was low (an ideal situation for the lawyer), a Value Factors Matrix might be used as follows:

Complexity/Value					
High	100	110	120	130	140
	90	100	110	120	130
Complexity/Value	80	90	100%	110	120
	70	80	90	100	110
Low	60	70	80	90	100
	High	Supply versus Demand			Low

In this case, a value of 140 percent of standard rates might be applicable. If, however, a reasonable result was obtained and the supply of experienced lawyers was very high in relation to demand, an 80 percent factor might be applicable.

COST/LEVERAGE DIFFERENCES

Costs per hour vary from two standpoints: total costs and annual chargeable hours. Obviously, compensation costs vary depending on lawyer experience, but they also can vary by areas of law, e.g., malpractice insurance premiums and cost of docketing systems. Similarly, annual chargeable hours also can vary by area of law, e.g., litigators working ten hours per day, seven days a week, 52 weeks a year will produce more annual chargeable hours than, say, tax lawyers who may have to stay abreast of rapidly changing tax laws and work on many relatively small matters. Profit per hour will vary, therefore, unless billing rates are adjusted to take into account these differences.

In addition to the above, profits per partner, as mentioned earlier, also can vary as the number of profit contributors per partner vary. Similarly, profits per matter also can vary based on the relationship of matter-responsible partner hours to other profit-contributor hours. These can vary because of a number of factors such as case size, matter complexity, client preferences and choice of the responsible partner. While it may be needless to say, profits will be greater (if all other factors remain equal) if more profit contributors per responsible partner are used on any particular matter.

To take into account these types of differences, a Cost Factors Matrix might be used as follows:

Leverage					
Low	100	110	120	130	140
	90	100	110	120	130
Leverage	80	90	100%	110	120
	70	80	90	100	110
High	60	70	80	90	100
	Low	Costs Per Hour			High

If we have a situation that allows high chargeable hours per day but also requires a very high ratio of partner to associate hours, 100 percent of standard billing rates might be used. On the other hand, with matters allowing only a small number of hours to be charged per day but making it possible to use a large number of associates or legal assistants, a 100 percent value also might be used.

VARIATIONS AND COMBINATIONS

Of course, other types of matrices can be used, such as client's ability to pay and preclusion from other work. Each firm should consider whether they are significant in their practice and if use of a matrix can be applied.

Additionally, the matrix technique should be thought of as additive when multiple matrices are used, i.e., the value derived from use of a matrix should be considered the 100 percent value when applying a second or third matrix.

A FINAL THOUGHT

Earlier, the matrix technique was referred to as a "tool." Like other tools, the effectiveness of its use is dependent on the professional or artisan using the tool.

Professional judgment must be applied when using this tool; its effective use can result in more profit to the practitioner.

CHAPTER 16

Milton W. Zwicker, *who practices in Orillia, Ontario, with Zwicker Evans and Lewis, writes a monthly column in the Canadian Bar publication* The National. *Always innovative, Zwicker suggests that the charge made for legal services should be the "price" not a "fee" because of the changed connotation that the word "price" implies. He argues that a new approach should be taken in "pricing." In the second article, he explores a "value added" approach, where each step is analyzed from the standpoint of what "value" from the client's point of view resulted from that step. He questions whether traditional attitudes toward the charging of fees are appropriate in today's legal marketplace.*

Legal Pricing Strategies Require a Great Deal of Skill and Knowledge

by Milton W. Zwicker

What part do legal fees play in the success or failure of lawyers and their firms? Probably more than most of us know or would like to believe. Lawyers are just beginning to learn what it means to be market driven. The competitiveness of the marketplace is forcing not only lawyers but many other service providers to do a better job of pricing. This means we must better understand the meaning and importance of legal fees. It appears that we have a long way to go to gain this understanding. Well-known Halifax lawyer, Peter Green, in a speech to the Nova Scotia Education Society, said: "The lawyer's fee is one of the least-understood aspects of the practice of law, both within the profession and by the general public."

Fee Versus Price

The way some lawyers freely quote legal fees to real estate agents and potential clients would lead you to believe these lawyers regard price as their only basis for competition. They also lend truth to Green's belief. Unfortunately, these fee-quoting lawyers do not realize that pricing strategies require a great deal of skill and knowledge.

These lawyers remind me of how Oscar Wilde defined a cynic in his most-often-quoted epigram, "A cynic is one who knows the price of everything and the value of nothing."

At the same time, this approach is understandable because of a dichotomy we face. On the one hand, we must remain competitive; on the other hand, we are bound by the traditions and rules of professional conduct.

Most rules of professional conduct, for example, forbid us "to provide legal services at reduced rates for the purpose of attracting clients."

The traditions of our profession permeate many aspects of our lives. These traditions surround the discussion of legal fees with a type of taboo. It is tradition that causes us to continue to call our charges "fees" instead of "price." There is an image of commercialism connected to the word *price* that we believe is not true of the word *fee*. The idea that lawyers perform legal services for satisfaction and not profit, covertly, if not overtly, permeates much of management thinking about pricing legal services. It is time we did a better job of analyzing and examining the role of legal fees, from our firms' and our clients' points of view. A successful marketing plan will force you to consider the role of fees as a practice development tool.

Perhaps it is time we got in step with the commercial world and called our charges "our price" instead of "our fee." This is more than a cosmetic change, because the word *fee* attempts to hide what is in truth a commercial transaction. In addition, the word *price* carries a lot of weight in economic theory. Undoubtedly, you will recall that economic theory directly links the price, value and utility of a product or service. Price is value, expressed in terms of dollars and cents. Fee, on the other hand, is a payment for service rendered by a superior. We must ask: What is the underlying effect on clients of a word that lacks a concept of value?

Theodore Levitt, renowned Harvard marketing professor, reminds us in *The Marketing Imagina-*

Reprinted with permission of the ***Canadian Bar Association.***

tion: "Price is, of course, powerful." Price plays a substantial part in determining the competitive position of your firm. This concept is easy to state, but we lack the research and knowledge to know how to price our services in ways other than by fixed fees and hourly rates.

PRICING GOALS

If you want to do a better job of pricing your services, first decide what you want your price structure to accomplish. Goal setting is as important in pricing as it is in any other part of your management success. Major pricing goals may be to:

- Earn a set percentage for draws over all firm costs;
- Get a target share of a market;
- Maximize profits; and
- Meet competition.

Very few firms, however, consciously establish pricing goals or clearly state their specific price policies. Without pricing goals, firms will continue to follow traditional fee-setting practices. In goal setting, you should be aware of some well-established facts and principles of pricing. For instance, clients rely heavily on price as an indicator of a service's quality. A number of studies have consistently shown that consumers' perceptions of quality vary directly with price. You can find a summary of some of these studies in the February 1973 issue of the *Journal of Marketing Research.* Our rules of professional conduct rule out the freedom of price flexibility found in most other businesses. The fundamental need for any organization, except governments, is to ensure that revenue, as a minimum, covers costs.

FEE DETERMINATION

It is only after you have determined your goals that you are in a position to determine what your fees should be. You now have the opportunity to consider carefully one of the primary elements of leverage in achieving firm profitability—pricing. There are five major methods you may wish to consider in setting your fees. Your actual fees, depending on the types of law you practice, may be one or a combination of these methods:

- Fees based on your total costs plus a desired profit (drawings). This method has one drawback. It does not take into account market conditions. If your costs are out of line, your fees may be much higher then your competition. You will need something else, besides price, to differentiate your services.
- Contingency fees.
- Fixed fees. These are fees that some outside body sets. Legal-aid tariffs are a good example of this type of arrangement.
- Contract fees are those that you establish by negotiation.
- Value-based billing. In essence, this means what the market will bear. This type of pricing is particularly suitable for new cutting-edge areas of the law. In the product-pricing field, this is known as "skim-the-cream pricing." This means the product or service you offer is relatively insensitive to price.

You no longer can ignore the demands of the marketplace with your fee-setting strategies or lack of them. A law firm must be market-oriented when it sets fees. This means you must consider your existing client relationships. You should examine your policies to be sure that the methods you use to set fees are meeting your clients' needs as well as your own. Fees are an important tool to help you obtain and retain clients. Remember, most clients are more value sensitive than they are fee sensitive. Give them value and they will continue to beat a path to your door.

Value-Added Pricing of Legal Services

by Milton W. Zwicker

A system that promises 20 to 50 percent increases in direct and indirect labor productivity bears close examination by every serious practitioner of management. I, too, could not avoid the temptation to examine just such a system, despite its use in manufacturing. Is there something from this system that I could put to use in my office? "Just-In-Time" manufacturing is spreading throughout corporate North America. Management consultant Edward J. Hay describes this system in his new book, *The Just-In-Time Breakthrough.* According to Hay, "JIT is a methodology for removing large amounts of nonvalue-adding activities from manufacturing, purchasing and distribution."

THE JIT PHILOSOPHY

Hay believes that you can apply JIT techniques to nonmanufacturing companies.

The dramatic changes taking place in the legal profession dictate that we must be alert to any system that will help us deliver legal services better, faster and cheaper. Especially, better from our clients' points of view. For me, this is the exciting promise: We can apply parts of the JIT philosophy to the practice of law. Hay reports "improvements in service to customers" is one of the obvious benefits realized by those who use this process. If you read Hay's book, you surely will find some sound management principles to apply to your practice. The legal profession is a sector of the economy crying out for the application of good management principles. If we want to explore and blaze new trails in the management of professional services, we must be willing to look beyond the borders of our own profession.

JIT will take you beyond those borders. Those borders begin with the idea that each step in the manufacturing process should add value to a product. To accomplish this, the JIT philosophy challenges many standard manufacturing concepts and procedures. We need to challenge many of our own standard operating procedures. We must prepare ourselves for change; otherwise, the marketplace will impose its own changes.

Our method of billing clients using time and hourly billing rates is being questioned and challenged by some clients and lawyers. The November 23, 1987, issue of *The National Law Journal* contained a special report on billing. The *Journal* article is proof of the need for change and the challenge we face:

> **Hourly rates, for decades the mainstay of law firms' fee structures, continue to be gradually supplanted by more creative ways of putting a price tag on a case. Task-based or value billing—a system in which lawyer and client negotiate an agreed-on fee for a case—is meeting broader acceptance by many firms and corporate in-house counsel.**

The concept of value billing forces us to think hard about every step or procedure we take on behalf of our clients. The JIT philosophy of value contains several important lessons that we can apply in the legal profession. We can adapt the JIT principle that requires listing each step in the manufacturing process for the purpose of a value-added analysis. If a step does not add value, eliminate it if at all possible. In his book, Hay gives an example of how this works as he describes the efforts at Xerox to adapt to JIT production. "The next step for Xerox was to realize that packaging does not add value. The original practice was to receive the product in corrugated

Reprinted with permission of the ***Canadian Bar Association.***

boxes, which were cut or ripped open and thrown away. Xerox developed returnable, recyclable plastic containers. . . ."

Value—What Is It?

Our attempt to adapt value billing to meet clients' needs is a good opportunity to think about value-added services. You cannot attempt value billing without value-added services. Value billing in the legal profession will not work until we come to grips and accept what value means to our clients. Our attempt at value billing merely reflects the demand by clients for value. Most of us, no matter what we are buying, don't mind paying a fair price so long as we receive value. What is value? There is no easy answer to this question, but the question, itself, is a challenge to the common wisdom of timekeeping. JIT contains not only a value message, but it marches in tune with the fundamental principles of marketing. This means in the long run we must satisfy our clients' needs.

If we are to think in terms of value, we must analyze every legal transaction and document the steps necessary to solve legal problems. On paper, some transactions will involve hundreds of steps or procedures. A value-added analysis will force us to look at each step, to determine if it is necessary and to set a value. Here is how a value-added analysis might look on paper:

Step No.	Activity	Standard Time Value	Actual Time Value	Added Value
1.	Client instructions	$125	$100	$ 75
2.	Prepare affidavit	$ 75	$ 75	$250

This example demonstrates that an activity can provide substantially more value to a client than time at normal billing rates or it can provide less value. This approach opens up the opportunity for you to discuss a particular activity with a client and demonstrate its value. Every legal transaction will not lend itself to such a process; however, this is no reason not to try. We must look for new and better ways to deliver legal services. The words of Hay about the challenges facing manufacturers can apply to our profession. "The most successful companies are trying to move to a JIT environment in order to meet challenges: to gain or hold onto market share, increase quality and lower price. These companies seek to make their manufacturing a strategic tool in the marketplace."

The Concept of Adding Value

If we are to think in terms of value, we must adapt new value statements and policies that encourage the concept of adding value. Clients frequently are concerned about the slow process of legal proceedings. Clients want us to provide reliable estimates of the time frames to complete legal transactions. Anything you can do to provide your services ahead of schedule, in a client's eye, is added value. If you, for example, promise a client that you will have an agreement on the fifteenth of the month and you provide it on the thirteenth, you have added value. Clients will pay for what they consider special service. Anytime you can exceed your own promises, you add value to what you have to offer. Knowing this, why not encourage such performance as standard practice within your firm? Turn the concept of just-in-time to always-on-time. A law firm that adopts "always-on-time" as a marketing strategy and carrys it off can easily differentiate itself from the competition.

And you can easily use computers to carry out this policy. Every time you make a promise, enter the promise into your computer tracking system. I do this and add the initials VA to each entry. These initials are a reminder that I am delivering a value-added service. These changes are not easy to make. Hay reminds us, "Many behavioral scientists contend that if change is to occur, it must be preceded by an unfreezing of the current climate that provides the basis for current behavior and attitudes."

Summary

In today's economy, clients are value-conscious and those lawyers who figure out what value is, and deliver it with imagination, will have no trouble succeeding. In the words of *The National Law Journal:* "There are many practical problems that make these and other similar approaches very difficult to implement. There is no easy solution to the problem of providing economic incentives for firms to minimize costs. Nevertheless, the ability of clients and law firms to devise some innovative fee arrangements represents the best hope for short-term improvements in the cost of legal services."

CHAPTER 17

***Geoffrey C. Hazard, Jr.**, and **W. William Hodes** describe some of the existing rules and decisions that heavily impact any approach to billing. These materials are reprinted from,* The Law of Lawyering: A Handbook on the Model Rules of Professional Conduct, *by Geoffrey C. Hazard, Jr., and W. William Hodes.*

The penultimate consideration is whether innovative approaches to billing fit within the parameters of the existing Rules of Professional Conduct. The ultimate issue is whether those rules should be changed for the good of both the lawyers and the clients.

A Look at the Ethical Rules; Fee Shifting in the Federal Courts

by Geoffrey C. Hazard, Jr. & W. William Hodes

RULE 1.5: Fees

(a) A lawyer's fee shall be reasonable. The factors to be considered in determining the reasonableness of a fee include the following:
  (1) The time and labor required, the novelty and difficulty of the questions involved and the skill requisite to perform the legal service properly;
  (2) The likelihood, if apparent to the client, that the acceptance of the particular employment will preclude other employment by the lawyer;
  (3) The fee customarily charged in the locality for similar legal services;
  (4) The amount involved and the results obtained;
  (5) The time limitations imposed by the client or by the circumstances;
  (6) The nature and length of the professional relationship with the client;
  (7) The experience, reputation and ability of the lawyer or lawyers performing the services; and
  (8) Whether the fee is fixed or contingent.

(b) When the lawyer has not regularly represented the client, the basis or rate of the fee shall be communicated to the client, preferably in writing, before or within a reasonable time after commencing the representation.

(c) A fee may be contingent on the outcome of the matter for which the service is rendered, except in a matter in which a contingent fee is prohibited by paragraph (d) or other law. A contingent-fee agreement shall be in writing and shall state the method by which the fee is to be determined, including the percentage or percentages that shall accrue to the lawyer in the event of settlement, trial or appeal, litigation and other expenses to be deducted from the recovery, and whether such expenses are to be deducted before or after the contingent fee is calculated. On conclusion of a contingent-fee matter, the lawyer shall provide the client with a written statement stating the outcome of the matter and, if there is a recovery, showing the remittance to the client and the method of its determination.

(d) A lawyer shall not enter into an arrangement for, charge or collect:
  (1) Any fee in a domestic-relations matter, the payment or amount of which is contingent on the securing of a divorce or the amount of alimony or support, or property settlement in lieu thereof; or
  (2) A contingent fee for representing a defendant in a criminal case.

(e) A division of fee between lawyers who are not in the same firm may be made only if:
  (1) The division is in proportion to the services performed by each lawyer or, by written agreement with the client, each lawyer assumes joint responsibility for the representation;
  (2) The client is advised of and does not object to the participation of all the lawyers involved; and
  (3) The total fee is reasonable.

OVERVIEW

Setting and collecting fees for professional services inevitably creates a conflict between lawyer and client. The conflict may be muted and nonantagonistic; frequently, it goes unspoken. But it can never be made to disappear.

In addition to being professionals, lawyers are business people. They must meet substantial overhead costs and are entitled to compensation for their labor and a return on their intellectual capital. A lawyer's acceptance of employment, therefore, always is based, in part, on its profitability. The lawyer must decide whether the fees to be earned are

---

Reprinted from *The Law of Lawyering: A Handbook on the Model Rules of Professional Conduct,* by Geoffrey C. Hazard, Jr., and W. William Hodes.

worth the effort and will outbalance the fees foregone in not taking some other client's case. This calculus impels a lawyer to impose some kind of limit, however flexible, on the amount of time committed to a case.

A potential conflict of interest under Rule 1.7(b) therefore attends the commencement of *every* client-lawyer relationship, for "the lawyer's own interest" may color or "materially limit" the representation. It is not surprising, therefore, that the loyalty-related concepts of communication and consent have been imported into Rule 1.5.

For example, the best way to minimize the risk that a client will find his or her bill an "unpleasant surprise" is openly to discuss fees in advance. For unsophisticated clients in particular, this kind of communication and "counseling" may be as important as the lawyer's preliminary legal advice. A lawyer should disclose a fair estimate of the likely total fee and explain any respect in which it is contingent or uncertain. Only after such disclosure is given can a client's consent to pay a certain fee be considered truly voluntary.

Rule 1.5(b) now *requires* such discussions. Its use of the term *communication* is a reminder that Rule 1.4 is implicated as well as Rule 1.7. Under Rule 1.4, a client must be given sufficient information so that he or she is able to intelligently direct the lawyer's actions. An important consideration for many clients is whether the services received will be worth the price. Similarly, a client's decision to continue pressing a legal matter may be heavily influenced by the prospective costs involved.

The explicit requirement of communication about fees is an improvement over the Code, which dealt with the question only in the Ethical Considerations. However, Rule 1.5(b) does not flatly require that the communication be in writing, and in this respect it does not go far enough. The Proposed Final Draft had imposed a general requirement of a writing, which would have further reduced disagreements or misunderstandings over fees and would have made it more difficult for unscrupulous lawyers to create misunderstanding. Unfortunately, the ABA House of Delegates thought this proposal represented too much of an infringement on a lawyer's freedom of action and deleted it; only *contingent* fees must be described in writing (Rule 1.5(c)).

A fee must not only be explained to the client; it also must be objectively reasonable. Rule 1.5(a) therefore prohibits unreasonable fees without regard to whether the client consents. The Rule then lists a number of factors to be used in determining the reasonableness of a fee. These factors, substantially taken from DR 2-106(B), can be used by a lawyer conscientiously trying to set a reasonable fee and by a disciplinary authority later evaluating the fee charged.

Although the list in Rule 1.5(a) is derived from the similar list in DR 2-106, the focus of that Disciplinary Rule was not so clear as that of the Model Rule. Under the Code, the question was not whether a fee was "reasonable," but whether it was "clearly excessive," although the Disciplinary Rule also did refer to "reasonableness." The Code's formulation thus suggested somewhat greater leeway for the lawyer. Furthermore, under the Code, the listed factors were not objective determinates but subjective factors that would lead "a lawyer of ordinary prudence" to conclude that the fee was excessive. Rule 1.5(a) adopts many of the same factors, but treats them as components of an objective criterion.

The first two subsections of Rule 1.5 lack an important definition that must be read into both. Both speak of the "fee" to be charged, but do not make clear enough that the explanation to a client should also address potential expenses as well. The typical client does not distinguish between legal fees and out-of-pocket expenses associated with the lawyer's handling of a legal matter. Lawyers who intend to guide rather than mislead must therefore assume that a discussion of "fees" also includes expenses.

Rule 1.5(c), dealing with contingent fees, adverts separately to the question of fees and expenses and requires written communication as to both. If this subsection is read in isolation, however, it can be misinterpreted to mean that *any* contingent fee is appropriate and *any* allocation of expenses is acceptable, so long as it is set forth in writing. That interpretation is incorrect, for contingent fees also must be reasonable, in conformity with Rule 1.5(a).

Rule 1.5(d) continues the traditional ban on charging contingent fees in criminal and certain domestic-relations matters.

Rule 1.5(e) represents a subtle but significant change in the law. Under traditional norms, fee splitting by lawyers has been curtailed to prevent payment of "referral" fees to lawyers who have done little or no legal work but act as case finders for other lawyers. Lawyers were permitted to split fees only if they shared the work or the "responsibility." In practice, this limitation was purely formal. Rule 1.5(e) now legitimizes fee splitting, so long as each lawyer assumes joint responsibility and the client agrees. Hence, lawyers will be able to profit as finders or forwarders merely by agreeing to share potential liability in the unlikely event of a later disciplinary proceeding or malpractice action.

Fee Shifting Under § 1988

Although the "American Rule" is that each party in litigation must pay its own lawyers, win or lose, there now are a very large number of statutory exceptions. The best-known and most-litigated of these is 28 U.S.C. § 1988, sometimes referred to as the Fees Act of 1976. Under the Act, a court "may allow" "reasonable" attorneys' fees to the prevailing party in certain civil-rights actions.

The legislative history is clear that Congress became concerned that many meritorious lawsuits, involving vindication of federal statutory and constitutional rights, would go unlitigated because they would not generate sufficient fees to attract competent counsel from the private bar. If these suits involved injunctive or declaratory relief, the fear was that plaintiffs would not be able to afford flat or hourly rates; if they involved money damages, the fear was that the chance of a substantial award was still too slim to attract counsel under normal contingent-fee arrangements. Yet Congress believed that federal policy would be served if such suits were brought by a series of "private Attorneys General." Encouraged by Congress, each of these lawyers would act for a small number of individuals, but in the aggregate they would lighten the federal government's enforcement load and also send the appropriate message to potential wrongdoers.

The Fees Act, therefore, provides the missing incentive: If a lawyer takes on such a case and wins for the plaintiff, the losing defendant will be required to pay a fee reasonably approximating market rates. The fee award thus may be thought of as a special kind of contingent fee. The lawyer gets paid only if the case is won (thus creating an appropriate *disincentive* for bringing weak cases), but the fee generally comes out of the pocket of the defendant, rather than cutting into the damages (if any) awarded the plaintiff.

Over the years, the statute has been interpreted to make such an award all but mandatory to a plaintiff who substantially prevails, either by judgment or favorable settlement on the merits. Normally, the fee award is calculated by multiplying the number of hours reasonably spent on the case by a reasonable hourly rate, taking into account market rates in the area, the experience of the lawyer, the results obtained and a number of other factors. The figure thus calculated is called the "lodestar" amount and in rare circumstances it can be increased or decreased. *Hensley v. Eckerhart*, 461 U.S. 424 (1983). Although the fee award has a pronounced contingent factor built in, the Supreme Court recently held that it would not permit any generalized "enhancer" or "multiplier" to be applied to the lodestar amount, although some adjustment to the hours or rates charged in the case might be permitted. *Pennsylvania v. Delaware Valley Citizens' Council for Clean Air*, 107 S. Ct. 3078 (1987).

The courts also have held that the right to an award accrues notwithstanding that plaintiff's counsel has served without charge to the plaintiff. Accordingly, awards are made routinely to plaintiffs represented by public-interest law firms and legal-services offices, on the theory that such awards replenish the budgets of these organizations, allowing them to free up resources to serve other clients. Furthermore, because lawyers from these organizations are acting as "private Attorneys General" as much as any other lawyers, to deny them the normal fee award would present a losing defendant with a windfall. *Blum v. Stenson*, 465 U.S. 886 (1984).

A perplexing set of problems has arisen where the plaintiff is proceeding on a normal (percentage) contingent-fee basis, rather than hourly rate or through legal aid or *pro bono* representation. If the plaintiff prevails, there can be a difference between the amount that would have been due the attorney under the contingent-fee contract and the lodestar amount that would have been awarded by the court.

A number of views have been advanced at various times. One view (the so-called "bright prospects" rule) was that because the plaintiff *had* been able to attract private counsel, there was no need for the statutory award and the lawyer should be left with the contracted-for percentage, while the client should accept the percentage decrease in his or her damages award, as normal tort plaintiffs do. This view ignored the fact that the plaintiff's lawyer almost certainly had weighed the possibility of receiving a statutory fee in the balance in deciding to take the case at all. Furthermore, to deny an award would provide a windfall to a proven wrongdoer.

Another view of the situation simply was that the statutory fee *supersedes* the contingent-fee agreement. Once the plaintiff prevails, the contingency has been removed and the plaintiff's lawyer should be compensated as Congress intended, without creating a windfall or "double payment," but also without creating disincentives by compensating the attorney at less than the lodestar amount. Still another view was that the fee award simply is part of the overall damages to be awarded to the plaintiff and is part of the amount that the attorney had in mind when entering into the contingent-fee contract with the plaintiff. Depending on the wording of the contract, the fee award will be either a separate earmarked amount to be paid to the lawyer or will be part of the recovery to which the contracted-for contingent-fee percentage will apply. These different conceptions play out differently according to whether the statutory fee obtained by award or negotiation is higher or lower than the amount that would result from applying the contingent-fee percentage.

In *Cooper v. Singer*, 719 F.2d 1496 (10th Cir. 1983), the Tenth Circuit first refused the defendant's invitation to use the private contract amount as a ceiling on the statutory award and then held that the lodestar amount, as independently determined by the court, would control. If the lodestar was *less* than the contingent fee, the lawyer would be required to reduce his or her fee to that amount on the theory that anything more was by definition not "reasonable." If the statutory fee was *more* than the contingent fee would have been, the lawyer would be entitled to all of it. In both situations, it appears to be contemplated that the plaintiff will not pay anything out of pocket. In effect, the court makes two awards against the defendant in favor of the plaintiff, one for damages and one for attorneys' fees, but commands the plaintiff to hand over the second award to his or her lawyer, dollar for dollar. The lawyer, in turn, is required to accept that award and to seek no further sum from the plaintiff. The court's power to rewrite the private contract in this fashion was said to spring from its inherent power to control lawyers appearing before it and to ensure that they received only such fees as are reasonable.

The Third Circuit took a slightly different tack in *Sullivan v. Crown Paper Board Co.*, 719 F.2d 667 (3d Cir. 1983). The court agreed that the lodestar amount should be determined independently and that if the award was higher than the contract amount, the plaintiff's obligation would be discharged by turning it over to the lawyer. But when the statutory fee is *lower* than the contracted-for amount, the plaintiff should be required to make up the difference, rather than forcing the lawyer to reduce his or her fee. In *Hamner v. Rios*, 769 F.2d 1404 (9th Cir. 1985), the Ninth Circuit reached the same result, but added one more twist: Where the lodestar amount is lower than the contracted-for amount, the court should decide on a case-by-case basis whether the plaintiff should make up the difference or whether the lawyer should be satisfied with the lower amount.

In *Kirchoff v. Flynn*, 786 F.2d 320 (7th Cir. 1986), the Seventh Circuit tried a different conceptual approach altogether. The lower court had used the privately set contingent rate of 40 percent to award a $10,000 fee in a case in which the plaintiff recovered $25,000 (the entire $35,000 to be paid by the defendant). The plaintiff claimed that the much-higher lodestar amount should have been awarded. At first glance, the trial court's method seems to generate the best possible approximation of market rates—the 40 percent rate was the actual product of an arm's-length negotiation and it generally is not an uncommon rate for tort cases. If the suit is successful, the lawyer receives what he or she bargained for, the defendant pays it and the vindicated civil-rights plaintiff keeps the entire damages award.

On appeal, however, the Seventh Circuit reversed the award precisely because it was linked too closely (and uncritically) with the contract. Judge Easterbrook's sophisticated opinion first demonstrated that the client-lawyer contract cannot be allowed to *control* the amount the defendant will pay, for the defendant did not participate in the market. If the plaintiff knows that the defendant will pay the entire freight, the plaintiff might as well agree to a 100 percent rate—attracting the best-possible counsel, doubling what the defendant must pay, but actually costing the plaintiff nothing.

This part of the opinion helps solve the puzzle left by the cases just discussed, for it separates the contract from the statutory fee and strongly implies that, as between the lawyer and the client, both should be bound by the contract because *as between them* it was freely negotiated. Thus, if the court-awarded fee is low, the plaintiff should *not* be able to force the lawyer to reduce the fee and should be required to pay the difference; however, if the fee awarded by the court is higher than the contract amount, the plaintiff should be able to pay the contract amount *and keep the balance*.

This perhaps surprising result seems to be consistent with *Evans v. Jeff D.*, 106 S. Ct. 1531 (1986). That case makes it clear that the fee award "belongs" to the client, not the lawyer, and is therefore subject to being waived or compromised by the client. By the same token, the "owner" of the eventual fee award should be allowed to use it as a bargaining chip in negotiations with lawyers who are considering taking the case. This reading of the statute still carries out the basic Congressional policy, for if civil-rights plaintiffs will in general receive additional "damages" in the form of a fee award, that will enable them to make this kind of case more attractive to private lawyers. That does not mean, however, as some civil-rights lawyers have argued, that the lawyer has an independent or vested right in the fee as against the defendant. Otherwise, a lawyer who had been fired by his or her client early in the litigation could demand the accrued fee to date from the defendant.

In the remainder of his *Kirchoff* opinion, Judge Easterbrook advanced what might be called a "specific market" approach. Although he had just demonstrated why the private fixed contingent fee could not be applied in order to fix the defendant's liability for fees, he argued that *some* percentage fee might, indeed, be superior to the lodestar approach where money damages, rather than injunctive relief, was sought. But because civil-rights plaintiffs face many procedural hurdles and substantive defenses that ordinary tort plaintiffs do not, a higher percentage rate might be appropriate in this particular market, and the case was remanded for such a determination. In *Kirchoff*, where there was a 40 percent contingent-fee contract, one must presume that if a higher percentage rate were approved on remand, the overall award to the plaintiff would be increased and the existing contract would then dictate that the lawyer receive 40 percent of that increment, *not* all of it.

The *Kirchoff* opinion concluded with the thought that while the lodestar approach best approximates the normal market where injunctive or declaratory relief is sought, it can lead to disproportionate fees in cases where only modest damages are likely to be awarded. To award hourly fees in this specific market might encourage counsel to invest time that even wealthy clients could not afford to pay for. This part of the opinion does not survive *Rivera v. City of Riverside*, 106 S. Ct. 2686 (1986), which was pending when *Kirchoff* was decided. In *Rivera*, the plaintiffs received a damages award of only $33,000, yet their lawyers spent almost 2,000 hours on the case over a period of four years. The lodestar was calculated to be $245,000, and this award (presumably all earmarked for the lawyers) was upheld.

What Is "Reasonable" Fee?

Ultimately, the clash in all of these cases is about what fee is "reasonable," and *Rivera* reflects the different philosophies very well. The dissenters argued vehemently that a fee more than seven times the damages award was by definition unreasonable, for no reasonable client would pay such hourly fees in pursuit of such a modest claim. But the plurality argued that it is precisely because private counsel would not otherwise invest the requisite time in such cases that the fee must be awarded in order to carry out the Congressional mandate to encourage the filing of meritorious but not lucrative civil-rights claims. In this view, the amount "won" by the plaintiff cannot be measured only in terms of the damages awarded; the plaintiff's lawyer is, in effect, being recruited as a salaried lawyer for the government, with the special conditions that the salary is contingent on success and that it will come from the losing defendant to the plaintiff and then from the plaintiff to the lawyer, according to whatever contract is in effect.

In any event, taking the situation as a whole—the statute, the assumption that there will be contingent fees and the complications of trying to impose the statutory award on top of a contingent-fee agreement—it makes more sense to hold that the statutory award simply augments plaintiff's damages and that the contingent-fee agreement applies to the recovery according to the agreement's terms. It should be open to plaintiffs and their lawyers to negotiate over the method of dividing up the damage and fee awards. For example, an agreement simply could provide that all damages go to the client and all amounts awarded as fees go to the lawyer. Or, as indicated earlier, the parties could agree to treat all amounts received by the plaintiff as equally subject to a fixed or bracketed percentage.

The plaintiffs' ability to seek a variety of fee arrangements on the market should ensure that counsel will be forthcoming in meritorious cases and that the (losing) defendant will pay the lion's share of the fee. By the same token, lawyers will be able to negotiate for sufficiently high percentages to protect them against the contingency of not prevailing. Because that contingency is what drove both the lawyer and the client to proceed on a contingent-fee basis in the first place, each should enjoy whatever benefits came from their bargain. If a court tries to superimpose its calculation of what is fair as between plaintiff and plaintiff's lawyer, it would undermine their allocation of risk.

Of course, the fee provided for in the agreement still must be "reasonable" so far as the law of lawyering is concerned. In this limited sense, the courts *should* exercise a supervisory role. But the term *reasonable*, as used in Model Rule 1.5 or its predecessor DR 2-106, does not necessarily have the same meaning as it does in a statutory provision for awarding "reasonable" fees. When a court assesses a "reasonable fee" against the defendant and turns that amount over to the plaintiff, it is exercising an adjudicatory function and must take into account a whole range of policies and must consider also what effect its ruling will have on other would-be market participants. Because the defendant is forced willy-nilly to "hire" the plaintiff's lawyer (after the fact) at roughly market rates, this might be called an application of market reasonableness.

In contrast, the term *reasonable* in Rule 1.5 requires the application of regulatory reasonableness. It is invoked to determine whether the actual lawyer-client fee contract properly may be enforced. In a case such as *Rivera v. City of Riverside*, both conceptions of reasonableness can be satisfied. While it would, of course, be unreasonable for private clients to spend $245,000 to gain $33,000 in damages, it is not unreasonable for society to acknowledge the public value of the many hours spent and to tax the defendant for it. As between the clients and the lawyer, it also is reasonable to uphold their agreement, giving the larger sum to the lawyer. Because the client's stake was ultimately rather small, and all agreed that the lawyer would not take the case unless assured the chance of a compensatory fee, why should the lawyer not enjoy the fruits of his or her labors?

NEGOTIATING SETTLEMENTS

Another series of difficult problems has involved the problem of negotiating settlements when potential Fees Act awards are in the game. For example, in a case involving a substantial claim for money damages, a defendant may indicate a willingness to settle but demand that the total settlement (including the attorney's fees the plaintiff will seek) be negotiated as a "package deal." The defendant then offers a total settlement figure, expressing indifference as to how the plaintiff and his or her lawyer split it. Or in a case in which a legal-services office is litigating a case involving injunctive relief only, the defendant offers to change its conduct to conform to the relief sought, but only on the condition that the plaintiff waive his or her right to attorney's fees under § 1988.

For a time, some courts and disciplinary authorities barred the first kind of negotiating tactic on the part of defendants on the theory that it created a conflict of interest between the plaintiff and his or her lawyer, forcing them to compete for shares of a fixed sum. The leading case was *Prandini v. National Tea Co.*, 557 F.2d 1015 (3d Cir. 1977). This prohibition against "tying" might have been commendable in theory, but it was unrealistic in practice.

The defendant knows that if he or she agrees not to contest liability, he or she will be liable for some attorney fees; he or she has a legitimate need, therefore, to know the approximate size of the award so that he or she can frame settlement offers accordingly. Such information may be critical to the defendant's willingness to settle at all, for some fee awards have far exceeded the amount claimed by the plaintiff on the merits, as in *Rivera*. By settling on the basis of a single lump-sum figure, defendants can eliminate the risk of indeterminate liability for fees.

At the same time, the plaintiff's attorney has better information than the defendant's attorney of the evidence that can be offered as to what would be a reasonable fee and therefore as to what fees a court probably will award. He or she can therefore assess whether the defendant's total offer will leave an acceptable sum for the client, once the fee award is subtracted. The plaintiff's attorney, of course, has an independent duty to recommend acceptance of only such offers as will benefit his or her client, but the client retains ultimate authority as to whether to settle on these or any other terms (see Rule 1.2(a)).

The *Prandini* court recognized all of this, but also recognized that defendant's tactics put pressure on the plaintiff's lawyer to seek a smaller award, so that the package is more attractive to the client. (A good analogy is a real estate broker who cuts a commission at the last moment to facilitate the closing of a deal.) Superficially, the pressure might seem to be "unfair," for the plaintiff's lawyer is under a duty to advance his or her client's interests and may not permit his or her own self-interest to "materially limit" the advice given (see Rule 1.7(b)).

The court in *Prandini* lost touch with the reality of the situation, however, by failing to acknowledge that where a plaintiff is represented by compensated counsel, there is *always* a conflict between them concerning distribution of the asset realized or protected through the attorney's assistance, whether the proceeds are from a settlement or from a judgment. Despite high-toned appeals to professional duty, in the end the exact worth of the lawyer's assistance only can be resolved by bargaining between the client and the lawyer, subject, of course, to the rule required that the attorney take no more than is "reasonable."

Although negotiation sometimes is awkward, it is perfectly proper for a lawyer to negotiate with a client in advance for a reasonable fee, to insist on being paid that fee and to let the client accept or reject the defendant's offer accordingly. (Compare Rule 1.5(b), which notes that fee arrangements normally should be made in advance of the representation, preferably in writing.) If the plaintiff's lawyer refuses to make a contribution to the plaintiff's recovery by cutting the fee, Rule 1.4 (governing communication with a client) is satisfied and so is Rule 1.7(b). This follows because the attorney's representation has *not* been materially impaired—the attorney has elicited an offer from the defendant and has accurately noted that the client must discount it by the client's legal obligation to pay the agreed-on fee. If the client is not satisfied with the net amount that remains, the client can reject the offer and attempt to obtain more from his or her adversary, rather than from his or her lawyer.

Of course, there are many situations in which the plaintiff's lawyer will agree to contribute to the settlement by accepting a smaller award than he or she would otherwise be entitled to. Under the *Prandini* regime, parties who were prohibited from engaging in overt simultaneous negotiation of fees and merits developed a set of tacit negotiating strategies to reach compromise in such situations.

As noted earlier, the amount of the fee to be awarded is central to all negotiated settlements where the Fees Act or a similar statute is in play. That amount, however, is influenced by the presentation that the prevailing lawyer makes to the court. Under *Prandini*, the plaintiff's lawyer may reveal to the defendant the proof he or she intends to offer (chiefly a log of hours worked) and may tacitly agree to offer no other proof (such as special difficulties encountered in the case, which might entitle him or her to a so-called "multiplier"). A lawyer also could tacitly agree to present *less* than all of the available proof. The court still would retain discretion in the matter and still would have final authority to set the amount of the award. Package deals were therefore similar to a negotiated stipulation that a court could reject if manifestly untrue or unjust. Still, rather than countenance the continued use of such tactics, which require that a mild deception be practiced on the court, the United States Supreme Court has disapproved the *Prandini* rule and authorized the overt simultaneous negotiation of fees and merits. See *Marek v. Chesney*, 105 S. Ct. 3012 (1985) (by implication) and *Evans v. Jeff D.*, 106 S. Ct. 1531 (1986).

The second negotiation scenario (demand that all fees be waived) is that involved in the *Jeff D.* case just cited. That situation differs from *Prandini* and many other "package-deal" cases in two ways. First, the case involved injunctive relief only; second, the lawyer was not a private attorney but worked for a legal-services office.

In *Evans v. Jeff D.*, the Supreme Court interpreted the Fees Act as vesting the right to recover fees *in the client*, although it acknowledged that the ultimate beneficiary would, of course, be the lawyer. That interpretation seems to be clearly correct, as is the Court's logical conclusion that what is owned by the client may be waived or negotiated away by the client. That conclusion is especially sound in light of the fact that Congress rejected a proposal that would have made some award mandatory and not waivable by the client.

The fact that *Jeff D.*, involved injunctive relief at first glance might seem to enhance the pressure on the plaintiff's lawyer: Because the plaintiff had no expectation of receiving any money on account of his substantive claim, it would be cost-free for him to use as a bargaining chip money that he was only going to pass along to his lawyer anyway. But this is illusory. In the case of compensated counsel, the difference between settlement damages and a consent-decree injunction is negligible, so far as the fee is concerned. The attorney will require the client to pay a certain fee for obtaining either form of relief. If the client is willing to pay the lawyer that sum in exchange for a quick settlement on the merits, the deal is a good one for all concerned. If the client is unwilling to pay the lawyer's fee, he or she will reject the defendant's demand for a fee waiver and then may have to accept less on the merits.

The fact that the attorney involved in *Jeff D.* was not private-compensated counsel but a salaried lawyer from a legal-services office also might be thought to drive an unfair wedge between the plaintiff and the lawyer. But this, too, is largely illusory. It is true that the plaintiff's lawyer legally cannot obligate a client to pay a fee, either because of Legal Services Corporation regulations or because of the tax-exempt status of the organization employing the lawyer. When the defendant conditions a settlement on a fee waiver, the lawyer still is bound to present the offer to the client, but the client now has no *financial* incentive to resist. There are other incentives, however. The plaintiff is, in effect, being asked to "trade" the legal services given him or her for legal services that could be given to *some other* legal-aid client. This follows because a fee award would replenish the legal-service organization's budget and allow it to serve others (including perhaps the very client whose case was foregone in order to serve the plaintiff involved in the settlement negotiation). If no award is made, the present plaintiff preempts the available legal services to the extent of the cost of the services already provided.

The underlying tension is not the ordinary two-party tension between lawyer and client regarding fees. Instead, it is a multiparty conflict over allocation of the lawyer's services as between competing indigent clients. A legal-aid lawyer has discretion to make this allocation; indeed, exercise of that discretion cannot be avoided. Furthermore, under Rule 1.2(c), lawyers and clients may agree to "limit" the services to be provided. Thus, while the client of a legal-services organization has no direct financial stake in the matter, provision of service can be limited in a way such that he or she *is* obligated to take into account the allocation of resources described previously. The fact that most legal-aid lawyers would be uncomfortable with such an explicit discussion of the actual cost of their services does not create an impermissible conflict of interest. To the contrary, such a frank discussion would be the legal-services analogue of private discussions about fees, now required by Model Rule 1.5(b).

Although the Supreme Court's statutory construction in the *Jeff D.* case appears to be sound, it may have ironic long-term effects that Congress did not foresee. Defendants routinely will demand fee waivers in all cases in which the plaintiff is represented by legal-services attorneys, whether the cases involve damages or injunctions or both. Whenever such settlements are effected, the legal-services office will have to swallow all costs of the successful action and will sooner or later have to forgo bringing other meritorious cases because of lack of funds. The irony, of course, is that these are federal funds and that the defendants will have received a windfall because they were sued by plaintiffs represented by "free" rather than private lawyers.

Jeff D. will not have an impact in all cases, of course. In many situations, the defendant will feel sufficiently confident of winning at trial that he or she will offer no settlement at all. Or the defendant may offer a settlement that the plaintiff considers inadequate without regard to attorney's fees. And there may be other cases in which plaintiffs will refuse to agree to a fee waiver out of moral obligation rather than financial pressure or specific undertaking. They may consider that because they have received the benefit of "free" legal services, the defendant (who was responsible for their having to seek counsel in the first place) should be required to replenish the legal services budget.

CHAPTER 18

The Honorable **Sidney C. Volinn** *is Bankruptcy Judge, United States Bankruptcy Court, Western District of Washington, in Seattle, Washington. Over the past decades the federal courts have moved toward the "Lodestar system," in approving attorney fees. The initial computation is to multiply a reasonable number of hours by a reasonable hourly rate, and then adjust that calculation based on factors that the court deems relevant. The quest for an objective method for setting fees, as bankruptcy judges regularly are required to do, has not been easy. There is a wide range of decisions. The courts wrestled with such questions as: what is overhead that is included in the hourly rate of the attorney; what and whose hours are not only reasonable but "necessary," what to do about perceived duplication of effort; what subjective factors are properly considered in adjusting the original time-based computation, and countless other issues. Judge Volinn's article, was prepared for his presentation at a seminar for bankruptcy judges in Santa Fe, New Mexico, on April 22, 1988. Note that the twelve factors to be considered in fee setting as noted in the* Johnson *case have been virtually eliminated, as subsequent court decisions declared them "subsumed" in the hourly rate.*

While the profession is moving in the direction of value billing, which involves subjective factors with less emphasis on the time-required factor, the federal courts are moving in the opposite direction with less recognition of these subjective criteria illustrated by the Johnson *rule.*

In the last sentence of his article, Judge Volinn holds out some hope for consideration, such as "the need for the work, the benefit to the estate and the reasonableness of the charge."

The Role of Lodestar in the Setting of Attorney Fees

by Sidney C. Volinn

Before proceeding to the primary subject, it would be appropriate to briefly comment on the role or perspective of the judge to whom is entrusted the task of considering and allowing fees. It has been said that "looking over the shoulders of attorneys to examine their charges is not a task welcomed by judges. . . . Even though our competence to undertake this scrutiny is limited at best, we must assume the burden because at present no other bearer is available." *Planned Parenthood of Cent. & Northern Arizona v. Arizona*, 789 F.2d 1348, 1351 (9th Cir. 1986), *aff'd sub nom. Babbitt v. Planned Parenthood of Cent. & Northern Arizona*, ____ U.S. ____, 107 S. Ct. 391 (1986).

Thus, it falls to the trial judge to hear and review fee applications. It is the province of the trial court to review and allow fees in a setting where the inhibitions pertaining to the usual attorney-client relationship do not prevail. Counsel for a debtor or a trustee represent a bankruptcy estate that is not the typical client. This is so because the ultimate cost or payment of the fee is borne by creditors who have no direct or contractual relationship with counsel. While, theoretically, the attorney-applicant may be subject to the constraints attendant to the creditors' interests as represented by the trustee or counsel, it is a rare occasion when creditors will make their views known. In the overwhelming majority of cases, the only review of fees is conducted by the bankruptcy judge, possibly with the involvement of the U.S. Trustee where there is one.

It is the obligation of the bankruptcy judge to critically examine fees whether there is opposition or not. *In re Goldenberg*, 2 F. Supp. 727, 727 (D.C. E.D.Pa. 1933); *In re First Software Corp.*, 79 B.R. 108, 111 (Bankr. D. Mass. 1987); *In re S.T.N. Enterprises, Inc.*, 70 B.R. 823, 831 (Bankr. D. Vt. 1987); *In re Malden Mills, Inc.*, 42 B.R. 476, 479 (Bankr. D. Mass. 1984). This independent obligation on the part of the judges to examine fees that may be charged against parties or entities where the ordinary or usual attorney-client relationship does not prevail is not unique to bankruptcy. Courts are required to set fees independently and objectively in probate matters, divorce or dissolution proceedings, as well as in many and varied fee-shifting situations permitted by agreement or statute (including the Bankruptcy Code in cases involving 11 U.S.C. §§ 506(b) and 506(c), where fees may be charged by or against secured creditors).

As indicated, the purpose of this paper is to provide a focus on the principal element in review of applications for attorney's fees. This element is expressed primarily in terms of hours multiplied by an hourly rate. This concept, came to be known as the "lodestar" test, originated in the Third Circuit in *Lindy Bros. Builders, Inc. v. Am. Radiator & Standard Sanitary Corp.*, 487 F.2d 161 (3d Cir. 1973) *[Lindy I]* and 540 F.2d 102 (3d Cir. 1976) *[Lindy II]*.

BILLING FACTORS

Prior to lodestar, the predominant method of evaluation involved consideration of various factors of which the hourly rate was but one variable. *Johnson v. Georgia Highway Express, Inc.*, 488 F.2d 714, 717-719 (5th Cir. 1974), a Title VII matter, is the leading case in this area. It listed twelve factors, the first of which is the time and labor involved. The additional factors are: (2) the novelty and difficulty of the problems; (3) the skill required to perform the legal services; (4) preclusion of other employment; (5) customary fees in the type of work involved; (6) whether the fee is fixed or contingent; (7) time limitations composed by the client or the circumstances; (8) the amount involved and the results obtained; (9) experience, reputation and ability of counsel; (10)

undesirability of the case; (11) nature and length of the professional relationship with the client; and (12) awards in similar cases.

Application of this array of variables is cumbersome and difficult. This was articulated in *Pennsylvania v. Delaware Valley Citizens' Council for Clean Air*, 478 U.S. 546, 92 L.Ed. 2d 439 (1986) (*Delaware I*), in which the Supreme Court stated:

> This approach *[Johnson]* required trial courts to consider the elements that go into determining the propriety of legal fees and was intended to provide appellate courts with more substantial and objective records on which to review trial-court determinations. This mode of analysis, however, was not without its shortcomings. Its major fault was that it gave very little actual guidance to District Courts. Setting attorney's fees by reference to a series of sometimes subjective factors placed unlimited discretion in trial judges and produced disparate results.

92 L.Ed. 2d at 455 (citation omitted).

Thus, lodestar has been employed with increasing frequency in recent years. The transition is illustrated by *In re Yermakov*, 718 F.2d 1465 (9th Cir. 1983), which, while alluding to the various criteria set forth in *Johnson*, stated, "The primary method used to determine a reasonable attorney fee in a bankruptcy case is to multiply the number of hours expended by an hourly rate." 718 F.2d at 1471. As in *Yermakov*, criteria employed by courts in considering attorney fees in nonbankruptcy settings now are applied in bankruptcy cases. *See In re Baldwin-United Corp.*, 79 B.R. 321 (Bankr. S.D. Ohio 1987); *In re Kero-Son, Inc.*, 59 B.R. 630, 633-634 (Bankr. D. Conn. 1986); *In re Jensen-Farley Pictures, Inc.*, 47 B.R. 557 (Bankr. D. Utah 1985).

Delaware I considered the propriety of an attorney's fee award pursuant to section 304(d) of the Clean Air Act (42 U.S.C. § 7604(d)), which provides that in any action to enforce the Act, the court may award costs of litigation, including a reasonable attorney's fee. The *Delaware I* Court stated:

> [In *Hensley v. Eckerhart*, 461 U.S. 424 (1983)] We . . . adopted a hybrid approach that shared elements of both *Johnson* and the lodestar method of calculation. . . .
>
> We further refined our views in *Blum v. Stenson*, 465 U.S. 886 (1984). *Blum* restated that the proper first step in determining a reasonable attorney's fee is to multiply "the number of hours reasonably expended on the litigation times a reasonable hourly rate". . . .
>
> *Blum* also limited the factors that a district court may consider in determining whether to make adjustments to the lodestar amount. Expanding on our earlier finding in *Hensley* that many of the *Johnson* factors "are subsumed within the initial calculation" of the lodestar, we specifically held in *Blum* that the "novelty [and] complexity of the issues," "the special skill and experience of counsel," the "quality of representation" and the "results obtained" from the litigation are presumably fully reflected in the lodestar amount, and thus cannot serve as independent bases for increasing the basic fee award. Although upward adjustments of the lodestar figure are still permissible, such modifications are proper only in certain "rare" and "exceptional" cases, supported by both "specific evidence" on the record and detailed findings by the lower courts.
>
> A strong presumption that the lodestar figure – the product of the reasonable hours times a reasonable rate – represents a "reasonable" fee is wholly consistent with the rationale behind the usual fee-shifting statute, including the one in the present case.

92 L.Ed. 2d at 455-456 (citations omitted).

In *Blum v. Stenson*, 465 U.S. 886 (1984), the Court held that virtually all of the *Johnson* elements were subsumed into lodestar except for the factor of contingency. *In re Powerine Oil Co.*, 71 B.R. 767 (9th Cir. BAP 1986), decided prior to *Pennsylvania v. Delaware Valley Citizens' Council for Clean Air*, _____ U.S. _____, 97 L.Ed. 2d 585 (*Delaware II*), affirmed allowance of a substantial increment to the lodestar figure because of a strong element of contingency, despite the absence of a contingent-fee agreement as provided for by 11 U.S.C. § 328. In a bankruptcy setting, this element still can be applicable, although there may now be reason to reexamine this issue because of *Delaware II*. This case, by a bare plurality (four justices), may have folded the remaining unsubsumed element, that of contingency, into lodestar, stating:

> It may be that without the promise of risk enhancement some lawyers will decline to take cases; but we doubt that the bar in general will so often be unable to respond that the goal of the fee-shifting statutes will not be achieved. In any event, risk enhancement involves difficulties in administra-

> tion and possible inequities to those who must pay attorney's fees; and in the absence of further legislative guidance, we conclude that multipliers or other enhancement of a reasonable lodestar fee to compensate for assuming the risk of loss is impermissible under the usual fee-shifting statutes.

Delaware II, 97 L.Ed. 2d at 599.

It should be noted, however, that taking into account the four justice dissents and Justice O'Connor's partial concurrence, it is arguable that the majority of the court has not as yet subsumed the element of contingency into lodestar. The dynamics of this problem are discussed by Judge Newsome in *Matter of Baldwin-United Corp.*, 79 B.R. 321, 344-346 (Bankr. S.D. Ohio 1987).

Powerine discussed the various Supreme Court cases then applicable, as well as *Chalmers v. City of Los Angeles*, 796 F.2d 1205 (9th Cir. 1986), *modified and reh'g denied*, 808 F.2d 1373 (9th Cir. 1987). *Chalmers*, following *Blum v. Stenson*, stated,

> We begin with the Supreme Court admonition that if "the claimed rate and number of hours are reasonable, the resulting product is presumed to be the reasonable fee contemplated by section 1988." The Supreme Court decision in *Blum* further holds that an upward adjustment of an award of fees by use of a multiplier is justified only in rare, exceptional circumstances.

Chalmers, 796 F.2d at p. 1215 (citations omitted). Thus, the Ninth Circuit clearly subscribes to lodestar. As stated above, this standard is applicable in bankruptcy.

The following cases deal with attorney's fees and discuss the key cases in this paper, as well as other cases:

- *Riverside v. Rivera*, 477 U.S. 561, 91 L.Ed.2d 466 (1986) (lodestar analysis appropriate in civil-rights cases, even though plaintiff receives only monetary damages that may be less than attorney's fees. Fee awards under 42 U.S.C. § 1988 do not necessarily have to be proportionate to the amount of damages civil-rights plaintiff actually recovers).
- *In re Agent Orange Product Liability Litigation*, 818 F.2d 226 (2d Cir. 1987), *cert. denied sub nom. Schwartz v. Dean*, 108 S. Ct. 289 (1987) (upheld trial court's exercise of discretion in allowing "quality" multiplier and denying "risk multiplier" (perhaps anticipating *Delaware II*)).
- *In re Seneca Oil Co.*, 65 B.R. 902 (Bankr. W.D. Okla. 1986) (recognized that *Johnson* factors or a good number of them now are used in determining the hourly rate for the lodestar calculation).
- *In re AOV Industries, Inc.*, 43 B.R. 468 (Bankr. D. D.C. 1984) (concluding, after reference to a number of attorney's fees cases in other statutory contexts, that lodestar analysis was proper in the bankruptcy context).

Another case of interest is *Mares v. Credit Bureau of Raton*, 801 F.2d 1197 (10th Cir. 1986). The *Mares* case is a detailed study of the activities of the lawyers, which resulted in the reduction of their fees and costs not only by the trial court but by the circuit court. The court stated in its conclusion:

> Our instructions to district courts regarding their evaluation of tasks, hours, rates and other matters were never meant to cause a subtle shift in the burden of proof from counsel to court. The burden is not for the court to justify each dollar or hour deducted from the total submitted by counsel. It remains counsel's burden to prove and establish the reasonableness of each dollar, each hour, above zero. In the process and especially in the end result, district courts must continue to be a court of wide latitude.
>
> In exercising their considerable discretion within proper guidelines, district courts should above all be directed by the Supreme Court's caution that:
>
>> *These statutes were not designed as a form of economic relief to improve the financial lot of attorneys, nor were they intended to replicate exactly the fee an attorney could earn through a private fee arrangement with his or her client. Instead, the aim of such statutes was to enable private parties to obtain legal help in seeking redress for injuries resulting from the actual or threatened violation of specific federal laws. Hence, if plaintiffs, such as* Delaware Valley, *find it possible to engage a lawyer based on the statutory assurance that it will be paid a "reasonable fee," the purpose behind the fee-shifting statute has been satisfied.*

801 F.2d at 1210 (citing *Delaware I*, 106 S. Ct. at 3098). The foregoing language sets forth a current concern with rising costs of litigation and a perception of the role of courts in dealing with it.

CONCLUSION

It is clear that lodestar has become the baseline for consideration of fee awards. In reviewing the discretionary distance for departure from that line, the Supreme Court appears to hold that the *Johnson* variables are substantially "subsumed" within the reasonable hourly rate. But there still remain the crucial areas for discretionary review within the margins of lodestar that would include considerations attendant to the need for the work, the benefit to the estate and the reasonableness of the charge.

CHAPTER 19

Charles Hansen *is Senior Vice President, Secretary and General Counsel of the Emerson Electric Co. in St. Louis, Missouri. In response to the inquiry by the Task Force, he has furnished us with the documents being presented here. In conversation with Hansen, we inquired how the Litigation Cost Control Matrix System has worked in the two years it has been used. Prior to adopting this system, which is used in products-liability cases only, Emerson Electric went back and analyzed a substantial number of closed cases handled over a three-year period by outside counsel. Certain ranges and practices were noted, both as to legal costs and ultimate disposition of several types of product-liability claims. The concept is to develop a plan, assuming the case will go to trial, even though 50 percent of the cases are settled before trial. The outside lawyer is required to set a budget. Advantages that are claimed are: (1) a case plan is developed within an agreed budget; (2) from the corporation's standpoint, there is a time-line budget for the fiscal year; (3) the system does not impinge on the outside lawyer's control of the case; and (4) both the lawyer and the client become cost conscious throughout the duration of the case. The following items provide greater information about the Litigation Cost Control Matrix System. They are:*

—a letter announcing the system;

—an article from the November 16, 1987 issue, Of Counsel, written by **Larry Smith;** *and*

—a copy of the Litigation Cost Control Matrix.

Hansen indicated that outside counsel are paid on an hourly basis during the preliminary stage of the litigation while the case is being evaluated in order to develop a case plan and agreed-on budget.

Cost Containment—Or a Route to Greater Client Satisfaction through Increased Efficiency

EMERSON ELECTRIC CO.
8000 W. Florissant
P.O. Box 4100
St. Louis, MO 63136
(314) 553-3798

CHARLES HANSEN
Senior Vice President
Secretary and General Counsel

August 11, 1986

To: All Trial Lawyers Handling Emerson Product Liability Cases
Re: Product Liability—Litigation Cost Control

The cost of defending Emerson in product-liability litigation has been escalating rapidly. For example, at the end of the first nine months of FY 1986, our fees, costs and expenses in product cases were $2,275,000 or 83 percent above the figure for the comparable nine months of FY 1985. Even more significantly, under our current cost-control system, we could not determine with any degree of accuracy why these fees and expenses had increased the way they did.

Obviously, something had to be done, but done in a way that would not impact adversely the dedication and performance of Emerson's trial attorneys.

One approach we quickly rejected was to resort to the techniques of a typical insurance company that involve, as we understand them, the imposition of stringent limitations on various facets of litigation. In our opinion, these techniques impact too much on the professional responsibility of the trial attorney.

What we did decide to do was to launch a joint effort among our trial attorneys and the lawyers managing product-liability litigation at Emerson—Ken Ross, Mike Keating and Linda Wuestner—to achieve cost-effective litigation management by simple and direct means. This program will go into operation on October 1, 1986, the start of our 1987 fiscal year.

One further word. The current monthly billing system provides, in our view, no meaningful control of litigation costs whatever. About the only thing we can determine from looking at a monthly bill is whether there has been duplication and whether or not lawyers in the firm have taken trips to Hawaii on a case being tried in Joplin, Missouri. Under this arrangement, it is possible (and in fact has happened) that when you add up all the monthly bills at the end of a case that has lasted three years, you may have paid legal fees of $150,000 in a $50,000 piece of litigation.

The ideal arrangement from the buyer's point of view would be to revert to the old-time system wherein the fees for a piece of litigation were paid only at the end of the case. The advantages of this system from the buyer's viewpoint are obvious, for only when the case is over can you really assess the worth of the legal services. We recognize, however, that reversion to this system is not possible today and in fact would be unfair to the trial attorneys who in effect would be asked to finance our litigation. However, some elements of the old system have been incorporated in our approach.

What we have developed is the "Litigation Cost Control Matrix System." A copy of the Matrix is attached hereto as Exhibit A.

Under this system, at the beginning of a case, a budget will be established through trial between trial attorney and one of the Emerson managing attorneys. To aid in this process, we have computerized the legal fees, costs and expenses actually incurred for all of our closed cases for the past two and one-half years. This, unfortunately, is a large universe. The work has been done by case category, e.g., "Pitman crane electrical contact," "chain saw," "table saw," "LP gas valve," et al. From this data we have developed average costs per case per category. As a result, we believe we now have meaningful guidelines as to what the average case by category has cost Emerson. The next step will be to spread the total case budget through four phases of litigation—First Evaluation Point, Formal Discovery, Ready for Trial and Trial and Post Trial. We think the First Evaluation Point is particularly important because we want to have some definitive system that forces both us and our trial attorneys to evaluate each case early on (say six months from the time a complaint is filed) to decide whether or not we should make a meaningful effort to settle before moving into formal discovery. We, of course, recognize that at the first evaluation point, we both will not have the kind of detailed information that will be developed during discovery, but given our knowledge of the product and certain key additional data learned during the First Evaluation Point Stage (how did the accident happen, what are plaintiff's injuries and medical prognosis, et al.), we should be able to decide together whether settlement efforts are appropriate.

Once the budget has been established in total and by Case Stage, how will the Matrix work?

First, we will request each of our trial attorneys to submit bills to us no more frequently than once per quarter per case. Such bills should include not only legal fees, but costs and expenses. We will no longer pay bills for fees, costs and expenses for $100, $200, and the like, that trickle to us at odd times. In addition, we will require that the trial attorney include in his quarterly bill for each case, a completed Litigation Cost Control Matrix. Incidentally, a reason for one bill per case per quarter is to focus our attention on a complete and accurate financial status of the case at that time. In the Matrix, the attorney must complete the box for "Fees to Date" (as defined in the Matrix), as well as completing the box for "Percent of Stage Completed." We recognize that there may be more than one Stage in progress (e.g., "First Evaluation Point" and "Formal Discovery"), so that completing the Matrix may require multiple entries.

When the Matrix is received here in St. Louis, we carefully will review it.

If the trial lawyer indicates that 50 percent of the First Evaluation Stage has been completed, but that he or she has spent $6,000 of an $8,000 budget, the managing lawyer will contact the trial attorney to find out why he or she is $2,000 over budget before paying the bill. Going on, if when the First Evaluation Stage is 100 percent complete, the attorney has spent $10,000 and the budget for that Stage is $8,000, unless we have approved the overage of $2,000, we will pay only the $8,000 and put the $2,000 into a suspense account for possible payment when the case is finally terminated either by settlement, trial or otherwise. Payments of amounts in the suspense account will be based on results.

The foregoing describes how new cases will be handled. Some variation, of course, is required for existing or open litigation. In the case of such litigation, we will consider money spent to date as sunk funds, but establish a budget for the remainder of the case. In order to do that effectively, we will need the following information from the trial attorney for each open case:

1. Total fees, costs and expenses paid to date;

2. An estimate as to the percent completion of the case as of such date; and
3. An estimate as to total fees, costs and expenses that might be incurred (assuming case is tried).

One of the Emerson managing attorneys will be contacting you shortly to get this information.

For example, assume the budget for a given case (as a new case) would have been $48,000. Assume also that the trial attorney tells us that he or she has spent $48,000 and the case is 50 percent complete. Based on these facts, we will establish a budget for the remainder of the case at $24,000, unless the trial attorney and the managing attorney otherwise agree.

We really need your input in this program. We believe no trial lawyer working for Emerson wants us to needlessly spend money. We must cut legal fees, costs and expenses, and the approach we have outlined is our way of doing this.

We know these fees, expenses and costs can be cut and the cases managed without impacting the professional responsibilities of our trial attorneys and the high quality of services you have provided us to date.

Sincerely,

Charles Hansen

Avoiding Line Item Review: Emerson Electric's Approach to Litigation Budgeting

by Larry Smith

Emerson Electric Co. in St. Louis has adopted a new approach to controlling litigation costs that, with its relative simplicity, may offer an innovative alternative to the methods most inside managers rely on to monitor outside costs. The plan was put into effect on October 1, 1986, at the start of the company's last fiscal year; now, a year later, general counsel Charles Hansen reports a 15 percent reduction—around $1 million—in the cost of outside counsel in product-liability cases.

These savings stand in marked contrast to a 68 percent increase in two comparable periods of 1985 and 1986. Not only was Hansen troubled by that volcanic cost run-up, but he couldn't even be sure why it had happened. He determined to correct the trend and likewise track exactly where the money was going. The urgency of his task was increased by the insurance liability crunch of 1985–86. "When we had a maximum deductible of [only] $4 million [on any litigation], in-house counsel could more easily swallow rising attorney fees," he says. "But now that figure is up considerably and the need for cost control is thus [commensurately] greater."

A New Matrix-System Approach

Hansen calls his new approach "the litigation cost control matrix system," because it is based on a simple matrix chart. The client begins by establishing a budget for an upcoming case, determined in consultation with outside counsel. To establish a dollar amount, case categories are used and guidelines extrapolated. For example, there may be a category for, say, traumatic electric shocks. Data on past cases from that category is reviewed, inflation or other variables taken into consideration and, based on those past costs, new cost parameters are established.

Once the budget is established, the matrix is drawn up. Four stages are contemplated: first evaluation, formal discovery, ready for trial and trial/post trial. Three figures are included in each stage: the total allotted budget, the fees total incurred to date (including all disbursements and expenses) and the percentage of the stage completed.

Consider a report listing a $5,000 budget for first evaluation and $7,500 in fees to date for that evaluation—with 100 percent of that stage completed. That means, outside counsel is $2,500 overbudget. Emerson will pay only the $5,000, not the $2,500 surplus. Instead, the money is put into a suspense account and applied toward future stages. If, in the next stage, outside counsel is $2,500 underbudget, there's a clean wash and Emerson will go ahead and pay the total bill. Anything that remains in the suspense account at the end of the case—in other words, the firm's total overage—is paid by Emerson only after an assessment of the firm's performance. The company reserves the right not to pay that overage at all.

NO MORE MONTHLY BILLS

Emerson wants to see bills no more frequently than every quarter and—what is particularly significant—those bills are not to segregate fees from expenses. This client simply will not pay the kind of supplemental expense bills that typically trickle in at other companies: $100 for a dinner here, $200 for a trip there. (And nothing gets paid at all if outside counsel doesn't bother to fill in the matrix chart, so that the department can assess it relative to the budget and the progress of the case.)

"I don't care what that dollar number on the bill means, whether it's mainly fees or includes a million lunches," Hansen says, "so long as the job's getting done within budget and we'll be ready to proceed to the next stage."

The system generally is flexible, because outside counsel still can get any unavoidable and justifiable overage approved by contacting the client beforehand. Moreover, if the exigencies of open litigation require a new budget, the client usually will agree to set one, using additional data and projections supplied by outside counsel.

Hansen contrasts this tracking method to two more prevalent approaches:

First, the insistence of some general counsel on approving every expenditure. This, Hansen suggests, may work at companies such as Xerox, where General Counsel Robert Banks has pioneered just such a tough-minded approach. But the total litigation load at Xerox is not quite so formidable as at Emerson, where product liability is a persistent issue. Hansen is extremely wary of hampering talented litigators or cramping the sometimes unorthodox styles of lawyers who know how to produce results. "By checking and approving only the final [cost] figure, I give outside counsel all the leeway they need to practice law however they see fit," he says. "Either they succeed within budget or they don't. That's all I care about."

And second, the insistence on detailed monthly bills. Hansen believes that these bills are utterly meaningless because there is no standard against which to measure them. "Maybe outside counsel will account for every penny they spent traveling to Hawaii to talk to an expert witness," says Hansen. "So what? How can you tell how important that witness really is or whether a telephone call might have sufficed?" By the same token, a heavily itemized bill is hard to balk at; when many inside managers see outside counsel explain their expenses so well, they naturally just pay the bill. But the real value of the time, that bang for your buck, can slip right through the cracks.

SUMMARY

Hansen adds that the matrix system restores some of the virtues of the old way of paying litigators, when inside lawyers were able to assess performance and results, then negotiate payment afterward. Now, with expenses mounting at every stage of a litigation, that's not possible, for it would put outside counsel in the unfair position of having to subsidize their clients' cases. Yet, without imposing that burden, Hansen's approach does give inside management the benefit of paying for completed tasks.

Furthermore, the system also helps outside counsel to manage better. Obviously, if a case is overbudgeted in discovery and that overage is not approved by the client, outside counsel then can assess what's ahead and try to cut costs in the pretrial or trial stages. Likewise, if outside counsel is underbudget for first evaluation, it may want to invest a little more time and money in discovery than it otherwise might have.

Finally, Hansen believes that his system can only prove a golden opportunity for the smaller firms to win more of his business. "Those firms know what good marketing it is to show enthusiasm about a system like this," he says. It's mutually understood that "their cost structures are more easily managed than the megafirms. So when they promise to stay within budget for each stage, I believe them." On the other hand, the megafirms may pay lip service to Hansen's system because they have to if they want his work, but, he says, "they find it more difficult to meet the goals."

Case Name: ______________________ v. ______________________

Attorney: ______________________ Date Prepared ______________________

Litigation Cost Control Matrix

Case Stage	First Evaluation Point	Formal Discovery	Ready For Trial	Trial and Post Trial	Total
Budget					
Fees to Date (including all Costs and Expenses)					
Percent of Stage Completed					

CHAPTER 20

Harold A. Feder, *of Feder, Morris, Tamblyn & Goldstein, P.C., Denver, Colorado, practices primarily in the general civil-litigation field and plaintiffs' personal-injury matters. In Chapter 19, it was pointed out that at an early stage, a case plan and budget were required. Naturally, the plan will vary from case to case. Here Feder shares with us his approach to the development of a case plan. The obvious implication of the case-plan approach is to enforce a discipline of early thought and evaluation of what you are trying to accomplish and how you are going to achieve the desired goals. Having determined this, the lawyer should become more efficient, should eliminate wasted effort and should have a better chance of obtaining good results. Where the client understands and adopts the plan, the lawyer-client relationship will be strengthened. Where there is agreement in advance as to the goals to be reached and what will be perceived by the client to be a benefit, it will be possible to place a value on the services, that is, to evaluate the extent to which the client's objective has been reached or to measure "value" or "benefit." In the development of the case plan, incentives can be built in and risks can be shared if the lawyer and the client so agree.*

In a follow-up exchange with Feder, we asked, "What is value from the client's point of view? Feder's response was, "It is money, principle, test of wills, vindication, anger or just bringing closure to a life's chapter."

No matter what the method of billing, it is important for lawyers to go through the process of determining what needs to be done to reach the objectives of the client. This is one of the emerging principles of the billing process.

Now for the Feder case plan.

What Is a Case Plan—And How Do You Go About Making One?

by Harold A. Feder

How Do You Make A Case Plan?

Gather the following information:

1. Client's name ____________________
   Address ____________________
   Phone ____________________
2. Type of case: ____________________
3. Opposing parties and lawyers: ____________________
4. Clients' objectives: ____________________
5. Rationale of the case—why this case makes sense: ____________________
6. What information is needed? ____________________
7. What are the subcategories of documents, exhibits and witnesses that are to be developed in preparation? ____________________
8. How are we going to get the information needed? ____________________
9. What are the legal issues and what research is needed? ____________________
10. What is our overall strategy? ____________________

11. Develop a time frame: ______

12. What resources will we need—people, support centers, materials? ______

13. The estimated number of hours we will devote to this case: ______

14. Who are the available staff people? ______

15. What outside resources, consultants, experts, technicians, space and equipment do we need? ______

16. What is the importance of this case as to legal issues, amounts involved, complexity, importance to the client or importance to society and the profession? ______

17. An analysis of the claims of plaintiff—law/fact amalgamation: ______

18. An analysis of the defenses and counterclaims—law/fact amalgamation: ______

19. Liability of nonparties: ______

20. Develop a budget for funds/hours/expenses: ______

21. Goals/Action Plan, including specific task assignments: ______

22. Action plan monitoring and follow-up: ______

23. Periodic evaluation: ______

24. Conclusion—by trial, settlement or alternative dispute-resolution technique: ______

CHAPTER 21

Edward P. Liebensperger *practices in the Boston, Massachusetts, firm of Nutter, McClennen & Fish. Although a discussion of alternate billing methods has relevance for firms of all sizes, from the solo to the megafirm, Liebensperger's frame of reference reflected by his work in the Litigation Section's Subcommittee on Billing Practices (of the Committee on Corporate Counsel) is the relationship between corporate counsel and outside counsel. He shares an outline of a presentation that he made at the 1987 Section of Litigation Fall Meeting. Following is the December 1985 Report on Alternative Billing Practices Survey.*

A Proposal for Improving Litigation Team Management: Task-Based Billing

by Edward P. Liebensperger

I. Inside and Outside Counsel Share the Common Goals of Achieving the Best Result at a Reasonable Cost
   A. The assumptions for this statement are the following:
      1. Counsels' ethical and professional obligations and motivations.
      2. Counsels' economic interest in satisfying the corporate client.
   B. Accomplishment of goals will be enhanced by cooperative, team approach between inside and outside counsel.
      1. Significant communication at the outset, and throughout litigation, will clarify corporation's goals, provide for exchange of substantive knowledge and aid the planning process.
      2. A detailed litigation plan and budget, revised continually, will act as the agenda for communication between inside and outside counsel.
      3. Litigation costs will be controlled by providing incentives for counsel to work efficiently and to seek early resolution. In addition, litigation costs will be controlled if outside counsel bears the risk of its own inefficiency.

II. The Problem: Hourly Rate Billing Is Inconsistent with Effective Team Management
   A. Hourly rate billing creates the wrong "mind set."
      1. Inside counsel is subject to:
         a. Becoming a "minder" rather than a participant;
         b. Abdicating responsibility to outside counsel, while nitpicking over hours spent and disbursements;
         c. Communicating only regarding keeping the bills down rather than developing a sound litigation strategy; and
         d. Becoming an adversary with outside counsel rather than a team member dedicated to a mutually beneficial result.
      2. Outside counsel is subject to:
         a. Allowing hourly rate billing to reward inefficiency; little incentive for effective case management;
         b. Thinking that advanced communication and case planning with inside counsel is not essential;
         c. Feeling that relationship with inside counsel is damaged by being "nickel and dimed" or otherwise criticized for hours spent; and
         d. Not properly managing lawyers in firm when billing on hourly basis.
   B. Hourly rate billing may discourage early settlement.
      1. Lawyers are bound ethically to achieve the best result and not intentionally to delay.
      2. However, there may be subtle, even unconscious, decisions, priorities and con-

duct by both inside and outside counsel that cause delay.

3. If there were a financial incentive to the outside lawyer for achieving an early settlement, then more creativity and aggressive pursuit of early settlement might result.

C. Hourly rate billing does not encourage team litigation planning that might reduce costs.

1. Without active management, hourly rate billing allows the case to progress with little planning.

D. There are many advantages of task-based billing.

1. Requires early coordination (negotiation) between inside and outside counsel to develop a litigation plan, budget and "price" for each task.
2. Unifies goals of inside and outside counsel so that they become a team rather than potential adversaries over hourly rates, disbursements, etc.
3. Gives outside lawyer the freedom and responsibility to effectively manage staff.
4. Corporation can more accurately predict litigation costs.
5. Requires intense communication and team relationship between inside and outside counsel throughout the litigation.

E. Alternative Billing Practices Survey of Committee on Corporate Counsel (1985).

1. One-third of corporate counsel reported willingness to try billing on a task-based basis.
2. However, nonhourly rate billing amounted to less than 10 percent of legal fees paid by corporations that had experimented.
3. Substantial number of corporate inside lawyers indicated a fundamental suspicion of outside lawyers' billing on an hourly basis. Inside counsel believed there was inefficiency, overstaffing and padding of hours by outside counsel. This suspicion cannot be healthy for effective team management of litigation.

Report on Alternative Billing Practices Survey

Departure from billing based on an hourly rate multiplied by the number of hours worked has been widely discussed in the legal press and in bar groups. So-called alternative billing practices have been rumored to be on the increase. Given the fundamental importance of the subject to lawyers working for and representing corporations, the Committee on Corporate Counsel of the American Bar Association's Section of Litigation undertook to survey lawyers from corporate law departments and law firms to obtain detailed information regarding the use of alternative billing practices and the prospects for future use of such methods in corporate litigation.

In the fall of 1984, a detailed questionnaire was sent to the members of the Committee on Corporate Counsel. Approximately 300 lawyers working in corporate law departments ("inside counsel") and 140 lawyers in law firms ("outside counsel") responded. The approximately 440 responses were tabulated by computer except for the narrative responses to the question, "What is the one thing that concerns you most about outside (inside) counsel's billing practices?", which were summarized by the Committee.

It is important to keep in mind the scope of the survey. The questions concerned billing practices only in corporate litigation matters. Also, the primary focus of the survey was to explore the following alternative billing methods: contingent fee, modified contingent fee (reduced, guaranteed hourly rate with additional fee calculated as a percentage of the result), flat fee, standard hourly rate plus bonus (based on result), piecework fee (e.g., $500 for a set of interrogatories) and value-based fee (fee based solely on an agreement reached at the end of the matter as to the overall "value" of the services performed).

Responses came from corporations throughout the country. More than 75 percent of the responses were from law departments with ten lawyers or less and about one-half of the companies grossed more than $1 billion in sales.

Outside lawyers' responses ranged from "megafirms" with more than 200 lawyers (8 percent) to lawyers in firms with less than 50 lawyers (57 percent). The lawyers were located throughout the United States, primarily in major urban centers.

While the results of the survey do not purport to be statistically valid, the responses are from a wide segment of the bar and constitute the only survey of this kind known to the Committee.

What follows is a summary of the findings of the

survey and a discussion of several of the individual comments.

Findings

Billing based on other than a standard hourly rate is relatively rare. Nearly half (46 percent) of inside counsel require, *in all instances*, standard hourly rate billing. For 82 percent of the companies, nonhourly rate billing accounted for less than 10 percent of total legal fees. Similarly, 88 percent of the outside lawyers reported that nonhourly rate billing amounted to no more than 25 percent of their total fees. Thirty-six percent of the outside lawyers bill, in all instances, on the basis of a standard hourly rate.

It is clear, however, that there is experimentation occurring with alternative billing methods. One-fourth of the inside lawyers reported using a contingent-fee arrangement in the past year. (Nearly half (44 percent) of the outside lawyers reported doing so.) Thirty-eight percent of the inside lawyers reported using a flat-fee arrangement in the past year. (Nearly half (46 percent) of the outside lawyers reported doing so.)

A small but consistent percentage (under 16 percent) of corporations reported experimenting with other billing methods, such as standard hourly rate plus bonus, piecework rates, "value" billing or modified contingent-fee arrangements. Outside lawyers' responses reflected this incidence of alternative billing arrangements, with the exception that a higher percentage (approximately one-third) of the ouside lawyers reported rendering bills on a modified contingent-fee arrangement and a standard billing rate plus bonus.

For the corporations reporting the use of flat-fee billing, 9 percent stated that they paid more than half their bills on that basis. However, the vast majority of companies (generally more than 90 percent) reported that if any of the alternative billing methods were used, the incidence of such bills was less than 10 percent of the companies' total bills. Outside lawyers responses reflected about the same incidence.

Several outside lawyers reported that fees based on hourly rates with a bonus paid based on result or on negotiations at the conclusion of the matter based on the "value" to the company were a common occurrence. Approximately 8 percent of the outside lawyers reported billing on an "hourly rate plus bonus" basis more than 50 percent of the time.

Prospects for Use of Alternative Billing Practices

Receptivity to alternative billing methods is high in certain cases. There was agreement that money, in the form of bonus fees for good results, provided extra incentive over and above a lawyer's ethical duty to achieve the best possible result for his or her client. Two-thirds of both inside and outside lawyers agreed that a bonus arrangement tied to the result will provide lawyers with a greater incentive to obtain superior results. Moreover, as described in the next section, serious concerns were expressed regarding standard hourly rate billing practices.

Perceptions of both inside and outside lawyers were that alternative billing arrangements are more appropriate when the company is a plaintiff. Approximately 70 percent of the inside lawyers would be willing to agree to a contingent fee, modified contingent fee or flat fee in a case where the company is a plaintiff. Where the company is a defendant, the only alternative billing method that garnered the approval of a majority (52 percent) of the responding inside counsel was a flat fee.

The most popular alternative billing arrangement favored by outside counsel—whether representing plaintiff or defendant—was an hourly rate plus bonus.

If the client company is a plaintiff, approximately 65 percent of the outside lawyers were willing to take the risk of a contingent fee or value-based billing. A larger percentage (90 percent) would agree to a modified contingent fee.

Only one-third of the outside lawyers would agree to a piecework basis for fees (notwithstanding whether they are representing plaintiff or defendant). Inside lawyers expressed about the same willingness to experiment with this fee basis.

Major disagreement occurred on flat fees. Outside counsel generally were cool to the concept of flat-fee billing. Only 33 percent would agree to such a fee arrangement if the company were a defendant and a slightly larger percentage (44 percent) would agree to a flat fee if the company were a plaintiff. Two-thirds of the outside lawyers agreed that it was not feasible to use flat fees because of the risk that a lawyer may not be compensated adequately for time expended.

On the other hand, more than two-thirds of the inside lawyers affirmed their belief in the feasibility of flat fees. Yet, the same percentage (66 percent) of inside lawyers disagreed with the proposition that in exchange for agreeing to a flat fee the outside lawyer should be assured of a steady flow of work. Outside lawyers, conversely, felt strongly (74 percent) that a steady flow of work should be assured in exchange for a flat-fee arrangement. A majority (57 percent) of inside counsel felt that a flat-fee arrangement would cause outside lawyers to work more efficiently and institute cost-cutting measures. A majority (55 percent) of outside lawyers disagreed.

A majority of both inside and outside lawyers opined that flat fees would not result in lower overall legal fees for companies. The perceived advantage of flat fees was that companies would be able to budget legal fees with more certainty and outside lawyers might increase their compensation by performing the tasks in less time than what was anticipated by the flat fee.

A majority (52 percent) of inside lawyers felt that flat fees for consultation time would encourage "preventive maintenance." Sixty-two percent of outside lawyers disagreed with that statement.

Major Concerns Regarding Billing Practices

The survey called for a narrative response to the question, "What is the one thing that concerns you most about outside (inside) counsel's billing practices?" More than 230 inside counsel and approximately 90 outside lawyers responded. The results reflected some misunderstanding, poor communication and, perhaps, mistrust in the relationship. In large part, it appeared that many of the problems in the relationship were because of billing based on the traditional hourly rate method.

Outside lawyers' most common concern was the belief that inside counsel did not fully comprehend the hours required to handle a case the way it should be handled. While inside counsel harped on keeping the bills down, they expected, nevertheless, superior results. There was a feeling that good results are unappreciated and that outside counsel's ability to perform the highest-quality work was hampered by inside counsel's nitpicking over hourly rates, number of hours spent, associate time, disbursements, etc. Frequently noted concerns were inside counsel's excessive concerns with budgeting, detailed billing and hourly rates. Of course, if the law firm were not billing based on standard hourly rates, these concerns would be eliminated.

By far the most frequently cited concern of inside counsel about billing practices was the lack of billing detail provided by outside counsel. Inside counsel strongly desired detailed billing, showing the number of hours expended, by date, personnel and description of what was done. Hourly rates per lawyer were requested, as well as supporting detail for disbursements. Clearly, the greatest source of irritation to corporate counsel was outside lawyers who failed to provide such detailed billing.

Perhaps the basis for inside counsel's desire for detailed billing can be inferred from another frequently cited major concern of corporate counsel. More than 75 inside lawyers expressed a fundamental mistrust of outside lawyers' billing practices. They believed there was "churning" of hours, "padding" of time sheets, overstaffing and inappropriate training of young lawyers included within outside lawyers' bills. A frustration with inside counsel's inability to verify bills was expressed and, presumably, their insistence on detailed billing stems from this frustration.

Comments and Conclusions

While alternative billing practices are not commonly used, at present, in corporate litigation, there is significant interest in trying some of the alternative methods. Moreover, the significant concerns, primarily of inside counsel, over the standard hourly rate billing method augurs for more experimentation with alternatives. Law firms that recognize the frustrations of corporations with the standard hourly rate for billing may develop innovative approaches that could be effective marketing tools. Because the law firm-client relationship is diminished by inside counsel's worry that the law firm is working inefficiently or, worse, padding hours on the bill, and outside counsel's concern that his or her professional judgment is impaired by the client's questioning of the hours needed to do a superior job, the relationship might be improved by moving to an alternative billing basis.

CHAPTER 22

Here we have grouped ideas on value billing as submitted by outstanding lawyers who practice in small firm settings. Their contributions appear in the order shown below.

Edna R. S. Alvarez, Los Angeles, California, *writes from the personal perspective of a solo practitioner who has a highly specialized practice in an urban community that has a high density of attorneys. Her comments with respect to value billing follow.*

Demetrios Dimitriou, *a sole practitioner in the financial district of San Francisco, California, deals with value billing in the sense of a truly subjective determination of a fee based on the perception of value by both lawyer and client.*

Ronald W. Del Sesto, *is with the Ronald W. Del Sesto Law Corporation in Providence, Rhode Island. His approach is to stress that the marketplace must accurately reflect value, but when third-party payor or the court sets fees, other factors than the marketplace can cause distortions.*

Lowell E. Rothschild, *of Mesch, Clark & Rothschild, P.C., Tucson, Arizona, has shared the firm's retainer agreement with an add-on that delineates specific time minimums. Note that there are three departures from hourly billing: (1) a minimum fee; (2) the adjustment of the final fee based on six additional factors set forth in the last paragraph on page 2; and (3) the minimum time charges specified in the add-on page. We have reproduced this retainer agreement, which illustrates the combined approaches to billing.*

J. Harris Morgan, *of Morgan & Gotcher, Greenville, Texas, recognizes that a small law office which utilizes technology and the team approach, primarily bases fees on the actual cost of the service plus a reasonable profit for the firm. He calls his approach "component billing."*

Value Billing—Five Approaches from Small-Firm Practitioners: First Approach

by Edna R.S. Alvarez

My sense is that the term *value billing* is intended to reflect a method of billing centered on capturing the full value to the client of services rendered by a law firm and communicating to the client that value. My experience tells me that effective billing must be bilateral. It must reflect the perspective of the producer, i.e., the attorney, and the perspective of the consumer, i.e., the client. One measurement of effective billing is billing that reflects what the attorney perceives is a fair fee, given the services rendered; results in full payment of the bill within a short period of its receipt; and leaves the client satisfied with the services rendered and with the professionalism of the attorney.

Two-Step Billing Method

Each attorney must develop his or her own system for effective billing. I would like to share with you one such system. Whenever legal services involve a "framework" document, consideration should be given to using a two-step method of billing—namely, "hourly" fee and "documentation" fee. The hourly rate is used for services rendered in order to arrive at a blueprint, i.e., a plan, which will be used to draft the necessary document. The hourly rate also is used for major document modifications requested by the client after the initial draft of the document has been prepared by the attorney in accordance with the blueprint. The documentation fee is a flat fee that is charged for producing the individualized (i.e., customized) framework document, which is based on the blueprint.

The documentation fee is a composite of variables such as complexity of document, uniqueness of document, tax-sensitive nature of document, tax benefit of document, expertise required, priority timing required, risk aspect of document, client attitude and desire to perform a particular service at a particular time. The documentation fee is not established until the plan framework is worked out in detail. The services for developing the plan are billed on an hourly basis.

This two-step billing method has been used successfully in my estate-planning practice. This method is explained to new clients, in writing, prior to our first appointment. Once the blueprint is arrived at, the client is asked to sign a fee agreement and to pay one-half of the documentation fee in advance. By this action, the client is reflecting a commitment to the plan from the beginning. The retainer amount is placed in my Client Trust Account until a draft of the documents is sent to the client, at which time the amount is withdrawn and placed in my business account. The balance of the documentation fee is due at the time of signing. This fact is reflected in the fee agreement and is confirmed in the cover letter that is sent to the client with the draft documents. Out-of-pocket costs for items such as photocopying are billed separately from the documentation fee.

The results of this system are as follows:

1. If a potential client does not feel that my proposed fee for preparing a document is

fair, we never get past the initial phase.

2. If documents are prepared, the client is highly motivated to complete the project because a significant investment already has been made, i.e., one-half of the documentation fee already has been paid.

3. Because payment is due on signing of the documents, receivables are minimal.

This bifurcated system of billing could be used in any area of practice involving framework documents such as incorporations, deeds, leases, buy-sells and employment agreements.

Value Billing—Second Approach

by Demetrios Dimitriou

I believe that there are three separate issues involved with respect to value billing. They are: (1) the mechanics of determining the criteria to use in arriving at an appropriate bill based on the services rendered; (2) is the lawyer the "right kind of lawyer" to make use of value billing as a means of payment for professional services rendered; and (3) what are the appropriate characteristics a client should have in order to be receptive conceptually to value billing and therefore willing to pay for the services based on such rationale.

MECHANICS

As to the first issue, mechanics, there is the need to establish how much it costs you to produce the services. The concept also requires that more than the usual amount of focus be placed on defining the scope of services for which the client is to be charged. Also, the lawyer's office needs to be able to identify and allocate costs and expenses of various necessary services and other firm assets used in producing the end product. It is necessary that accurate costs be established so that the true costs and expenses incurred in rendering the legal services for the client are known. To the extent that there has been misuse of firm assets (either through false starts, misguided activities or other ineffectual use of office assets), there is no value to the client and therefore should not be billed. For this reason alone, it becomes imperative that there be a clear understanding of the services that are to be performed. The time and effort expended in clarifying the scope of legal services to be rendered is beneficial not only to the firm, by minimizing wasted or misdirected efforts and resources, but also focuses the client on the scope of legal services that are to be rendered and communicates the value of those services to the client. From the attorney's perspective, unless the costs are accurately determined, the attorney runs the risk of either not receiving payment for services rendered or alternatively charging too much and becoming uncompetitive as a result. Thus, the attorney must have a clear and accurate idea as to true costs in rendering services. This procedure also minimizes the risk of unproductive expenditure of services on behalf of the client.

THE LAWYER

With respect to the second issue, the lawyer, it is my belief that the attitude of the attorney toward the statement sent to the client is critical. It does little good to accurately determine costs, arrive at an appropriate statement and then find that the attorney is not prepared to render such a statement. My point is that the attorney must be convinced that the value-billing approach is valid, fair to the client and the attorney and reflects the true value of the services rendered to the client. In going through the exercise of determining true costs, the attorney will become educated as to how much value is being given to the client. By spending the time to accurately diagnose the issues and either chart a course of action with the client or agree on services to be rendered and expected results, the client is given the opportunity to appreciate the value of the services rendered. In the final analysis, the attorney must know that the statement rendered is fair and reasonable.

THE CLIENT

With respect to the third issue, the client, an analysis should be made to determine that the client is an appropriate client for value billing. If the client perceives legal services as being indistinguishable, treated like a "commodity" that can be weighed or timed or otherwise treated as being interchangeable from one purveyor or another, then the concept of value billing will fail. You need a client who either appreciates the value of the services being rendered or can be shown and is willing to accept the value concept of the services being rendered in order for value billing to succeed. You need to have a qualified client.

In summary, you need to know your true costs, be comfortable with the concept and apply it to clients who can appreciate the value of the services rendered.

Value Billing—Third Approach

by Ronald W. Del Sesto

I suppose the starting point is to determine what billing method most accurately calculates the amount that the marketplace is willing to pay lawyers for rendering legal services. In the terminology of economists, this is determining what method is the most efficient.

On answering that question, the next stage would be to adapt the most theoretically efficient method for use in our day-to-day dealings with the three groups that are most involved with our fees:

1. Our clients, the group that is most directly affected, and the ones that most accurately reflect the marketplace as they can negotiate with us in advance, leaving them the freedom to use us or to hire others;

2. Third-party payors, i.e., nonclients who are obligated by law or contract to pay our fees even though they have not negotiated for our services; and

3. The courts, which frequently must either set the amount of our fees or pass on the "reasonableness" of our proposed fee.

The Courtroom

A digression: The courts are ill-equipped to serve a meaningful role in the fee-setting process. This is to say, judges seldom can accurately reflect the marketplace because judges are not—and generally never have been—consumers of legal services. Some of them were once the purveyors of such services. I say "some" because many judges come from careers in government service or the world of academia and thus have had little exposure to the marketplace. Frequently, those judges who were in the private practice of law came from large firms where they individually had little to do with the day-to-day financial aspects of the law practice. Or they have been judges for such a duration of time that their private-practice experience is of little relevance in today's days of rapid changes in office technology, these days of "megafirms" and "boutique" practices, days that now require heavy capital expenditures by lawyers, a radical departure from just ten years ago.

More so, many judges equate legal fees to their own salaries and thus ignore the operational costs of their entire office: employees (clerks, sheriffs, secretaries, etc.), their space (including utilities), their pension and health benefits and their staff's pension and health benefits, and the costs of equipment—all of which are as necessary a part of their courthouse world as those elements are to the world of lawyers.

By way of illustration to highlight the distortion that can arise: In Rhode Island, our chief justice recently stated that it costs the state $250,000 annually for each trial court judge, in addition to the judge's salary. Assume then, that a judge's salary is $60,000. In setting a lawyer's fee, a judge easily could think that $50 an hour is what the judge earns ($60,000 divided by 1,200 hours), so a fee much more than that would be excessive. Put differently, that a $100-an-hour fee would be a real "decent" fee. A judge who is more attuned to economics would gauge his or her cost at more than $300,000, including the judge's salary plus overhead and fringe benefits, not even taking into account the obsolescence factor of the capital expense for office equipment. Such a judge would appreciate the fact that his or her hourly cost approximates $250 an hour or about four times more than gross salary (an 80 percent overhead factor). Two judges, then, both from the same jurisdiction, coming from different vantage points, could compute their own hourly cost and differ by a factor of four, which would impact proportionately on their setting of legal fees.

Without belaboring the point, the complexity of the fee-setting process becomes unmanageable in the courtroom environment where there is little understanding or appreciation of today's actual cost of running a modern, technologically oriented, efficient law office.

The Marketplace

In my mind, the starting point for the setting of legal fees is the marketplace. And for each of us, our marketplace value already is established in the most efficient, distortion-free manner: by our day-to-day dealings with our very own clients, those who have had the opportunity to accept or reject us and chose to accept the agreed-to fee structure. As the D.C. Circuit Court of Appeals stated in *Laffey:*

> **Proceeding presumptively with the firm's own rates allows the court to avoid the essentially impossible task of selecting one rate over another from a wide range of "market" rates, it limits the power of the trial judge arbitrarily to reward or punish attorneys by setting rates virtually at will and it allows the parties and the court to avoid a "second major litigation" over the rate-making process. *The marketplace best measures "Market Value";* appraisal by no other method has as much claim to veracity and objectivity . . . [emphasis added]**

And the *Laffey* court concluded, "(i)n almost every case, the firm's established billing rates will provide fair compensation."

Any court engaged in the fee-setting procedure that departs from the marketplace-established fees will create distortion, with one of three results:

1. The court will award a below-marketplace fee and thus "reward" the payor by forcing the lawyer to subsidize the payor's operations;

2. The court will "reward" the lawyer for factors the free marketplace ignores and thus unfairly take money from the payor; or

3. By happenstance, the court will match the marketplace (at random, so that the court's next fee-setting proceeding again will offer the court two out of three opportunities to distort the marketplace).

Let's reflect a moment on the two court-created distortions. One compels the lawyer to subsidize the payor's operations because the court awards a fee lower than that which the marketplace would pay that lawyer. Thus, if by contract (e.g., a promissory-note collection case) the losing party has to pay legal fees, the court distorts the marketplace when it awards less-than-marketplace fees; in essence, the court is forcing the lawyer to "contribute" to the loser's operations ("contributing" in the sense of noncompensated time, the lost-opportunity curve, etc.).

A lawyer can insulate himself or herself from such results by billing the difference to the client (after all, it was the client in the first instance that contracted with the losing party; so it is the client and not the attorney that should bear the ill consequences of that relationship) or by refraining from accepting those types of cases and letting the marketplace forces take over (presumably those new to the bar would take over that type of practice, to be continually replaced by newcomers). Though society is ill-served if lawyers refrain from accepting fee-shifting cases that promote the common good, e.g., civil rights, I suppose everyone else involved (judges, sheriffs, clerks, etc.) would be getting full pay, so why should the lawyer be the only one suffering a financial loss? The other side of the coin is that there is no reason to underpay an attorney in a fee-shifting-by-contract case, especially one that is business oriented, for to do so would make the lawyer a nonparticipate-in-the-profits "partner" of the parties.

(Perhaps the Supreme Court has such a dilemma in mind when in *Blum v. Stenson* it applied a "prevailing market rate" standard to awarding fees to private nonprofit "legal services" organizations—the corollary to *Laffey's* awarding the lawyer's already-existing rate in dealing with profit-making attorneys.)

The other court-created distortion—and the one that is most prevalent today—is for the court to "reward" the attorney for those factors the marketplace ignores. This situation dramatically distorts the marketplace and is best illustrated by the experience of the past fifteen to twenty years. In their quest to find a simplistic, routine method of arriving at fees, the courts have more and more relied on time spent as the sole or major factor. The very simplicity of the mathematics is seductive: hours consumed multiplied by hourly rate.

Time Billing—The Norm

What effect has court-induced time billing had on the marketplace? The primary effect is that time billing has become the norm, and in some jurisdictions, the *only* acceptable method of billing. Time billing, by its very nature, penalizes the efficient, organized, systems-oriented attorney. It is a great disincentive to early settlements. It inherently causes "churning," for to maximize profits, one has to maximize costs, the amount of hours consumed.

That said, time billing has had a profound effect on the practice of law over the past fifteen years. It is largely responsible for the creation of megafirms because time billing allows some (the partners) to enjoy the profits created by those whose take-home pay is lower than their billings. Geometric nonpartner growth creates lots of profit—at least for the moment; the crunch comes tomorrow when the "juniors" become partners and the billings and take-home pay begin to approximate each other. That is when some firms shrink and others disintegrate; in either case, the lawyers disperse, a common phenomenon today that was totally unheard of, say, twenty years ago.

It would seem then, with ballooning overhead resulting in spiraling hourly rates, that the consumer has not reaped a benefit from time billing. The courts continue to be befuddled. The only ones pleased with the situation are those that capitalize on the value added, the partners of large law firms (and I guess the new lawyers at such firms who start off their professional careers being very well compensated).

The solo practitioner and those in small law firms are ill-served by time billing. These attorneys generally do all their own work, and time billing discourages such old-fashioned concepts. Time billing does not recognize, and consequently does not pay for, ingenuity, imagination, experience, productivity. In short, all the virtues one needs to practice alone are totally ignored in the world of time billing. So the ultimate marketplace distortion is achieved when a nontime-biller who is quite successful (meaning the marketplace has recognized his or her unique worth) is required by the court to accept a time-based fee, a billing method that truly has no relevance to the marketplace and certainly no relevance to the solo or small-firm attorney.

For those who reap what they alone sow, product billing—fees based on the project itself (the responsibility assumed by the attorney, the experience required of the attorney) and the value added by the attorney to the client's exposure to the law (because of the lawyer's talent and productivity)—is the most efficient billing method, for that is how the marketplace is willing to pay such attorneys.

Editor's Comment:

Six months after Ronald Del Sesto submitted his materials, the United States Court of Appeals for the First Circuit came down with its decision in *United States of America v. Metropolitan District Commission, et al.* (No. 87-1956, May 19, 1988). Here are some interesting quotes from this fee-approval case.

—"In certain cases, these objectives may be better met by concentrating on what was necessary to be accomplished rather than on a welter of time sheets."

—"Thus, the private market can at best 'afford relevant comparisons'."

—"It is precisely because there is no external market-based check on the scope of counsel's efforts . . . that it falls to the court to act as the guarantor of fairness."

—"Because the amount of time that an attorney reasonably requires to do a piece of work depends to some extent (often, to a great extent) on the qualifications and work ethic of the attorney, the court gauged reasonably necessary time by 'us(ing) the yardstick of a single, competent, industrious lawyer, knowledgeable in environmental litigation, supported by adequate staff' over the relevant time frame."

—"The trial bench need not feel handcuffed by counsel's submission of time records, no matter how elaborate."

Value Billing—Fourth Approach

by Lowell E. Rothchild

RETAINER AGREEMENT

I hereby retain MESCH, CLARK & ROTHSCHILD, P.C. as my attorneys to represent me in all matters relating to:

____

____

____

____

Should my attorneys advance any costs in this case, including costs of investigation, court fees, depositions, witness fees, photographs, exhibits, copying, long distance calls, travel, postage fees or any other expenses necessary to a proper prosecution of my case, I agree that all of these charges will be paid by me promptly on being billed.

In consideration of my attorney's agreement to represent me, I agree to pay a minimum fee of $_________. I understand that this is a minimum fee only and that I will be billed for services in excess of the minimum fee. I understand I will be charged a base charge for legal services on an hourly fee basis of $_________ per hour and paralegal services on an hourly fee basis of $_________ per hour and that charges will be made for all telephone calls, letters, documents or materials reviewed, pleadings, travel, depositions, court hearings and any and all other activities related to the matter.

In the event I desire to terminate the services of my attorneys pertaining to this matter, I shall pay them all costs that have been advanced and their fee for services to date of termination of this Agreement. I understand I will not be entitled to a refund of the minimum fee; however, such amounts paid will be credited toward the hours worked on my matter should the hourly charge exceed the minimum fee paid. I hereby grant my attorneys a lien on all my papers, documents, materials or other items that my attorneys may have possession of to secure payment of their fee. I agree all amounts paid to my attorneys for fees (advance, minimum or otherwise) may be deposited in their regular account and need not be held in trust.

I realize the hourly fee quoted above is subject to increase from time to time and that my attorneys will notify me in writing thirty days prior to any increase in their hourly fee. If I do not wish to be charged at the new fee, I agree to pay my attorneys in full for their services up to the date of the expected increase and terminate our relationship. I understand that if my attorneys continue to represent me past the date of the increase, the new fee will be in effect and I agree to pay said fee for all services rendered thereafter.

I am aware that payment for services rendered and costs disbursed will be considered due and payable when a statement is rendered. Normally, statements will be rendered on a monthly basis; however, some matters will not be billed until conclusion. Interest at the rate of 18 percent annually

continued →

or $1^1/_2$ percent per month will be charged on the unpaid balance of all unpaid statements more than thirty days overdue from the date the statement is rendered.

I agree and understand that on my failure to pay any statement for costs or services rendered within thirty days, my attorneys may withdraw from further representation of me in any matter.

I further agree and consent to execute any documents that may be necessary to effect such a withdrawal.

I acknowledge my responsibility for fees incurred and understand that, if appropriate, my attorneys will attempt to have the court award attorney's fees to me from the adverse party. If my attorneys are able to collect either all of the fees or a portion thereof pursuant to court order or by agreement with the adverse party, I will receive credit against fees for all such sums collected. Should it become necessary for my attorneys to proceed with collection measures against me to collect any due and unpaid fee incurred in this matter, I agree to pay reasonable attorney's fees and court costs incurred in such collection procedures.

I agree to keep my attorneys advised of my whereabouts at all times and to cooperate in the preparation and trial of my case, to appear on reasonable notice for depositions and court appearances and to comply with all reasonable requests made of me in connection with the preparation and presentation of my case.

All matters concerning the presentation of my case, such as its preparation, costs to be expended, witnesses to be interviewed and/or deposed, motions to be filed, stipulations and any other technical and/or legal matters are to be left to the discretion of my attorneys. Any questions concerning trial approach, appeals, settlement, etc., shall be determined jointly by my attorneys and myself.

I hereby grant my attorneys a lien on my cause of action and on all my funds, papers, documents, materials or other items that my attorneys may have possession of, in connection with this matter, to secure payment of their fee and advances. I hereby authorize and agree that my attorneys shall retain their fee and advances from any amounts recovered in this matter by settlement, judgment or otherwise. I agree that any such recovery may be applied by my attorneys to pay outstanding fees and costs in this matter or in any other matter they may be handling for me. My attorneys are hereby authorized to endorse my name to any checks or drafts payable to me for amounts recovered in this matter and to deposit same in trust to disburse such funds as provided in this agreement. I acknowledge that a lawsuit by its nature is unpredictable and that my attorneys have made no guarantee regarding the successful determination of any matter.

I also understand that the attorney fees for services are based on additional factors that are: (1) intensity of labor required; (2) novelty, complexity and difficulty of the questions involved; (3) special experience and skill necessary to perform the task; (4) responsibility assumed; (5) results obtained; and (6) extraordinary time limitations imposed by the circumstances. I understand that my final fee for legal services will be determined to be a percentage of the hourly base charges, depending on the foregoing additional facts, and that said charges for legal services will range between 100 to 300 percent of said hourly charges but can be higher. I understand that this fee system is based on the value of services and not only on hours expended on the matter.

DATED this ________ day of ______________, 19____.

____
Client

____
Client

Accepted:
MESCH, CLARK & ROTHSCHILD, P.C.
By: ______________________________

READ CAREFULLY:

This is your contract. It protects both you and your attorney and will prevent misunderstanding. If you do not understand it or if it does not contain all the agreements discussed, please call it to our attention.

MINIMUM TIME CHARGES

The undersigned has on the _____ day of _______________, 19_____, signed a written retainer agreement with Mesch, Clark & Rothschild, P.C., for legal services. Such contract provides for payment of services by the hour and it is understood that certain transactions and activities are billed with a minimum time regardless of the actual time spent. I understand that if the actual time spent on the task exceeds the minimum-time charge as set forth herein that I will be charged for the actual time spent. I hereby authorize such minimum-time charges and agree to pay such and acknowledge that such are reasonable charges under the circumstances. Such minimum-time charges are set forth herein as follows:

Preparation of any pleading	.3
Preparation of any letter or document	.3
Preparation of complaint	1.5
Preparation of answer	1.0
Review of any letter or document	.2
Review of any pleading	.2
Telephone	.2
Conference	.5
Court appearance	.7

DATED this _____ day of _______________, 19 _____.

____
Client

____
Client

Accepted:
MESCH, CLARK & ROTHSCHILD, P.C.
By ______________________________

READ CAREFULLY:

This is part of your retainer agreement and contract. It protects both you and your attorney and will prevent misunderstanding. If you do not understand it, please call it to our attention.

Value Billing—Fifth Approach

by J. Harris Morgan

The component-billing idea is a practical approach to the new pricing required for the production of legal service through teams of various functions. By including a charge for the use of a log to avoid dictation, for example, you have plugged in a charge for the development of a system. The machine costs were once an important item, but as the costs of computers has been reduced, this input is retreating. When we use word-processing equipment that costs in excess of $24,000, the 100 hours that the equipment was actually used in a month had a considerable value. In order to justify it and let it produce revenue, the multiple of three was applied. This meant that a $24,000 machine that ran 100 hours per month was charged out over the life of the machine at about $8 per hour. When computers began to cost less than $1,500, including software for word processing, this machine charge was greatly reduced. On the other hand, the expertise required for the team production of legal service increases the people cost and the people cost becomes more and more important. This extrapolates into the need to recover a profit on receptionists, word processors and secretaries. The legal-assistant battle, I think, has already been won as a charging factor.

My hope is that we will begin to define what we mean by value.

One of the current problems in billing is the enormous waste under our Rules of Civil Procedure applicable to court actions. Centralized dockets still exist in the United States and one of them is in Greenville, Texas. We have some judges who do not waste lawyers' time and on a time basis the fees for handling matters in those courts are much less than the fees for handling the same matter in another judge's court sometimes in the same jurisdiction. Is it fair for a client to be charged for the inadequacy of a court procedure? Is it fair for the law firm to be asked to bear the costs of an inadequate and antiquated system? Whose value are we talking about?

The Harris Morgan Budgeting Formula

In the budgeting process, the place to begin is to ascertain your costs. The second step is to determine how much you are worth on an annual basis. Twenty-five percent of the time that is entered into your system will not be charged for, will not be billed or will not be collected. So add 25 percent to your billing goal.

Annual Billing Goal

$100,000	**for you**
+$ 75,000	**overhead**
$175,000	**TOTAL**
+$ 43,750	**(25 percent written off)**
$218,750	**TOTAL BILLING GOAL**

Our estimate of time is *the* major factor that determines the fee in a bill. Initially, only the partners' time was billed. After 1910, some law firms started billing for associates' time. In the early 1970s, some law firms started billing for legal assistants' time.

The production of legal services is a team operation, including:

(1) Lawyering;
(2) Word processing;
(3) Administration; and
(4) Delegation.

The delegation function is vital for the efficient production of legal services. For example, where there are written procedures, or a quality staff person or legal assistant, the lawyer can delegate a substantial amount of work without the necessity for detailed supervision by the lawyer.

Every person in the law firm is entitled to a billing rate. If you need to increase your gross income, it can be done in much smaller bites when everyone in the office has a billing rate. The bill is more accurate because the client pays for the services actually rendered.

THE MORGAN SYSTEM

Determine your gross expenses by the aforementioned method. For a given person in your office, determine how many chargeable hours he or she will work in a year. Each person must produce three times what they are earning.

EXAMPLE

$15,000 (annual salary)
× 3
$45,000

$45,000 divided by 1,000 hours/year = $45/hour (billing rate of that person)

The cost to develop a substantive system can be determined and charged back to the clients who benefit from it.

Log To Avoid Dictation To Produce a Will
$125 (Your rate)
× 10 (# of hours)
$1,250 to produce the log
$1,250 divided by 20 usages = $62.50 Log Use Charge

Use the same method to bill for the use of your equipment.

AGREEMENT FOR LEGAL SERVICES

The Law Office of Morgan and Gotcher agrees to provide legal services in the ________________ matter discussed by the undersigned attorney and client and the client agrees to pay the following:

(A) $_________

OR

(B) $_________ per hour for attorney's time, $40 per hour for support-staff time, $10 per hour for machine time plus log, duplication and mail costs,

whichever (A) or (B) is **greater,** plus expenses.

Responsibility to provide legal services will be accepted and work will begin when we receive $_________.

Attorneys will not obligate client for any large expense without client's prior approval.

If and when it becomes apparent that the above amounts for fee or expenses will be expended under this agreement, an additional sum to be set by the attorney will be deposited by client.

Attorneys have the right to cease legal work and keep all funds received for legal services if client does not make additional deposits as requested by attorneys.

The base fee ((A) above) is a **minimum** fee and no part of it is refundable if client decides to discontinue the matter.

Each of the undersigned has read the above agreement and agrees to each of the terms and conditions stated above.

SIGNED this _____ day of __________________, 19_____.

LAW OFFICE OF MORGAN & GOTCHER

_________________________________ By: _________________________________

Client Attorney

CHAPTER 23

Samuel L. Reed, *of Defur, Voran, Hanley, Radcliff and Reed, Muncie, Indiana, is from a thirteen-lawyer firm. His article reflects a thoughtful analysis of the total lawyer-client relationship. A common thread in the chapters of this anthology is the importance of an understanding and agreement with the client as to what services are to be performed and how the client will be billed, no matter what method of billing will be used. Here Reed goes a step beyond, recognizing that billing is but one part, an important part, of the total relationship. Satisfied clients bring longtime relationships and breed additional clients for the ongoing success of the practice.*

Legal Fees—What's Fair?

by Samuel L. Reed

My goal is to discuss how legal fees can be fair to both client and lawyer, emphasizing that fairness to one does not preclude the likelihood of fairness to the other.

Clients are entitled to quality legal services for a reasonable price, while lawyers are entitled to be adequately compensated for our years of professional training and expertise.

Clients not only deserve fees that are reasonable and fair, but the fees must be *perceived* to be fair. The lawyer must provide the opportunity to discuss the rationale and basis for fees at the onset of the representation.

Fee Determination

The client is entitled to know what factors will be considered by a billing lawyer, although it is not reasonable for a client to expect a definite fee to be established in advance. The lawyer can quote an hourly rate normally charged for his or her work and also can explain that complete time records will be kept. The lawyer may be able to estimate the time necessary to complete the matter. He or she should indicate, however, that other factors may be considered in arriving at the fee. These factors are discussed later in this article. Even though clients may experience some uncertainty about what their final fees will be, they should be able to determine whether or not they have confidence in their lawyers and whether they want to be represented by their attorneys.

This author recommends a written letter of understanding concerning fees that the client should review, discuss and sign. Each party should keep a copy.

The lawyer must keep the client abreast of activities performed. The client should be sent copies of correspondence, pleadings and other documents, and the billings sent to the client should contain itemized entries showing what work was completed.

A well-done brochure also can help a client understand how fees are established. The brochure can be taken home, reviewed and kept by the client for study at a convenient time.

The relationship between the client and lawyer must be one of mutual trust and loyalty. The client must rely on the experience and knowledge of the lawyer. The lawyer must educate the client about court and law-office procedures.

What Is the Client Buying?

When a client buys the services of a competent, experienced and caring lawyer, he or she receives something unique. The client obtains an advocate who is dedicating energies, time, expertise and years of training and experience to assist the client in accomplishing an objective. Only a qualified lawyer can be such an advocate within the framework of our legal system. The client is even more satisfied if he or she believes the lawyer is an expert in his or her field.

In addition, the client is buying the services of a professional agent, one who counsels the client within legal, moral and ethical guidelines, but who reserves the right to withdraw from a case if the client cannot accept those conditions. Likewise, the client retains the right to discharge the lawyer and seek the services of someone else.

The client should feel that the lawyer is the "best money can buy." The client is more satisfied if he or she believes that he or she is better represented than his or her adversary. A lawyer's reputation takes years to establish. A winning lawyer, however, is not always better than a losing lawyer, because some clients have better cases than others. Yet, over a period of time, competent lawyers seem to establish enviable track records, which, in part, result from the fact that good lawyers fulfill their duty to advise a client when he or she is less likely than his or her adversary to prevail. In such a case, it is not in the client's best interest to proceed with a particular matter.

An accepting client considers the fees that are paid to be a good *investment,* which enables the client to accomplish his or her objectives. It also helps if the client and lawyer believe their relationship will be a continuing one. Most clients accept this principle: "you get what you pay for." It is when they don't understand what they are paying for that they question the size of fees. We can help them understand.

Surprisingly, a client often is not so concerned about the size of a fee, but rather that the lawyer really cares about him or her and his or her cause. Fee disputes seldom arise when a client truly feels that a lawyer "cares."

A client must understand that the lawyer's actions are in the best interests of the client and that they are not designed to increase the size of the fee. Whenever the client harbors even a hint of mistrust for the lawyer, the relationship suffers.

What a Client Deserves

A client wants a lawyer who *cares,* who respects the client, the client's position and the results the client seeks. The lawyer must be *accessible* to the client and must take the time to *communicate* with and keep the client aware of developments and activities in the client's case. Furthermore, a client is entitled to *timeliness* on the part of the lawyer. A client is not paying the lawyer to do things late or to do them slowly. The client is entitled to have his or her case expedited unless the lawyer and client agree that it is in the client's best interest to slow things down.

A client also expects the lawyer to work hard. Although a lawyer represents many clients, each client really is only interested in what the lawyer is doing for *him or her,* and what the lawyer has done for him or her *today.* Was something done today that will cause the client to be satisfied if he or she receives an invoice today?

In addition, a client has a right to expect the lawyer to be dependable, to be fair, to be honorable and to explain what the law is and how it applies to his or her case. Although a successful result generally is thought of as being the ultimate service a lawyer can perform, many other factors are involved in the practice of law—particularly when you want your client to accept your fee as fair.

Sometimes it may be necessary to explain to a client what goes into the overhead expenses of the lawyer's office. Some clients mistakenly think that most of the fee is profit to the lawyer, when normally more than 50 percent of fees paid is expended for office overhead.

Clients should be made aware of the costs of secretarial and paralegal help, as well as the costs of supplies, legal library and the technology needed to keep up with changing trends in the law. They may not be aware of the costs of mandatory continuing legal education, professional liability insurance and competition with other law firms for the best and brightest new lawyers. If clients want the best lawyers, they must pay a reasonable fee to obtain the highest level of professionalism.

The "Time-Expended" Trap

Over the past several years, lawyers have become better timekeepers, enabling them to properly bill clients for services performed. In the absence of good time records, lawyers often overlooked many things performed for the client and merely guessed at what was fair to the client (and to the lawyer). This method was not scientific, however, and sometimes was not fair to either the client or the lawyer.

Those lawyers who keep detailed time records earn more than those who do not, and it generally is agreed that keeping complete records also is good for clients, for the basic fee only covers time actually expended by the lawyer. Because most lawyers now use detailed billings, clients have become more interested in what the lawyer is doing and how much time is being spent by the lawyer on his or her behalf. Clients are able to multiply the "hourly rate" by the "hours expended" and carefully check the lawyer to see if the bill is "right."

Some lawyers now are wondering, however, if straight hourly billing is really fair. Does "hourly rate" multiplied by "hours expended" have anything to do with professionalism? Does it have anything to do with results obtained? What about experience? What about the reputation and expertise of the lawyer? What about the pressure and the need for an emergency representation? If the lawyer is a specialist in a certain field, having spent many hours and years to get there, should only the client benefit because the specialist can accomplish an assignment in a fraction of the time that it would take a general practitioner? Isn't the specialist entitled to be compensated for this expertise and ability to do something more quickly and more efficiently than someone not so trained and experienced? What is really of value to the client?

This author believes that a lawyer with experience, expertise, knowledge and the ability to get things done in an expeditious manner is worth more to a client than one who spends a great deal of time involving the client in complicated and slow-moving procedures.

"Hourly rate" multiplied by "hours expended" is not necessarily fair to the client or the lawyer. A lawyer must use his or her judgment in determining what is fair and must then communicate the explanation to the client.

Summary

A lawyer who "gouges" clients will not stay in business very long. Nor should he or she. Lawyers who do quality work and bill reasonably will continue to be the successful lawyers.

Clients should understand that more is involved in establishing a fair fee than multiplying the "hourly rate" by the "hours involved." The novelty of the legal question involved, as well as the detailed research necessary to "make new law" should be paid for by the client. The reputation of the lawyer or firm also is a factor to consider. The knowledge, expertise and experience of the lawyer truly is important, but probably most important is whether the lawyer cares.

In conclusion, legal fees must be fair and *perceived* as fair. We lawyers have a duty to spend time with our clients to help them acquire this perception. There should be less "mystery" about lawyers and the practice of law. Clients should feel that we are a part of their team and that they are making an investment in their future when we devote ourselves to them.

Clients need to be convinced that they are getting something no one else can give them. They are getting us as their representative, as their advocate and as a professional who cares about them and their cause. They need to be convinced we want to be, and will be, fair.

* * *

At the request of the Task Force, Samuel Reed expanded his comments on several specific points. His first-person response reflects the same kind of quiet, perceptive understanding of the total lawyer-client relationship that characterized his initial observations.

You have asked me to expand on how I believe we can get the client to consider fees as a good investment. Let me ramble a bit on that subject.

The client must understand that his or her lawyer truly is unique, in that the lawyer is devoting all of his or her energy and professional expertise on behalf of the client. The lawyer has devoted much of his or her life to professional training, experience and skill in preparing for this opportunity. The client needs to understand that the lawyer can get the client where the client wants to go. The lawyer is a means to an end. There may be no other way for the client to get to where he or she wants to go. The lawyer has the peculiar knowledge and the ability to get results for the client. The lawyer presents the opportunity for the client to receive "good" representation and the benefits of the technology and know-how from the offices of the lawyer.

How does the client understand this? We as lawyers must tell the client in a professional and unassuming way. Better yet, the client can hear it from other satisfied clients. We can make this information available in brochures and other printed material. Word of mouth probably is the best method to help the client understand the value of his or her investment. Praise certainly means more coming from others. Bankers and other successful and respected persons in the community can be our best salespersons.

Caring and Competent Attitudes

You also have asked me to provide illustrations on how a lawyer can present a caring and competent attitude. First, let the client know that you do care by telling him or her. Visit the client at his or her place of business or in a setting other than in your office. Do things with or for the client for which you do not intend to send a bill. Conduct free seminars on topics of interest. Attend social events, lunches and other meetings away from the office. Send letters of congratulations and thank yous. Take the client as a guest to athletic or dramatic events in your community. Ask the client to honestly critique your work and your firm.

In addition, you can periodically provide the client with written information on changing concepts and trends in the law, as well as on other matters that you believe will interest the client. Communicate with the client about nonlegal matters. Keep in touch with your client.

Alternative Billing Methods

You also asked me to discuss alternative billing methods. It is our normal practice to bill our clients monthly. They appreciate this, for it allows them to see how much of an investment they are making and whether it appears to be within their budget. On contingency-fee cases, however, we only bill monthly for costs and expenses advanced, unless we secure these at the time that they are incurred. We are flexible enough that if some clients want us to bill quarterly or semiannually, we are happy to do this. Some cases, for one reason or another, are not billed until the case is concluded. This probably should only be done if it is anticipated that the matter can be concluded within a six-month period of time.

We often deem it appropriate to secure a retainer, particularly if the client is from out of our area or is unknown to us. In some cases, although relatively few in number, you may recover from the other party or possibly opposing counsel. Some courts and legislatures now are making it possible to recover in such cases if litigation is deemed frivolous in nature.

I believe you should bill every client, even if the amount of your invoice is greatly reduced. I believe it gives the client a sense of pride and a sense of being "your client," even if the amount paid is less than the going rate.

Other alternative billing possibilities could include a concept of billing in accordance with the results. This would be slightly different from the contingency-fee arrangement, for you would be paid regardless of outcome, but you would be paid considerably more if the outcome is very good. This should be worked out in advance with the client.

I believe every invoice going to a client that I represent should be reviewed and given some thought by me. I have peculiar and personal knowledge about each client, his or her ability to pay, the results I have obtained and other numerous matters that should be programmed in when preparing and submitting an invoice for payment.

We also understand that some clients are unable to pay immediately on receipt of an invoice. We are willing to work out payment programs as long as we are convinced that the client is doing his or her best and paying according to his or her ability. We are willing to extend the time for payment if that is appropriate. In general, we are firm, yet reasonable, in our billing practices.

CHAPTER 24

Ezra Tom Clark, Jr., *is President of E. T. Clark, Inc., a consulting firm in Mesa, Arizona. Clark practiced law and later became the managing partner of a growing Arizona law firm. Mr. Clark, a well-known speaker and writer, particularly for his practical, straightforward approach to law-practice management, shares ideas here especially applicable to litigation.*

Getting Out of the Hourly Rate Quagmire—Other Billing Alternatives

by Ezra Tom Clark, Jr.

When it comes to billing, most lawyers are slaves to the time clock. In far too many firms, the only factor used to determine the fee is the amount of time spent performing the service. In addition, the extensive use of computers has perpetuated the time-billing mentality. Why have lawyers been sucked into an hourly rate quagmire that is having an adverse impact on lawyer's income? To find the answer to this question, we need to turn the clock back to the 1960s. During this period, few lawyers kept time records and most fees were based on uniform fee schedules approved by bar associations or the courts or the fee was determined by evaluating a number of different factors specified in the canons of ethics.

Far too often, lawyers were not sympathetic to the needs of the client and were insensitive to the client's concerns regarding how fees were determined and the affordability of legal services. Lawyers made a number of mistakes in setting fees, and failed to follow several important principles of billing that now are incorporated in the canons of ethics and are essential for maintaining a good client relationship.

Twenty years ago, few lawyers discussed the fee arrangement with the client in the first interview. In fact, many lawyers felt it was "unprofessional" to discuss fees, fearing the client would get the wrong impression. Only a handful of lawyers had written fee agreements or confirmed the fee arrangement in writing with the client. The client usually was billed when services were completed. There was no itemization of what services were provided, when they were provided or who performed them. There usually was a one-line description: "Professional Services Rendered" and the amount of the fee. This cursory billing approach, the failure to keep the client informed, escalating legal fees, more complex legal problems and the feeling that the client did not have control or a handle on legal costs, created the hourly rate environment that now permeates the legal profession.

Hourly rates have become the most commonly accepted manner of determining fees because a lawyer is paid for the time and effort expended regardless of the outcome. The client is able to control legal costs and can specify who will do the work at what price. This approach may be the only reasonable fee arrangement in difficult or complex cases.

There are some serious disadvantages to an hourly rate billing arrangement. A lawyer may be motivated to put in hours rather than focus on the results of the case. This method fails to recognize that some spectacular results may be achieved with little effort or time. There also is little incentive for lawyers to develop forms, systems and procedures that reduce the time necessary to provide a service. Furthermore, there is little incentive to delegate the work to other lawyers or legal assistants who may provide the service at a lower hourly rate or fee.

These disadvantages create a number of billing problems that lawyers deal with in a variety of ways. In many law firms, "billing units" or minimum-time entries for certain types of services are used extensively, particularly in insurance defense litigation where low hourly rates are common. Where a lawyer has become more efficient because of experience, expertise or the development of forms or systems, billing units or creative timekeeping techniques often are utilized extensively. This problem is not unique to the legal profession. Billing units or minimum-time charges are common in other service industries where services are based on a time charge. For example, most automotive-repair charges are calculated on the basis of a billing-unit charge for the type of service provided.

The purpose of this article is to provide an overview of some of the alternatives to hourly rates. Because hourly rates are used by most lawyers and will continue to be important in the near future, it is important to review how these rates should be determined and used.

Hourly Rates

In far too many cases, hourly rates are determined by what the market will bear or what the competition is charging rather than on the basis of the profit a firm wishes to realize. Information regarding market rates may be obtained from participation in economic surveys, informal discussions with other lawyers who provide similar work, advertised rates or rates disclosed in bids or requests solicited by public agencies and some businesses. A firm also may determine rates based on a historical analysis of billing rates adjusted for inflation, cost of doing business, expertise and other factors.

More and more firms are determining hourly rates on an actual cost basis with an adjustment for an appropriate level of profit for the firm. In order to determine what rates will need to be charged in order to obtain the desired level of income, the following information is needed:

1. Planned or budgeted expenses, excluding partner or shareholder compensation and benefits;

2. Anticipated billable time by partner or shareholder, associate and legal assistant;

3. Reasonable allocation of expenses by partner or shareholder, associate and legal assistant;

4. Firm collection rate—billings divided by cash receipts; and

5. Billing rate—billable hours or dollars (work-in-progress) divided by billed hours or dollars.

Some firms are using the same hourly rate or a "blended" or uniform rate for all lawyers. This approach enables clients who require billing budgets to more accurately estimate legal costs when the total hours for a legal task are known. It is also attractive to the client because more experienced lawyer's time is charged below normal rates. It also may be easier to market because only one rate is involved rather than the varied hourly rates that exist in many firms. On the other hand, some associate rates may be higher than normally would be justified.

If this method is used, it is important that the law firm reserve the right to determine which lawyers work on a matter, otherwise the client may always request senior or more-experienced lawyers. Some firms who use this approach charge one rate for routine legal services or up to a certain ceiling, with a higher rate for more complex or difficult cases. Other firms may have hourly rates based on a per diem charge for trial time or other types of legal services.

Most law firms that extensively use hourly rates have multiple and/or different hourly rates for partners or shareholders, associates, legal assistants and law clerks. There may be different hourly rates within these categories based on experience, expertise or legal specialty and seniority. Hourly rates may also vary by the type of client served, e.g., higher rates for larger corporate clients, lower rates for smaller businesses or clients who cannot afford higher rates. It is not uncommon to use a volume discount determined according to the amount and type of work a client brings to the firm. This type of discount often is used for routine work or insurance matters. A number of clients concerned with the fact that the clock keeps running in many complicated or protracted cases have attempted to require a cap on fees. Caps are dangerous and may be unfair unless they are higher than the estimated fee. Firms that consent to caps or ceilings are afraid that they may lose the client's business if they refuse or they will be placed in the embarrassing position of having to acknowledge that the firm does not place much faith in its own estimates.

Fixed Fee

In most firms, fixed fees are the best alternative to hourly rates. They are often used in routine cases or with matters where fees can be estimated fairly accurately. A modified fixed fee may be used for certain segments of legal services, e.g., pleadings, depositions, with an hourly rate for the trial or other services in the case. The minimum/maximum fee is another variation of the fixed fee. It may be used where results are important, such as in zoning cases and licensing or operating certificates. If the results are achieved, the maximum fee is charged. If the results are not satisfactory, the fee charged would not be less than the minimum.

A number of lawyers provide unlimited telephone consultation for routine matters for a fixed fee. Some firms are experimenting with fixed fees for certain types of legal services, e.g., legal research, discovery, legislative services and other routine litigation services.

There are some distinct advantages to this type of approach. A client knows how much the service is going to cost and can budget for this amount. The lawyer is motivated to work efficiently and economically to maximize results and profits. Accurate time records and computer-generated reports enable a firm to be more accurate in determining fixed fees and evaluating profitability by type of legal service performed. Because the fee is based on factors other than just the amount of time spent, there is an incentive for the development of forms and systems and the utilization of technology and legal assistants or other support staff to provide services.

A number of lawyers are hesitant to use fixed fees because it is difficult to estimate the fee in complex cases or in matters where the lawyer has little control over the activities of opposing party or counsel and the judge. Because many lawyers do not have accurate management or statistical information concerning the cost of providing certain types of legal services, there is a risk of losing money if the fee is too low. Furthermore, fixed fees require careful monitoring of time spent, results and profitability to make certain that the fixed fee is reasonable and provides an acceptable profit margin.

Fixed fees are commonly used in criminal matters, domestic or family-relations matters, estate planning, probate, routine corporate or administrative-agency work, tax and employee-benefit plans. Every law firm should have an internal fixed-fee schedule that should be developed by practice area. This schedule should be used as a guide to determine when the arrangement should be used and the amount of the fee to be charged.

Contingent Fee

Under this arrangement, the fee is based solely on the results or the outcome of the case, with the lawyer taking all of the financial risk. The amount of time spent should be carefully recorded to evaluate the profitability of the case, but time spent has nothing to do with the amount of the fee. This method is used primarily in plaintiff personal-injury cases, for clients who cannot afford to pay for the services provided and in subrogation and collection matters. Because of escalating litigation or collection costs, a number of business clients are becoming more interested in this method.

This arrangement usually results in higher fees than most other types of fee arrangements. It encourages a lawyer to be efficient and aggressive because time has no bearing on the amount of the fee. It also allows lawyers to represent clients who would otherwise not be able to afford legal counsel. In most instances, the lawyer's interest and the client's interest are the same. Unless contingent-fee cases are carefully screened and evaluated, they can be an economic disaster with serious impact on a firm's profits and cash flow. They may require significant out-of-pocket costs that may never be recovered or recovered after a lengthy time period. There is the risk of no fee if the case is lost or the services performed are not successful.

Listed below are some typical contingent-fee arrangements that are discussed in *Legal Fees & Representation Agreements*, published by the Section of Economics of the American Bar Association:

1. _____% of any and all sums recovered by way of settlement prior to instituting a lawsuit;
   _____% of any and all sums recovered either as a result of trial or by way of settlement after a lawsuit has been instituted;
   _____% of any and all sums recovered if any judgment is appealed, either on behalf of the client or by any adverse party, or if garnishment or any proceeding after judgment has to be brought to collect the judgment or any portion thereof;
   _____% of any and all sums recovered if the matter is the subject of a retrial as ordered by a trial or appellate court;
2. _____% on the first of any and all sums recovered by way of settlement in or out of court;

_____% on the next of any and all sums recovered by way of settlement in or out of court;

_____% on the next of any and all sums recovered by way of settlement in or out of court; or

_____% of any and all sums in excess of recovered by way of any settlement in or out of court.

Modified Contingent Fee

Under this method, the lawyer takes some risk but not all of the risk required in a contingent-fee case. The client agrees to pay a premium under certain conditions that have been agreed on in advance. The client's and lawyer's interest are usually the same with this type of arrangement.

The fee is determined as follows: The client pays the lawyer or law firm a small retainer to offset overhead and out-of-pocket costs. Instead of a retainer, the firm may charge on an overhead hourly basis. The bulk of the fee is determined on a percentage of the difference between the amount realistically at issue in the case and the final judgment. Example: For a $250,000 judgment or settlement in a $1,000,000 case, the lawyer would get a percentage of $750,000, plus the retainer. If the judgment is for $1,000,000 or higher, the lawyer only would get the retainer or the overhead hourly rate. As an alternative, the retainer or overhead hourly rates could be offset against the percentage fee.

Retainer or Cash Advance

This method may be used in conjunction with an hourly or per diem arrangement, when providing ongoing legal services as general counsel or when the client wants to assure availability of counsel and/or preclude counsel from representing other clients who may have competing interests.

There are a number of variations to this approach:

1. Fees to be earned: The client pays an initial retainer that is deposited in a trust or general account and a monthly bill is submitted. The client is expected to monthly reimburse the firm for services provided or to replenish the retainer when requested. Any unearned balance is returned to the client when the representation is completed.

2. Assuring counsel availability: A retainer is paid to assure counsel availability for a specified period. The retainer is applied to specified services to be performed or is nonrefundable if no services actually are performed. This may provide for an optional-fee arrangement in the event of more-extensive representation.

3. Fixed or periodic amounts for continuing services: A specified amount is paid monthly for specific services. The agreement usually provides for periodic review or adjustment in the event fees are lower or higher than the amount charged for the retainer.

OTHER BILLING ARRANGEMENTS

1. Small case program: The firm agrees to small cases to provide training for younger lawyers at a reduced fee. The client is spared the cost of more-experienced lawyers handling these cases.

2. Loaned or rented counsel: An attorney is assigned to work with a client at reduced rates, sometimes away from the office.

3. Loss leader: Reduced fees are offered for several types of services in the hope of obtaining other or future business, e.g., estate planning, probate, handling personal matters for corporate officer, etc.

CHAPTER 25

Donald S. Akins *is a Senior Vice President of Hildebrandt, Inc., management consultants in the Texas regional office. Over the years he has made substantial contributions to law-practice management in his numerous writings and speaking engagements. Here he approaches the subject of billing methods from the client's perspective. His theme is client acceptance of alternate pricing with emphasis on client education of what pricing is all about, client understanding of the ingredients of pricing, and client acceptance of the advantages of various pricing techniques.*

Client Acceptance of Alternate Pricing

by Donald S. Akins

Never before in the history of the legal profession have we experienced the amount of change currently taking place. These changes cover a broad spectrum—from firm structure to a very sophisticated use of all aspects of technology. Changes in the pricing of legal services, however, is more talk than action. Unless we revolutionize how legal services are priced, the legal profession will face even tougher times, many law firms will be unable to compete and will go out of business, and the average income for lawyers overall probably will decline. Too many firms are unwilling to accept this premise. Some of the key economic indicators, however, are beginning to illustrate that tough times are here and probably will get worse. We must change the focus of pricing from rates multiplied by hours to values and risks.

The theme of this article is client acceptance of alternate pricing with emphasis on client education of what pricing is all about, client understanding of the ingredients of pricing and client acceptance of the advantages of various pricing techniques.

IMPACT OF HISTORY

History has had a major impact on the current dilemma, making change more difficult. More than twenty years ago, only a handful of lawyers kept time records and billing followed no set pattern. Some billing was annually, some was at the completion of a matter, some was when the billing attorney felt like billing and a large percentage was when the firm was short of funds. Few, if any, records were kept to determine the cost of a particular service—but no one seemed to care.

Pricing generally followed four approaches:

1. **Job or package.** There was an agreed-on price from the outset for the legal work to be done. Even though the firm had no idea what the project would cost and few cost controls were in place, the concept was a sound one. How we let this slip away was criminal.

2. **Amount of the project.** These transactions were priced on the basis of the amount in question. This approach addressed value and risk but did not include the "difficulty" factor.

3. **Benefit conferred.** This approach was based on value and risk saved and/or increased value. This was a great idea. It was difficult, however, to enforce without written agreements because clients were unwilling to let lawyers make the rules as the matter unfolded. (Sound familiar?) Lawyers doing contingency work learned that they needed an employment agreement with the clients. It is a shame that all lawyers did not learn the value of fee agreements. (No client should employ a lawyer without a written fee agreement.)

4. **Hunch.** This approach was basically what the billing attorney thought a matter was worth, what the client would pay or what the client could pay. We must include "what the matter is worth" in our current thinking.

Most clients were comfortable with the pricing of their legal work and minimal complaints were made about legal fees. The average compensation of lawyers was below acceptable levels and most seminars and articles related to ways to improve the profession as opposed to the bottom line. Also, it was common for corporations to give most of their work to one law firm.

About twenty years ago, some of the most crucial surveys in the history of the profession were completed. They proved that lawyers who kept time earned more money than lawyers who did not keep time. This was a startling revelation and offered lawyers the opportunity to develop a cost mechanism to make their pricing more cost-effective. The stage was set—clients accepted pricing by the job, value of the project and benefit conferred. Time records were the missing link.

What happened next began to set a tone for a new approach to pricing. The survey results did not indicate that hours multiplied by rates was the best approach to pricing. Quite the contrary, the results indicated that with time records as guidelines, firms had a cost-analysis tool that would improve profitability using their present approaches to pricing. Lawyers overreacted to the survey results and took the easy way out.

This was the genesis for emphasis on the bottom line at the expense of professionalism. Most lawyers began to keep time records and lawyers spent the next ten to fifteen years educating clients that hours multiplied by rates is the best approach to pricing. Most clients ultimately agreed and we were off to the races. During these ten to fifteen years, lawyers had it too easy. As costs increased, lawyers would increase the rates to offset the impact. In the majority of cases, there was almost an open-end to the number of hours recorded and billed. We truly had squandered the opportunities presented by the surveys and the profession was on a collision course with reality—how high can billing rates go and when will clients want more information about expected fee parameters?

Many lawyers became complacent and did not address the effectiveness of the new pricing approach and made little effort to improve efficiency. The computer exacerbated the problem and many lawyers became lazy billers. They started to believe that the value of legal services should, in fact, be directly tied to hours multiplied by rates. The computer printouts listed all timekeepers and standard billing rates and produced an amount for billing-review purposes. In reality, there was little review and the invoices were prepared with the amount from the printout (a possible write-up in some cases). We had lost sight of the "value of a matter" and, in fact, clients now were being charged with all of the firm's inefficiencies and the training of the young lawyers.

Most lawyers always have believed that they knew what the clients wanted from their lawyers and what the clients were willing to pay for. A number of surveys, however, have shown that lawyers' perceptions of what clients want and what clients actually want are just the opposite. Historically, lawyers have been "results" oriented and clients have been "effort" oriented. This helps explain why "rates multiplied by hours" pricing has run into a dead end—it has absolutely no direct relationship to efforts or results. Many lawyers will take a strong exception to this premise. However, the number of recorded and billed hours illustrates only the ability of a lawyer to record and bill time. I am not advocating the abolition of recording billable hours. I am, however, strongly advocating that billable hours should be used more for calculating costs than for portraying the value of legal services.

Lawyers do not know enough about their clients or their clients' businesses. This includes products, services, leadership, growth and expansion and competition. It is difficult to discuss possible pricing alternatives without a thorough knowledge of all aspects of the clients and their businesses. This spills over into client concerns about lawyers; for example:

1. Unknown fee arrangement. Most clients no longer are willing to let the lawyers determine the fee arrangement without their knowledge or participation. The absence of a written fee agreement and/or a vague fee agreement often results in a grievance being filed against a lawyer. This destroys any opportunity to discuss alternate pricing and causes the nail to be driven a little deeper into the coffin.

2. Poor or lack of communication. Too many clients simply do not know what their lawyers are doing, are unaware of the status of their matters and are left to try and figure out what is going on. This is suicide. A formal approach to communication is an effective tool to show effort. Lawyers must be accessible and responsive.

3. Excessive staffing. Up until a few years ago, clients funded the training of young

lawyers. Recently, that door has begun to close and firms are scrambling to find ways to train young lawyers without sacrificing profitability. This is no easy task and must be considered when designing alternate pricing methods.

4. Technician versus counselor. Clients have varying needs. Some require a technician, some require a counselor. Clients are more likely to pay a premium for a counselor than they are for a technician. Proper use of technicians, however, is crucial for developing packages and systems that can be priced by the job. Too many compensation systems reward lawyers for being strapped to their desks and are not flexible enough to also reward a counselor who may save a client a million dollars with only a few billable hours. The trend has been (and continues today) for clients to use their accountants instead of their lawyers for business advice. We must reverse this trend.

5. Lack of preventive education and maintenance. Clients complain that their lawyers have a tendency to wait for the telephone to ring to receive the next assignment instead of keeping the clients abreast of developments that will impact on their businesses. Clients want to be told about expected governmental decisions, industry trends and surfacing competition. Clients are more than willing to pay for this information.

6. Lack of knowledge of needs and problems. Lawyers have more opportunities to discuss alternate pricing when they are aware of the crucial needs and major problems of their clients than when the client calls with the next assignment and the lawyers have to spend excessive time learning the scope of the problem, what caused it and possible ramifications.

History has allowed lawyers to play tricks on themselves. What goes around, ultimately comes around. This has now happened, as illustrated by the following:

1. Expansion of in-house legal staffs. During the past ten years, corporations have increased their in-house legal staffs in numbers and in expertise. While this trend is slowing, corporate counsel are developing ways to improve management of outside counsel, always with an eye toward cost control.

2. Spreading the work. Corporations are spreading their work among firms based on the reputation of specialists. This has increased the competition for business and resulted in firms being asked to make presentations of why they should be employed. This has put pressure on keeping the rates down. However, this presents opportunities to develop unique approaches to pricing (corporate counsel want to hear about new approaches).

3. Expanded and more-sophisticated marketing efforts. The rapid increase in competition for business has resulted in firms getting serious about their marketing efforts, including the pricing of legal services.

4. Pressure to keep rates down. Clients do not want the lawyers with the highest rates to do all their work. Except in larger matters with high exposure, clients would rather have lawyers and paralegals with lower rates do most of the work with their counselor (high billing rates) coordinating the assignment. Too many lawyers have developed a "my client" mentality, believing that the client wants only them to do all of the work. This simply is not the case in most situations. The key to marketing is addressing client, industry and practice-area needs and problems, not selling the firm as "full service."

Lawyers now are trying to figure out how to develop alternate pricing techniques and sell them to clients. In other words, what was available for the taking when the survey results were announced twenty years ago is now a tough assignment. It took years to convince clients that hours multiplied by rates was the best approach. Likewise, it will take years to convince clients that alternate approaches should be considered.

INTERNAL CONSIDERATIONS

The computer provides firms with the types of data necessary to determine the profitability of all types of matters. This data, however, must be used to improve efficiency through cost control and proper staffing.

Some of the key ingredients to consider are:

1. Billing rates. The unanswered question is what should be included in the billing rates and what should be billed separately. Certain clients will insist that all of their work be priced by the hour and some clients (insurance companies, for example) will set maximum rates far below the standard rates of all partners and many associates. The two key questions here are whether a firm should do this type work and how the matters should be staffed to make a profit. Lawyers should ask their clients what charges they will accept over and above the hourly rate.

2. Realization rate. The income side of a budget must be analyzed when calculating the cost of a matter. Most budgets are still a function of hours multiplied by rates with an adjustment for write-downs of time and write-offs of accounts receivables. The end result is a realization rate. The cost of a matter is increased when the realization rate is below the rate stipulated in the budget.

   Poor realization usually is the result of poor work-acceptance guidelines (firms should be more selective of the types of work they accept and should realize that they cannot do everything for every client), overstaffing, lack of supervision, ineffective collection procedures and bankruptcies.

   Alternate pricing techniques are easier to develop and sell when a firm's practice is focused (instead of accepting every piece of work that comes along).

3. Overhead cost per billable hour. It is important to know the overhead cost per hour, including the compensation of associates and paralegals.

   The realization rate and cost for a project must be projected and compared with the results. A key to pricing is analyzing similar projects to learn from mistakes.

4. Training time. The cost of training time must be factored into the equation. The firm must bear the cost of this time unless the client is aware of the situation and has approved it. Some clients are willing to pay for all or part of this time if it is being used to expand the expertise of one or more lawyers who will be members of a team working on a client's business.

5. Cost to develop forms, systems and procedures. Few firms have done a good job in developing forms, systems and procedures. One of the major obstacles has been the perception that you don't get credit for doing this type of work. The major obstacle, however, has been pricing by the hour. Until recently, there has been no incentive, for clients did not question the number of hours billed for a particular matter.

   A good set of forms, systems and procedures gives a firm the opportunity to price certain work by the job. The cost to develop this information should be recorded and allocated to future projects.

6. Use of technology. Technology is becoming a leverage tool. The cost must be built into the pricing techniques or the leverage will be eliminated and the cost will be substantial.

7. Partner appetite for compensation. This may be the toughest consideration. Without alternate pricing, partner compensation will bear the brunt. In the next five years, most firms that continue to use hours multiplied by rates pricing will see partner income levels shrink. This, more than anything else, probably will serve as the catalyst to encourage firms to address alternate pricing techniques.

Firms have access to the data necessary to determine the cost of producing each service, including acceptable compensation for partners. However, this is the easiest part. Clients (those that buy the services) must be convinced. This can be done, but it will take a lot of work. Most firms should plan for at least a five-year education process.

External Considerations

A shift to alternate pricing must be externally driven (what will be acceptable to clients). However, firms must do their homework and devise systems to sell the alternate approaches.

1. Hours multiplied by rates pricing. This will not disappear in the next five to ten years (maybe never). The key is to eliminate as much of this approach as possible. Litigation (especially defense) possibly will be the toughest to address. Some options should be considered.

    (a) Understanding of the employment. The responsible attorney must understand the assignment, what is expected, how to proceed with new facts, reporting requirements, etc. There should be an employment agreement spelling out all of the details.

    (b) Proper staffing. Staffing should be discussed with the client. Firms must realize that the cost of training young lawyers must be borne (at least shared) by the firm.

    (c) Tougher supervision. The responsible attorney must control the assignment. Each member of the team must understand the game plan and there should be weekly meetings to discuss all aspects of the case.

    (d) Use of in-house staff. The trend is increased participation by in-house lawyers and staff. This must be coordinated and the in-house people should be part of the team meetings (telephone works pretty well).

    (e) Defense contingency. Some clients would like the firm to share in their risks. Consider an assignment as a prototype—charge by the hour and compare the hourly charges with an agreed percentage of savings (possibly tied to certain thresholds). To illustrate:

Maximum exposure	$1,000,000
Acceptable exposure (agreed by client and firm)	500,000
Actual damages (50 percent of hourly charges or no fees at all)	750,000+
Actual damages (75 percent of hourly charges, possibly not to exceed X dollars)	500,000
Actual damages (hourly charges plus percent of $100,000, possibly not to exceed X dollars)	400,000
Actual damages (hourly charges plus percent of $500,000, possibly not to exceed X dollars)	-0-

    (f) Blended rate. All lawyers and paralegals will be charged at the same rate. Insurance defense and collections (hourly charges) are possibilities. To illustrate:

COSTLY APPROACH

Timekeepers	Hours	Firm Rates Rate	Firm Rates Bill	Client Rates Rate	Client Rates Bill	Difference
Partner A	5	$150	$750	$100	$500	($250)
Partner C	4	125	500	100	400	($100)
Associate X	6	80	480	75	450	($30)
TOTAL	15 hours		$1,730		$1,350	($380)
			NET LOSS			($380)

Points:
1. High billing rate partners did most of the work.
2. Associate utilization was minimal.
3. Legal assistants were not utilized at all.

MAJOR IMPROVEMENT

Timekeepers	Hours	Firm Rates Rate	Firm Rates Bill	Client Rates Rate	Client Rates Bill	Difference
Partner A	2	$150	$300	$100	$200	($100)
Associate X	3	80	240	75	225	($15)
Associate Y	10	60	600	75	750	$150
TOTAL	15 hours		$1,140		$1,175	$35
Gain						
Partner A	3	$150	$450			
Partner C	4	125	500			
Associate X	3	80	240			
NET GAIN (over Costly Approach) ($380 loss plus net gain of $1,225)						$1,605

Points:
1. Partner time was minimized, allowing the partners to spend their time on work at their standard rates.
2. Better utilization of Associate X's time.
3. Legal assistants still not utilized.

MORE IMPROVEMENT

Timekeepers	Hours	Firm Rates Rate	Firm Rates Bill	Client Rates Rate	Client Rates Bill	Difference
Partner A	1	$150	$150	$100	$100	($50)
Associate X	1	80	80	75	75	($5)
Associate Y	4	60	240	75	300	$60
Legal Asst. A	9	45	405	60	540	$135
TOTAL	15 hours		$875		$1,015	$140
Gain						
Partner A	4	$150	$600			
Partner C	4	125	500			
Associate X	5	80	400			
Associate Y	6	60	360			
	NET GAIN (over Costly Approach) ($380 loss plus net gain of $2,000)					$2,380

Points:
1. Further minimized partner time.
2. Reduced time of Associate X with higher billing rate.
3. Reduced time of Associate Y.

BEST APPROACH (BLENDED RATES)

Timekeepers	Hours	Firm Rates Rate	Firm Rates Bill	Client Rates Rate	Client Rates Bill	Difference
Partner A	1	$150	$150	$90	$90	($60)
Associate X	1	80	80	90	90	$10
Associate Y	4	60	240	90	360	$120
Legal Asst.	9	45	405	90	810	$405
TOTAL	15 hours		$875		$1,350	$475
Gain						
Partner A	4	$150	$600			
Partner C	4	125	500			
Associate X	5	80	400			
Associate Y	6	60	360			
	NET GAIN (over Costly Approach) ($380 loss plus net gain of $2,335)					$2,715

Points:
1. All timekeepers priced at same billing rate.
2. Other aspects are same as preceding example.

(g) Unit pricing. The client and firm agree on the amount of time to be charged for specified activities, such as filing answers, depositions, interrogatories, attending hearings, filing motions, etc. This is similar to how the medical profession schedules certain procedures and the cost for each.

(h) Package deal for all work in a city. Some insurance companies are exploring the idea of giving one firm all of their work in a city. This is an opportunity to develop a game plan to share the risks with the client. However, there are some opportunities to realize substantial premiums if the approach is well defined. *NOTE:* There is a major risk in staffing to handle this work and the firm must make sure there are protections if the client decides to move the work to another firm. The employment agreement is crucial.

2. Job/project pricing. This probably will be the easiest to sell of all alternate pricing. People are accustomed to buying on this basis. However, they still have to be sold because they also are accustomed to shopping for the best price and reputation for quality and service. The key is packaging.
   (a) Stay abreast of the needs and problems of your clients. Certain needs and problems will be repetitive. Also, clients will have similar needs and problems. Look for the opportunities to develop a package that can be priced accordingly.
   (b) In larger firms, the department heads should develop a list of assignments that can be packaged. In smaller firms, the list can be developed by a partner whose specialty is in the area being considered.
   (c) Analyze the cost to produce the services on five to ten prior assignments. Look for ways to improve staffing and efficiency.
   (d) Build forms, systems and procedures to develop a package. A partner should be assigned to develop each package.
   (e) Accumulate the cost to build the package and allocate to subsequent projects. The first two or three projects likely will cost more than the package price. The goal, however, should be to price the package in excess of the cost to produce.
   (f) Consider a prototype project for a financial institution (there are many possibilities) for handling real estate transactions (residential and commercial).
   (g) Use an engagement letter that accurately spells out what the client will receive as part of the package. Exceptions will be priced accordingly.
   (h) Project pricing can be developed for many aspects of a firm's business practice—real estate, tax, securities, bonds, etc. The amount of the transaction and corresponding risks may be built into the package price in some cases.

3. Benefit-conferred pricing. This approach to pricing is more acceptable to clients when the firm shares in the risks. Contingency pricing is a form of benefit conferred in that the firm's participation in fees is based on a positive result. There are several other approaches to benefit conferred—amount saved, increased value, etc.
   (a) As with project pricing, stay abreast of the needs and prob-

lems of your clients. Certain needs and problems may create large exposures or offer opportunities for the clients to reap substantial benefits. Look for opportunities to share the risks with the clients or to participate in the enhancement of a client's assets.

(b) Conduct an analysis of assignments handled during the prior two years in which a benefit-conferred approach could have been discussed with the clients. Categorize the assignments to develop a pattern.

(c) Based on the types of assignments, develop some general strategy for incorporating benefit conferred as part of your pricing discussion. This may include one or more of the following:

(1) Hourly rate base plus percentage of amount saved (possibly amount saved in excess of X amount).

(2) Percentage of amount saved.

(3) Hourly rate plus percentage of amount of value increased (possibly amount of value increase in excess of X amount).

(4) Percentage of value increase.

(d) A written fee agreement must spell out all of the details of how benefit conferred will be determined.

(e) Benefit-conferred pricing is not available in very many situations. However, it can be considered for discussion in certain securities and tax matters, acquisitions, zoning, bank chartering, etc.

4. Piece of the action. This approach to pricing carries substantial risk and requires the firm to "get in bed" with the client. This works best with start-up companies and weak or bankrupt companies being purchased by new owners. There are numerous legal issues and malpractice carriers are not particularly enamored with the idea. The major need usually is capital. Many of these companies welcome participation by their lawyers (business advice and legal fees based on company performance). A perfect example is the original relationship between Ross Perot and the firm of Hughes & Luce when Perot was establishing EDS. Neither side knew for sure where the venture was going and there was not a lot of available capital.

(a) You must be very selective of which clients you approach about this type of pricing. A committee composed of related practice disciplines should analyze each situation. If possible, the committee should be composed of the responsible attorney, a tax attorney, a corporate/banking attorney, a commercial litigator and a "deal maker."

(b) Compensation to the firm may be in stock (normally not acceptable), percentage of company earnings beyond X amount, equity interest, discounted hourly rates, discounted hourly rates plus one or more of the other vehicles, fees out of future earnings, possibly with a "kicker."

(c) The most likely candidates for this type of pricing are start-up businesses, small and emerging businesses and certain real estate ventures.

5. Financing/influence brokerage. Some lawyers are in a position to help clients/potential clients arrange financing for various projects. The risk is substantial unless proper care is taken not to actually make a recommendation to the lender. Giving the

introduction is all that is needed in some cases. The fee may be set as a percentage of the amount of the financing.

Effective influence is worth more than hourly rates. Firms should market the lawyers who can exert influence on decision making. Examples are former governors, congressmen, employees with the IRS and other branches of federal, state and local governments. Fees for this type of service should be priced in multiples of $25,000 to $100,000.

The most difficult aspect of this approach is marketing the capability. The easiest part is pricing for the value of the service rather than hours multiplied by rate.

Client Acceptance

After you have analyzed the cost structures, developed the packages and agreed on the pricing for each package, the hard job lies ahead—client education and acceptance. This will require:

1. Knowledge of your clients and your clients' businesses. You must stay current about:
   (a) Governmental forces that will impact a client's business.
   (b) Economic trends of the client.
   (c) Industry trends of the client.
   (d) Current and projected legal needs.
   (e) Geographic expansion—demographics of new location, industry trends in new location, leadership, etc.

2. Service/industry information about your major clients.
   (a) Identify opportunities for cross-selling additional work to existing clients and targeting new clients in the industry.
   (b) Gives firm a list of expertise needs.

3. Expertise/experience chart of lawyers. This will portray available expertise and the experience levels of all lawyers.
   (a) Specialization and reputation are keys to selling alternate pricing.
   (b) This chart will highlight a firm's recruiting needs—entry level, experienced associates or a partner with a recognized expertise.

4. Writing proposal letters, including proposed budgets of time and expenses.

5. Organizing client presentations.

6. More written employment agreements.

7. Internal education about the need for alternate pricing.

The best approach is to think small at first. Take one particular opportunity (package billing), develop the package, select a few clients to work with, try out the approach, modify where necessary, and finalize the approach. Then move on to the next opportunity. Use the same technique for the other pricing approaches. Your goal should be to develop some success stories.

You will be trying to unravel a great deal of what was messed up twenty years ago. The ball is in your court—the clients must be convinced.

CHAPTER 26

Luther J. Avery, *of San Francisco's Bancroft, Avery and McAlister, is always a provoker of thought. He has furnished the Task Force with materials that reflect the California requirement for a written-fee agreement. Some of these materials are reproduced here so that we can learn what has happened in California and thereby anticipate what may happen in other jurisdictions. These materials are organized as follows:*

Part 1. Article 8.5 Fee Agreements, Sections 6146, 6147, 6148 and 6149.
Part 2. The State Bar of California, Sample Written Fee Agreement Forms
Part 3. Sample Client/Lawyer Agreement
Part 4. Draft of a Fee Manual for In-Office Use.

What's Happening In California and How to Cope

The California State Bar Act Rules of Professional Conduct

Part 1. Article 8.5 Fee Agreements, Sections 6146, 6147, 6148 and 6149

[NOTE: Full text of Article 8.5 & Sections 6146–6148 are not presented here.]

ARTICLE 8.5 FEE AGREEMENTS

§ 6146. Limitations; Periodic Payments; Definitions

(a) An attorney shall not contract for or collect a contingency fee for representing any person seeking damages in connection with an action for injury or damage against a health care provider based upon such person's alleged professional negligence in excess of the following limits:

(1) Forty percent of the first fifty thousand dollars ($50,000) recovered.
(2) Thirty-three and one-third percent of the next fifty thousand dollars ($50,000) recovered.
(3) Twenty-five percent of the next one hundred thousand dollars ($100,000) recovered.
(4) Ten percent of any amount on which the recovery exceeds two hundred thousand dollars ($200,000).

The limitations shall apply regardless of whether the recovery is by settlement, arbitration, or judgment, or whether the person for whom the recovery is made is a responsible adult, an infant, or a person of unsound mind.

(b) If periodic payments are awarded to the plaintiff pursuant to section 667.7 of the Code of Civil Procedure, the court shall place a total value on these payments based upon the projected life expectancy of the plaintiff and include this amount in computing the total award from which attorney's fees are calculated under this section.

(c) For purposes of this section:

(1) "Recovered" means the net sum recovered after deducting any disbursements or costs incurred in connection with prosecution or settlement of the claim. Costs of

medical care incurred by the plaintiff and the attorney's office overhead costs or charges are not deductible disbursements or costs for such purpose.

(2) "Health care provider" means any person licensed or certified pursuant to Division 2 (commencing with section 500) or licensed pursuant to the Osteopathic Initiative Act, or the Chiropractic Initiative Act, or licensed pursuant to Chapter 2.5 (commencing with section 1440) of Division 2 of the Health and Safety Code; and any clinic, health dispensary, or health facility, licensed pursuant to Division 2 (commencing with section 1200) of the Health and Safety Code. "Health care provider" includes the legal representatives of a health care provider.

(3) "Professional negligence" is a negligent act or omission to act by a health care provider in the rendering of professional services, which act or omission is the proximate cause of a personal injury or wrongful death, provided that the services are within the scope of services for which the provider is licensed and which are not within any restriction imposed by the licensing agency or licensed hospital. (Added by Stats. 1975, 2nd Ex. Sess., ch. 1; Amended by Stats. 1975, 2nd Ex. Sess., ch. 2, effective September 24, 1975, operative December 12, 1975; Stats. 1981, ch. 714.)

§ 6147. Contingency Fee Contract: Contents; Effect of Noncompliance; Application to Contracts for Recovery of Workers' Compensation Benefits

(a) An attorney who contracts to represent a plaintiff on a contingency fee basis shall, at the time the contract is entered into, provide a duplicate copy of the contract, signed by both the attorney and the plaintiff, or his guardian or representative. The contract shall be in writing and shall include, but is not limited to, all of the following:

(1) A statement of the contingency fee rate which the client and attorney have agreed upon.

(2) A statement as to how disbursements and costs incurred in connection with the prosecution or settlement of the claim will affect the contingency fee and the client's recovery.

(3) A statement as to what extent, if any, the plaintiff could be required to pay any compensation to the attorney for related matters that arise out of their relationship not covered by their contingency fee contract. This may include any amounts collected for the plaintiff by the attorney.

(4) Unless the claim is subject to the provisions of Section 6146, a statement that the fee is not set by law but is negotiable between attorney and client.

(5) If the claim is subject to the provisions of Section 6146, a statement that the rates set forth in that section are the maximum limits for the contingency fee agreement, and that the attorney and client may negotiate a lower rate.

(b) Failure to comply with any provision of this section renders the agreement voidable at the option of the plaintiff, and the attorney shall thereupon be entitled to collect a reasonable fee.

(c) This section shall not apply to contingency fee contracts for the recovery of workers' compensation benefits. (Added by Stats. 1982, ch. 415. Amended by Stats. 1986, ch. 475.)

§ 6148. Written Fee Contract: Contents; Effect of Noncompliance

(a) In any case not coming within section 6147 in which it is reasonably foreseeable that total expense to a client, including attorney fees will exceed one thousand dollars ($1,000), the contract for services in the case shall be in writing and shall contain all of the following:

(1) The hourly rate and other standard rates, fees, and charges applicable to the case.
(2) The general nature of the legal services to be provided to the client.
(3) The respective responsibilities of the attorney and the client as to the performance of the contract.

(b) All bills for services rendered by an attorney to a client shall clearly state the basis thereof, including the amount, rate, basis for calculation, or other method of determination of the member's fees; and, upon request by the client, the attorney shall provide a bill to the client no later than 10 days following the request. The client is entitled to similar requests at intervals of no less than 30 days following the initial request.

(c) Failure to comply with any provision of this section renders the agreement voidable at the option of the client, and the attorney shall, upon the agreement being voided, be entitled to collect a reasonable fee.

(d) This section shall not apply to any of the following:

(1) Services rendered in an emergecny to avoid foreseeable prejudice to the rights or interests of the client or where a writing is otherwise impractical.
(2) An arrangement as to the fee implied by the fact that the attorney's services are of the same general kind as previously rendered to and applied for by the client.
(3) If the client knowingly states in writing, after full disclosure of this section, that a writing concerning fees is not required.
(4) If the client is a corporation.

(e) This section applies prospectively only to fee agreements following its operative date. (Added by Stats. 1986, ch. 475.)

§ 6149. Written Fee Contract Confidential Communication

A written fee contract shall be deemed to be a confidential communication within the meaning of subdivision (e) of Section 6068 and of Section 952 of the Evidence Code. (Added by Stats. 1986, ch. 475.)

Part 2. The State Bar of California, Sample Written Fee Agreement Forms

I. INTRODUCTION

Attached are five sample fee agreements, drafted in response to Business and Professions Code Section 6148, which requires California lawyers to have written fee agreements with their clients under most circumstances. That statute took effect on January 1, 1987.

The first three are short forms designed for use in relatively small, routine matters. They cover: (1) litigation on an hourly basis; (2) non-litigation on an hourly basis; and (3) non-litigation on a fixed fee basis. The remaining two are designed for use in more complex hourly matters and cover (4) litigation (5) and non-litigation.

II. OVERVIEW

A. DISCLAIMER

Neither the State Bar of California nor its Committee on Mandatory Fee Arbitration makes any representations or warranties of any kind, express or implied, concerning the legal adequacy or enforceability of any of the accompanying forms or any part of them. Nothing in these "Instructions and Comments" or in the forms shall be interpreted or construed as such a representation or warranty. These "Instructions and Comments" and the forms are intended for use only by lawyers admitted to practice in California, who are expected to utilize their own independent legal and business judgment when evaluating the forms and these comments.

B. INTENDED PURPOSE AND LIMITATIONS

The accompanying forms are samples only. They are not mandatory forms. They enjoy no preferred status. They create no minimum standards. They do not presume to address every setting in which the attorney-client relationship arises, nor do they contain every term a fee contract might include. In Part VI below, we discuss several additional clauses.

By enumerating certain charges and billing practices, we do not suggest that you must or should adopt them. We simply acknowledge that some lawyers follow them.

We have varied the samples in content and style. The short forms are written in formal, contractual language, while the long forms are more colloquial. We have made no effort to tailor the samples to any particular specialty nor to cover every variation. Lawyers are encouraged to mold the samples to fit their needs.

C. SUMMARY OF THE STATUTE

Section 6148 of the Business and Professions Code requires California lawyers to have written fee contracts with their clients whenever the client's total expense, including fees, will likely exceed $1,000.

The fee contract must state:

(1) The lawyer's hourly rate and other standard rates, fees and charges;

(2) The general nature of the legal services to be provided to the client; and

(3) The responsibilities of lawyer and client under the contract.

If a lawyer fails to comply with the statute, the fee agreement becomes voidable at the client's option, whereupon the lawyer is limited to a "reasonable" fee.

A written fee contract is not required when services are rendered in an emergency; when a writing

---

is impractical; when the client is a corporation; when the client, after full disclosure, makes a written waiver of the benefits of Section 6148, or when the fee agreement is implied in fact by a prior course of dealing between the lawyer and the client.

Finally, the statute requires lawyers to provide their clients with written billing statements. A client may demand such statements at minimum intervals of 30 days. The lawyer must provide a statement within 10 days after demand. All statements, whether requested by the client or not, must state ". . . the amount, rate, and basis for calculation or other method of determination of the [lawyer's] fees." (subd.(b)).

III. GUIDELINES FOR COMPLIANCE

Compliance with the statute is largely a matter of judgment for the individual lawyer. Forms alone cannot tell a lawyer how to comply. Rather, compliance will result from lawyers' understanding of the statute's provisions and the issues those provisions raise.

A. STANDARD FOR DISCLOSURE

Because it is undoubtedly consumer protection legislation, the statute must be examined in the light most favorable to the client. Disclosures required by the statute should be accompanied by all additional information necessary to make the disclosure complete, accurate, and not misleading. If a client could contend that omitted matter would have been material to the decision to retain the lawyer, then the matter in question should be disclosed to avoid the statute's penalties.

B. CONTRACT IN WRITING

To meet the statute's requirement of a contract in writing, the fee arrangement should be signed by both the lawyer and the client. A lawyer should be firm in requesting that the client sign the agreement before work commences.

C. DISCLOSURE OF STANDARD "RATES, FEES, AND CHARGES"

A lawyer should err on the side of inclusion when enumerating standard rates, fees and charges. In an hourly case, fixed charges for specific functions should be disclosed to avoid misleading the client. For example, most firms have a minimum billing unit; many charge a minimum number of hours for a court appearance; others routinely charge flat fees for the use of standardized documents developed over the years.

Costs and expenses that are passed through should be enumerated in enough detail to avoid misunderstanding. Charges passed through other than "at cost" should be listed to avoid omitting a "standard rate, fee or charge."

D. NATURE OF SERVICES/DUTIES OF PARTIES

When the statute requires disclosure of the nature of the services to be rendered and the respective duties of the lawyer and the client, it simply enumerates two of the indispensable terms of a contract. When the fee is on an hourly basis, these items can be covered in simple, short generalities. In flat or "premium" fee contracts, however, the scope of the lawyer's responsibilities should be defined carefully.

E. BILLS: AMOUNT, RATE, AND BASIS

Beginning on January 1, 1987, all bills must state the amount, rate and basis for calculation (or other method of determination) of the lawyer's fees. A bill that simply states "for services rendered" is no longer sufficient. In an hourly case, the bill would comply with this requirement if it simply listed the lawyers who performed services, the time each expended, their hourly rates and the resulting fee for each lawyer's time. In other types of cases, such as flat or premium fees, the bill should refer to the "basis of calculation," which should be set forth in the fee agreement. Nothing in the statute requires lawyers' bills to describe the services that were rendered.

F. EXEMPTIONS

Except for the provision exempting corporate clients from the required disclosures, the exemptions in the statute are relatively narrow. Lawyers should rely on these exemptions with extreme caution, if not at their peril.

G. EFFECTIVE DATE

Beginning January 1, 1987, all bills must comply with the statute, even if the attorney/client relationship predated 1987. The statute's provisions for written contracts and their contents apply only to attorney/client relationships that begin in 1987. Lawyers should take care, however, to comply with the statute whenever a pre-1987 agreement is superseded or modified in a material respect.

H. BREVITY AND CLARITY V. COMPLETE DISCLOSURE

The statute embraces two inconsistent goals: complete disclosure on the one hand, and providing information to clients in an understandable format on the other. Each lawyer should strive to strike a balance between these goals when drafting fee agreements.

IV. INSTRUCTIONS FOR SHORT FORMS

The short forms are lean contracts, intended for use in routine matters by lawyers with simple billing structures. They are written in the contractual language that many lawyers prefer for these short agreements. They are self-contained. Once lawyers draft a few inserts and fill in some blanks, these forms can be reproduced on their letterhead, ready to come alive when a client's particulars are inserted and the parties sign.

A. FORM NO. 1: HOURLY-LITIGATION

1. Conditions (Par. 1) and Effective Date (Par. 11) At the threshold, you must determine at what point the contract comes to life. Until it does, there is no written contract that complies with the statute. Once it does, you are obligated to render services, even if you have not been paid. If you perform services before the written contract takes effect, you will be limited to a "reasonable" fee. This form and the other samples embody one solution to these intertwined issues. It is not the only solution, nor will it always be the best solution.

Par. 1 (Conditions) interacts closely with par. 11 (Effective Date). Working together, the two clauses are designed to delay the lawyer's obligation to perform services until the client signs the contract and pays the deposit; however, the clauses also are drafted to bring within the contract any services performed before signing and payment. The delay in the lawyer's obligation to perform services is based on a cautious reading of the statute's written contract requirement. We assume that no written contract exists until both parties sign and perform the conditions precedent. At the same time, however, we recognize that lawyers frequently will (or must) perform services before signing and payment; they will often do so under circumstances that will not fall within the statute's exemptions for emergencies or impracticality. For that reason, we bring "premature" services under the contract's protection; upon signing and payment the contract will take effect, but *retroactively* to the date the lawyer first performed services. Without the retroactivity provision compensation for "premature" services would be limited to a reasonable fee, because the services were performed without a written contract in violation of the statute.

Of course, if the contract never takes effect (for failure to sign or pay), then the statutory penalty limits the lawyer to the reasonable value of any services performed.

If you expect to perform services before the contract is signed and the deposit paid, then document the facts in a writing, preferably one signed by the client. Likewise, document your reliance on any statutory exemptions, such as emergency or impracticality.

2. Scope and Duties (Par. 2) Fill in a brief description of the subject of the representation. This is a statutory requirement. Enumeration of the client's and lawyer's duties likewise are required by the statute.

3. Deposit (Par. 3) This is an optional clause. Fill in the amount of any deposit and the date by which it must be paid. A lawyer cannot withdraw funds from the trust account without the client's express authorization. We have provided for that authorization. If you prefer a more cautious approach to the authorization question, you could provide that sums will be withdrawn from the trust account only after they are invoiced to client and "x" days pass without client's protest of any of the charges.

4. Legal Fees (Par. 4) Add any standard or minimum time or dollar charges for specific functions—for example, "x" hours for any court appearance or "y" dollars for the "standard" first set of interrogatories. If you do not disclose such practices, you probably are misleading the client when you state that you charge by the hour.

5. Costs and Expenses (Par. 5) This

is not an inclusive list. You may include more or less. Additional items are included in the cost provisions of the long form agreements. You should disclose the rate or charge for any items not passed through strictly at cost; if you do not, you may violate the statute's requirement that standard rates, fees and charges be disclosed.

6. Statements (Par. 6) Nothing requires a lawyer to send periodic statements, unless the client demands a statement. Lawyers' statements *need not* describe the services rendered, but must state the "basis" of the charges, including the amount, rate, and basis for calculation or other method of determination of your fees.

7. Lien (Par. 7) This is an optional clause.

8. Discharge and Withdrawal (Par. 8) This is declaratory of applicable law and rules.

9. Conclusion of Services (Par. 9) Returning the file and other property is required under existing law and rules.

10. Disclaimer of Guarantee (Par. 10) This is an optional clause.

B. FORM NO. 2: HOURLY–NON-LITIGATION

With the exceptions and additions recited below, the comments on form 1 apply equally to form 2.

1. Scope and Duties (Par. 2) We have added an exclusion for litigation.

2. Costs and Expenses (Par. 5) We have deleted litigation-related costs.

3. Lien We have eliminated the lien, because it may sometimes be inappropriate in a non-litigation context.

C. FORM NO. 3: FIXED FEE–NON-LITIGATION

With the exceptions and additions recited below, the instructions for forms 1 and 2 apply equally to form no. 3.

1. Scope and Duties (Par. 2) Lawyers should take extreme care in defining what will and will not be done under the fixed fee agreement. Inattention to this point can result in a lawyer doing far more work than expected, all for a fixed fee.

2. Fixed Fee (Par. 3) The issue of nonrefundability raises the specter of an unconscionable fee. Lawyers should be aware that they may be required to refund all or part of the fixed fee, to avoid violating the prohibition against unconscionable fees.

3. Discharge and Withdrawal (Par. 7) If a lawyer withdraws before completing the contract, the client may be entitled to a refund, either because the fee retained would be unconscionable, or because the lawyer's withdrawal was not justified.

V. INSTRUCTIONS FOR LONG FORMS

A. FORM NO. 4: HOURLY-LITIGATION

With the exceptions and additions recited below, the instructions for form 1 apply equally to this form.

1. Scope of Services (Par. 2) Scope of services excludes appeal from the judgment and execution proceedings. You may exclude more, less or nothing. We have created a safety net, providing that this agreement will cover any future services. That clause will prevent inadvertent violations of the statute's requirement for a written fee contract. Some lawyers take the opposite approach, however, stating that they engage to perform only the services described in the agreement.

2. Minimum Fee/Deposit (Par. 4) You need not require a minimum fee or a deposit of any kind. This paragraph sets forth one way to handle the deposit if you opt for one.

We have provided that part of the initial deposit will be a minimum fee. That amount should not be so high that it will be considered unconscionable. We also have placed a ceiling on further deposits. Without a ceiling, the right to require further deposits is so open ended that it could be unenforceable for uncertainty. In addition we have provided for advance payment of all fees and costs to be incurred in preparing for and conducting trial or arbitration. Because it is calculated based on objective facts, we have placed no ceiling on the pre-trial deposit.

3. Legal Fees and Billing Practices (Par. 5)

In the second paragraph we have enumerated some of the billing practices that are frequently the subject of dispute.

4. Out of Town Travel (Par. 6 (b))

Many firms either do not charge for travelling time or charge at reduced rates. You may wish to address first class air travel.

5. Rate Schedule

In Part D of the Rate Schedule, we have listed charges that are not usually passed through strictly at cost. All such charges should be enumerated to comply with the statute's command that lawyers disclose their standard rates, fees and charges. We also have disclosed clerical staff overtime rates, even though they obviously are strictly at cost.

B. FORM NO. 5: HOURLY NON-LITIGATION

The comments on forms 1, 2, and 4 apply equally to form 5.

VI. Additional Provisions

There are innumerable additional provisions that a lawyer can include in a fee agreement. We will deal here only with three—attorney's fees, interest and arbitration.

An attorney's fees clause is permitted.

Although lawyers ethically may charge interest, we do not believe that most lawyers will want to comply with the rather onerous truth in lending regulations that must be honored before an interest provision will be enforceable. In some instances interest is recoverable by law (e.g., Civ. Code, sec. 3287).

Lawyers may include a general statement in their fee agreements to the effect that fee disputes between lawyers and clients are subject to arbitration at the client's election. However, we recommend against affirmative agreements to arbitrate, and/or to be bound. Such clauses will not be enforceable, in our opinion, without full disclosure to the client of the ramifications of those choices and the comparative advantages and disadvantages of other alternatives. To secure client's informed consent on this point and to document that process is an onerous undertaking.

VII. Conclusion

We have disseminated these forms in the hope that they will be useful to lawyers in their practices. We urge you to make any alterations in these forms so that they conform to your practice and the needs and requirements of you and your clients. We invite your comments and suggestions.

Sample Written Fee Contract #1
Hourly—Short Form—Litigation

HOBART, COLFAX & WHEELER
441 Bauchet Street
Los Angeles, CA 90012
(213) 680-9600

__________ _____, 19____

ATTORNEY-CLIENT FEE CONTRACT

This ATTORNEY-CLIENT FEE CONTRACT ("Contract") is entered into by and between William King ("Client") and Hobart, Colfax & Wheeler ("Attorney").

1. **CONDITIONS.** This Contract will not take effect, and Attorney will have no obligation to provide legal services, until Client returns a signed copy of this Contract and pays the deposit called for under paragraph 3.

2. **SCOPE AND DUTIES.** Client hires Attorney to provide legal services in connection with __________________. Attorney shall provide those legal services reasonably required to represent Client, and shall take reasonable steps to keep Client informed of progress and to respond to Client's inquiries. Client shall be truthful with Attorney, cooperate with Attorney, keep Attorney informed of developments, abide by this Contract, pay Attorney's bills on time and keep Attorney advised of Client's address, telephone number and whereabouts.

3. **DEPOSIT.** Client shall deposit $_________ by _________. The sum will be deposited in a trust account, to be used to pay:

__Costs and expenses only.
__Costs and expenses and fees for legal services.

Client hereby authorizes Attorney to withdraw sums from the trust account to pay the costs and/or fees Client incurs. Any unused deposit at the conclusion of Attorney's services will be refunded.

4. **LEGAL FEES.** Client agrees to pay for legal services at the following rates: partners- __/hour; associates- __/hour; paralegals- __/hour; law clerks- __/hour; and for other personnel as follows, ____________________________. Attorney charges in minimum units of __ hours.

5. **COSTS AND EXPENSES.** In addition to paying legal fees, Client shall reimburse Attorney for all costs and expenses incurred by Attorney, including, but not limited to, process servers' fees, fees fixed by law or assessed by courts or other agencies, court reporters' fees, long distance telephone calls, messenger and other delivery fees, postage, in-office photocopying at $_________ per page, parking, mileage at $_________ per mile, investigation expenses, consultants' fees, expert witness fees and other similar items. Client authorizes Attorney to incur all reasonable costs and to hire any investigators, consultants or expert witnesses reasonably necessary in Attorney's judgment, unless one or both of the clauses below are initialed by Client and Attorney.

______________ Attorney shall obtain Client's consent before incurring any cost in excess of $ _________.
______________ Attorney shall obtain Client's consent before retaining outside investigators, consultants, or expert witnesses.

6. **STATEMENTS.** Attorney shall send Client periodic statements for fees and costs incurred. Client shall pay Attorney's statements within _____ days after each statement's date. Client may request a state-

These sample written fee agreement forms are intended to satisfy the basic requirements of Business & Professions Code Section 6148 but may not address varying contractual obligations which may be present in a particular case. The State Bar makes no representation of any kind, express or implied, concerning the use of these forms.

ment at intervals of no less than 30 days. Upon Client's request Attorney will provide a statement within 10 days.

7. **LIEN**. Client hereby grants Attorney a lien on any and all claims or causes of action that are the subject of Attorney's representation under this Contract. Attorney's lien will be for any sums due and owing to Attorney at the conclusion of Attorney's services. The lien will attach to any recovery Client may obtain, whether by arbitration award, judgment, settlement or otherwise.

8. **DISCHARGE AND WITHDRAWAL**. Client may discharge Attorney at any time. Attorney may withdraw with Client's consent or for good cause. Good cause includes Client's breach of this Contract, Client's refusal to cooperate with Attorney or to follow Attorney's advice on a material matter or any other fact or circumstance that would render Attorney's continuing representation unlawful or unethical.

9. **CONCLUSION OF SERVICES**. When Attorney's services conclude, all unpaid charges shall become immediately due and payable. After Attorney's services conclude, Attorney will, upon Client's request, deliver Client's file to Client, along with any Client funds or property in Attorney's possession.

10. **DISCLAIMER OF GUARANTEE**. Nothing in this Contract and nothing in Attorney's statements to Client will be construed as a promise or guarantee about the outcome of Client's matter. Attorney makes no such promises or guarantees. Attorney's comments about the outcome of Client's matter are expressions of opinion only.

11. **EFFECTIVE DATE**. This Contract will take effect when Client has performed the conditions stated in paragraph 1, but its effective date will be retroactive to the date Attorney first provided services. The date at the beginning of this Contract is for reference only. Even if this Contract does not take effect, Client will be obligated to pay Attorney the reasonable value of any services Attorney may have performed for Client.

"Attorney"

HOBART, COLFAX & WHEELER

By: ______________________________

George Clinton

"Client"

____

William King

Address: ______________________________

____

Telephone: ______________________________

Sample Written Fee Contract #2
Hourly—Short Form—Non-Litigation

HOBART, COLFAX & WHEELER
441 Bauchet Street
Los Angeles, CA 90012
(213) 680-8600

__________ ____, 19____

ATTORNEY-CLIENT FEE CONTRACT

This ATTORNEY-CLIENT FEE CONTRACT ("Contract") is entered into by and between William King ("Client") and Hobart, Colfax & Wheeler ("Attorney").

1. **CONDITIONS.** This Contract will not take effect, and Attorney will have no obligation to provide legal services, until Client returns a signed copy of this Contract and pays the deposit called for under paragraph 3.

2. **SCOPE AND DUTIES.** Client hires Attorney to provide legal services in connection with ________________. Attorney shall provide those legal services reasonably required to represent Client and shall take reasonable steps to keep Client informed of progress and to respond to Client's inquiries. Attorney's services will not include litigation of any kind, whether in court, in administrative hearings or before government agencies or arbitration tribunals. Client shall be truthful with Attorney, cooperate with Attorney, keep Attorney informed of developments, abide by this Contract, pay Attorney's bills on time and keep Attorney advised of Client's address, telephone number and whereabouts.

3. **DEPOSIT.** Client shall deposit $________ by ________. The sum will be deposited in a trust account, to be used to pay:

__Costs and expenses only.
__Costs and expenses and fees for legal services.

Client hereby authorizes Attorney to withdraw sums from the trust account to pay the costs and/or fees Client incurs. Any unused deposit at the conclusion of Attorney's services will be refunded.

4. **LEGAL FEES.** Client agrees to pay for legal services at the following rates: partners- __/hour; associates- __/hour; paralegals- __/hour; law clerks- __/hour; and for other personnel as follows, ________________________. Attorney charges in minimum __ units of hours.

5. **COSTS AND EXPENSES.** In addition to paying legal fees, Client shall reimburse Attorney for all costs and expenses incurred by Attorney, including, but not limited to fees fixed by law or assessed by public agencies, long distance telephone calls, messenger and other delivery fees, postage, in-office photocopying at $________ per page, parking, mileage at $________ per mile, investigation expenses, consultants' fees and other similar items. Client authorizes Attorney to incur all reasonable costs and to hire any investigators or consultants reasonably necessary in Attorney's judgment, unless one or both of the clauses below are initialed by Client and Attorney.

____________ Attorney shall obtain Client's consent before incurring any cost in excess of $ ________.
____________ Attorney shall obtain Client's consent before retaining outside investigators or consultants.

6. **STATEMENTS.** Attorney shall send Client periodic statements for fees and costs incurred. Client shall pay Attorney's statements within ____ days after each statement's date. Client may request a state-

---

These sample written fee agreement forms are intended to satisfy the basic requirements of Business & Professions Code Section 6148 but may not address varying contractual obligations which may be present in a particular case. The State Bar makes no representation of any kind, express or implied, concerning the use of these forms.

ment at intervals of no less than 30 days. Upon Client's request Attorney will provide a statement within 10 days.

7. **DISCHARGE AND WITHDRAWAL.** Client may discharge Attorney at any time. Attorney may withdraw with Client's consent or for good cause. Good cause includes Client's breach of this Contract, Client's refusal to cooperate with Attorney or to follow Attorney's advice on a material matter or any other fact or circumstance that would render Attorney's continuing representation unlawful or unethical.

8. **CONCLUSION OF SERVICES.** When Attorney's services conclude, all unpaid charges shall become immediately due and payable. After Attorney's services conclude, Attorney will, upon Client's request, deliver Client's file to Client, along with any Client funds or property in Attorney's possession.

9. **DISCLAIMER OF GUARANTEE.** Nothing in this Contract and nothing in Attorney's statements to Client will be construed as a promise or guarantee about the outcome of Client's matter. Attorney makes no such promises or guarantees. Attorney's comments about the outcome of Client's matter are expressions of opinion only.

10. **EFFECTIVE DATE.** This Contract will take effect when Client has performed the conditions stated in paragraph 1, but its effective date will be retroactive to the date Attorney first provided services. The date at the beginning of this Contract is for reference only. Even if this Contract does not take effect, Client will be obligated to pay Attorney the reasonable value of any services Attorney may have performed for Client.

"Attorney"

HOBART, COLFAX & WHEELER

By: ______________________________
George Clinton

"Client"

____
William King

Address: ______________________________

____

Telephone: ______________________________

Sample Written Fee Contract #3
Fixed Fee—Short Form—Non-Litigation

HOBART, COLFAX & WHEELER
441 Bauchet Street
Los Angeles, CA 90012
(213) 680-9600

__________ ____, 19____

ATTORNEY-CLIENT FEE CONTRACT

This ATTORNEY-CLIENT FEE CONTRACT ("Contract") is entered into by and between William King ("Client") and Hobart, Colfax & Wheeler ("Attorney")

1. **CONDITIONS.** This Contract will not take effect, and Attorney will have no obligation to provide legal services, until Client returns a signed copy of this Contract and pays the fixed fee and deposit called for under paragraphs 3 and 5.

2. **SCOPE AND DUTIES.** Client hires Attorney to provide legal services in connection with ______________. Attorney shall provide the following services: ______________. Attorney's services will not include litigation of any kind, whether in court, in administrative hearings or before government agencies or arbitration tribunals. Attorney shall take reasonable steps to keep Client informed of progress and to respond to Client's inquiries. Client shall be truthful with Attorney, cooperate with Attorney, keep Attorney informed of developments, abide by this Contract, pay Attorney's bills on time and keep Attorney advised of Client's address, telephone number and whereabouts.

3. **FIXED FEE.** Client agrees to pay a fixed fee of $________ for Attorney's services under this Contract. The fixed fee is due by ____________. Attorneys shall have no obligation whatsoever to provide services to Client until the fixed fee is paid in full. Unless the fee retained would be unconscionable and except as provided in paragraph 7, the fixed fee will be earned in full and no portion of it will be refunded once any substantial services have been performed.

4. **COSTS AND EXPENSES.** In addition to the fixed fee, Client shall reimburse Attorney for all costs and expenses incurred by Attorney, including, but not limited to, fees fixed by law or assessed by public agencies, long distance telephone calls, messenger and other delivery fees, postage, in-office photocopying at $________ per page, parking, mileage at $________ per mile, investigation expenses, consultants' fees, and other similar items. Client authorizes Attorney to incur all reasonable costs and to hire any investigators or consultants reasonably necessary in Attorney's judgment, unless one or both of the clauses below are initialed by Client and Attorney.

____________ Attorney shall obtain Client's consent before incurring any cost in excess of $ ________.
____________ Attorney shall obtain Client's consent before retaining outside investigators or consultants.

5. **DEPOSIT.** In addition to the fixed fee Client shall deposit $________ by ____________. The sum will be deposited in a trust account, to be used to pay for costs and expenses. Client hereby authorizes Attorney to withdraw sums from the trust account to pay the costs Client incurs. Any unused deposit at the conclusion of Attorney's services will be refunded.

6. **STATEMENTS.** Attorney shall send Client periodic statements for fees and costs incurred. Client shall pay Attorney's statements within ____ days after each statement's date. Client may request a state-

These sample written fee agreement forms are intended to satisfy the basic requirements of Business & Professions Code Section 6148 but may not address varying contractual obligations which may be present in a particular case. The State Bar makes no representation of any kind, express or implied, concerning the use of these forms.

ment at intervals of no less than 30 days. Upon Client's request Attorney will provide a statement within 10 days.

7. **DISCHARGE AND WITHDRAWAL.** Client may discharge Attorney at any time. Attorney may withdraw with Client's consent or for good cause. Good cause includes Client's breach of this Contract, Client's refusal to cooperate with Attorney or to follow Attorney's advice on a material matter or any other fact or circumstance that would render Attorney's continuing representation unlawful or unethical. If Attorney withdraws before completing Attorney's duties under this Contract, Client may be entitled to a refund of some or all of the fixed fee, depending on the facts and circumstances.

8. **CONCLUSION OF SERVICES.** When Attorney's services conclude, all unpaid charges shall immediately become due and payable. After Attorney's services conclude, Attorney will, upon Client's request, deliver Client's file to Client, along with any Client funds or property in Attorney's possession.

9. **DISCLAIMER OF GUARANTEE.** Nothing in this Contract and nothing in Attorney's statements to Client will be construed as a promise or guarantee about the outcome of Client's matter. Attorney makes no such promises or guarantees. Attorney's comments about the outcome of Client's matter are expressions of opinion only.

10. **EFFECTIVE DATE.** This Contract will take effect when Client has performed the conditions stated in paragraph 1, but its effective date will be retroactive to the date Attorney first provided services. The date at the beginning of this Contract is for reference only. Even if this Contract does not take effect, Client will be obligated to pay Attorney the reasonable value of any services Attorney may have performed for Client.

"Attorney"

HOBART, COLFAX & WHEELER

By: ______________________________
George Clinton

"Client"

____
William King

Address: ______________________________

____

Telephone: ______________________________

Sample Written Fee Contract #4
Hourly—Long Form—Litigation

HOBART, COLFAX & WHEELER
441 Bauchet Street
Los Angeles, CA 90012
(213) 680-9600

____________ _____, 19_____

ATTORNEY-CLIENT FEE CONTRACT

This document (the "agreement") is the written fee contract that California law requires lawyers to have with their clients. We (Hobart, Colfax & Wheeler) will provide legal services to you (William King and King & Co., Ltd.) on the terms set forth below.

1. **CONDITIONS.** This agreement will not take effect, and we will have no obligation to provide legal services, until you return a signed copy of this agreement and pay the initial deposit called for under Paragraph 4.

2. **SCOPE OF SERVICES.** You are hiring us as your attorneys, to represent you in the matter described on the attached Rate Schedule. We will provide those legal services reasonably required to represent you. We will take reasonable steps to keep you informed of progress and to respond to your inquiries. If a court action is filed, we will represent you through trial and post-trial motions. After judgment we will not represent you on appeal or in execution proceedings. Unless you and we make a different agreement in writing, this agreement will govern all future services we may perform for you.

3. **CLIENT'S DUTIES.** You agree to be truthful with us, to cooperate, to keep us informed of developments, to abide by this agreement, to pay our bills on time and to keep us advised of your address, telephone number and whereabouts.

4. **MINIMUM FEE/DEPOSIT.** You agree to pay us an initial deposit of $__________ by __________. Of the initial deposit, $_______________ will be our minimum fee, paid in exchange for our agreement to represent you. The minimum fee is non-refundable, but our hourly charges will be credited against it. The remainder of the initial deposit, as well as any future deposit, will be held in a trust account. You authorize us to use that fund to pay the fees and other charges you incur.

Whenever your deposit is exhausted, we reserve the right to demand further deposits, each up to a maximum of $__________. Once a trial or arbitration date is set, we will require you to pay all sums then owing to us and to deposit the attorneys' fees we estimate will be incurred in preparing for and completing the trial or arbitration, as well as the jury fees or arbitration fees likely to be assessed. Those sums may exceed the maximum deposit.

You agree to pay all deposits after the initial deposit within ________ days of our demand. Except for the minimum fee, any unused deposit at the conclusion of our services will be refunded.

5. **LEGAL FEES AND BILLING PRACTICES.** You agree to pay by the hour at our prevailing rates for time spent on your matter by our legal personnel. Our current hourly rates for legal personnel (and other billing rates) are set forth on the attached Rate Schedule. The Rate Schedule also provides for periodic increases.

We will charge you for the time we spend on telephone calls relating to your matter, including calls with you, opposing counsel or court personnel. The legal personnel assigned to your matter will confer among themselves about the matter, as required. When they do confer, each person will charge for the time expended. Likewise, if more than one of our legal personnel attends a meeting, court hearing or other proceeding, each will charge for the time spent. We will charge for waiting time in court and elsewhere and for travel time, both local and out of town.

6. **COSTS AND OTHER CHARGES.**

(a) *In General* We will incur various costs and expenses in performing legal services under this agreement. You agree to pay for those costs and expenses in addition to the hourly fees. The costs and expenses commonly include process servers' fees, fees fixed by law or assessed by courts and other agencies, court reporters' fees, long distance telephone calls, messenger and other delivery fees, postage, parking and other local travel expenses, photocopying and

These sample written fee agreement forms are intended to satisfy the basic requirements of Business & Professions Code Section 6148 but may not address varying contractual obligations which may be present in a particular case. The State Bar makes no representation of any kind, express or implied, concerning the use of these forms.

other reproduction costs, clerical staff overtime, word processing charges, charges for computer time and other similar items. Except for the items listed on the Rate Schedule, all costs and expenses will be charged at our cost.

(b) *Out of Town Travel* You agree to pay transportation, meals, lodging and all other costs of any necessary out-of-town travel by our personnel. You will also be charged the hourly rates for the time legal personnel spend travelling.

(c) *Experts, Consultants and Investigators* To aid in the preparation or presentation of your case, it may become necessary to hire expert witnesses, consultants or investigators. We will not hire such persons unless you agree to pay their fees and charges. We will select any expert witnesses, consultants or investigators to be hired.

7. **BILLING STATEMENTS**. We will send you periodic statements for fees and costs incurred. Each statement will be due within ____________ days of its date. You may request a statement at intervals of no less than 30 days. If you do, we will provide one within 10 days.

8. **LIEN**. You hereby grant us a lien on any and all claims or causes of action that are the subject of our representation under this agreement. Our lien will be for any sums owing to us at the conclusion of our services. The lien will attach to any recovery you may obtain, whether by arbitration award, judgment, settlement or otherwise.

9. **DISCHARGE AND WITHDRAWAL**. You may discharge us at any time. We may withdraw with your consent or for good cause. Good cause includes your breach of this agreement, your refusal to cooperate with us or to follow our advice on a material matter or any fact or circumstance that would render our continuing representation unlawful or unethical.

When our services conclude, all unpaid charges will immediately become due and payable. After our services conclude, we will, upon your request, deliver your file to you, along with any funds or property of yours in our possession.

10. **DISCLAIMER OF GUARANTEE**. Nothing in this agreement and nothing in our statements to you will be construed as a promise or guarantee about the outcome of your matter. We make no such promises or guarantees. Our comments about the outcome of your matter are expressions of opinion only.

11. **EFFECTIVE DATE**. This agreement will take effect when you have performed the conditions stated in Paragraph 1, but its effective date will be retroactive to the date we first performed services. The date at the beginning of this agreement is for reference only. Even if this agreement does not take effect, you will be obligated to pay us the reasonable value of any services we may have performed for you.

HOBART, COLFAX & WHEELER

By: ______________________________
George Clinton

I/We have read and understood the foregoing terms and those set forth on the attached Rate Schedule and agree to them, as of the date Hobart, Colfax & Wheeler first provided services. If more than one party signs below, we each agree to be liable, jointly and severally, for all obligations under this agreement.

Address: ______________________________
____
Telephone: ______________________________

____
William King

Address: ______________________________
____
Telephone: ______________________________

KING & CO., LTD.
a Partnership
By: ______________________________
William King
General Partner

RATE SCHEDULE

A. Identification

Client: William King and King & Co., Ltd., a partnership
Matter: Dispute with Henry Wilson Co. and other related matters

B. Hourly rates for legal personnel

Senior partners	_____/hour
Partners	_____/hour
Associates	_____/hour
Paralegals	_____/hour
Law clerks	_____/hour

C. Standard charges

We charge for our time in minimum units of _____ hours.
[List any other standard charges or minimum time units]

D. Costs and expenses

In-office photocopying	_____/page
Mileage	_____/mile
Computerized legal research	_____/hour
Word processing	_____/hour
Other computer time	_____/hour

Clerical staff overtime will be charged at 1.5 times the base hourly rate or at the rates required by applicable law, whichever is greater. The base hourly rates for clerical personnel presently range between $___________ and $___________.

E. Subject to change

The rates on this schedule are subject to change on _____ days written notice. If you decline to pay any increased rates, we will have the right to withdraw as your lawyers.

Sample Written Fee Contract #5
Hourly-Long Form-Non-Litigation

HOBART, COLFAX & WHEELER
441 Bauchet Street
Los Angeles, CA 90012
(213) 680-9600

____________ _____, 19_____

ATTORNEY-CLIENT FEE CONTRACT

This document (the "agreement") is the written fee contract that California law requires lawyers to have with their clients. We (Hobart, Colfax & Wheeler) will provide legal services to you (William King and King & Co., Ltd.) on the terms set forth below.

1. **CONDITIONS.** This agreement will not take effect, and we will have no obligation to provide legal services, until you return a signed copy of this agreement and pay the initial deposit called for under Paragraph 4.

2. **SCOPE OF SERVICES.** You are hiring us as your attorneys, to represent you in the matter described on the attached Rate Schedule. We will provide those legal services reasonably required to represent you. We will take reasonable steps to keep you informed of progress and to respond to your inquiries. Our services will not include litigation of any kind, whether in court, in administrative hearings or before government agencies or arbitration tribunals. Unless you and we make a different agreement in writing, this Agreement will govern all future services we may perform for you, other than litigation.

3. **CLIENT'S DUTIES.** You agree to be truthful with us, to cooperate, to keep us informed of developments, to abide by this agreement, to pay our bills on time and to keep us advised of your address, telephone number and whereabouts.

4. **MINIMUM FEE/DEPOSIT.** You agree to pay us an initial deposit of $__________ by __________. Of the initial deposit, $_______________ will be our minimum fee, paid in exchange for our agreement to represent you. The minimum fee is non-refundable, but our hourly charges will be credited against it. The remainder of the initial deposit, as well as any future deposit, will be held in a trust account. You authorize us to use that fund to pay the fees and other charges you incur.

Whenever your deposit is exhausted, we reserve the right to demand further deposits, each up to a maximum of $__________. You agree to pay all further deposits within ________ days of our demand. Except for the minimum fee, any unused deposit at the conclusion of our services will be refunded.

5. **LEGAL FEES AND BILLING PRACTICES.** You agree to pay by the hour at our prevailing rates for time spent on your matter by our legal personnel. Our current hourly rates for legal personnel (and other billing rates) are set forth on the attached Rate Schedule. The Rate Schedule also provides for periodic increases.

We will charge you for the time we spend on telephone calls relating to your matter, including calls with you or opposing counsel. The legal personnel assigned to your matter will confer among themselves about the matter, as required. When they do confer, each person will charge for the time expended. Likewise, if more than one of our legal personnel attends a meeting, or other proceeding, each will charge for the time spent. We will charge for waiting time and for travel time, both local and out of town.

6. **COSTS AND OTHER CHARGES.**

(a) *In General* We will incur various costs and expenses in performing legal services under this agree-

---

These sample written fee agreement forms are intended to satisfy the basic requirements of Business & Professions Code Section 6148 but may not address varying contractual obligations which may be present in a particular case. The State Bar makes no representation of any kind, express or implied, concerning the use of these forms.

ment. You agree to pay for those costs and expenses in addition to the hourly fees. The costs and expenses commonly include fees fixed by law or assessed by public agencies, long distance telephone calls, messenger and other delivery fees, postage, parking and other local travel expenses, photocopying and other reproduction costs, clerical staff overtime, word processing charges, charges for computer time and other similar items. Except for the items listed on the Rate Schedule, all costs and expenses will be charged at our cost.

(b) *Out of Town Travel* You agree to pay transportation, meals, lodging and all other costs of any necessary out-of-town travel by our personnel. You will also be charged the hourly rates for the time legal personnel spend travelling.

(c) *Consultants and Investigators* To aid in the preparation or presentation of your case, it may become necessary to hire consultants or investigators. We will not hire such persons unless you agree to pay their fees and charges. We will select any consultants or investigators to be hired.

7. **BILLING STATEMENTS.** We will send you periodic statements for fees and costs incurred. Each statement will be due within ____________ days of its date. You may request a statement at intervals of no less than 30 days. If you do, we will provide one within 10 days.

8. **DISCHARGE AND WITHDRAWAL.** You may discharge us at any time. We may withdraw with your consent or for good cause. Good cause includes your breach of this agreement, your refusal to cooperate with us or to follow our advice on a material matter or any fact or circumstance that would render our continuing representation unlawful or unethical.

When our services conclude, all unpaid charges will immediately become due and payable. After our services conclude, we will, upon your request, deliver your file to you, along with any funds or property of yours in our possession.

9. **DISCLAIMER OF GUARANTEE.** Nothing in this agreement and nothing in our statements to you will be construed as a promise or guarantee about the outcome of your matter. We make no such promises or guarantees. Our comments about the outcome of your matter are expressions of opinion only.

10. **EFFECTIVE DATE.** This agreement will take effect when you have performed the conditions stated in Paragraph 1, but its effective date will be retroactive to the date we first performed services. The date at the beginning of this agreement is for reference only. Even if this agreement does not take effect, you will be obligated to pay us the reasonable value of any services we may have performed for you.

HOBART, COLFAX & WHEELER

By: ____
George Clinton

I/We have read and understood the foregoing terms and those set forth on the attached Rate Schedule and agree to them, as of the date Hobart, Colfax & Wheeler first provided services. If more than one party signs below, we each agree to be liable, jointly and severally, for all obligations under the foregoing agreement.

Address: ________________________________
____
Telephone: ______________________________

____
William King

Address: ________________________________
____
Telephone: ______________________________

KING & CO., LTD.
a Partnership
By: ____
William King
General Partner

RATE SCHEDULE

A. Identification

Client: William King and King & Co., Ltd., a partnership
Matter: Sale of 200 N. Spring St., Los Angeles

B. **Hourly rates for legal personnel**

Senior partners	_____/hour
Partners	_____/hour
Associates	_____/hour
Paralegals	_____/hour
Law clerks	_____/hour

C. **Standard charges**

We charge for our time in minimum units of _____ hours.
[List any other standard charges or minimum time units.]

D. **Costs and expenses**

In-office photocopying	_____/page
Mileage	_____/mile
Computerized legal research	_____/hour
Word processing	_____/hour
Other computer time	_____/hour

Clerical staff overtime will be charged at 1.5 times the base hourly rate or at the rates required by applicable law, whichever is greater. The base hourly rates for clerical personnel presently range between $__________ and $__________.

E. **Subject to change**

The rates on this schedule are subject to change on _____ days written notice. If you decline to pay any increased rates, we will have the right to withdraw as your lawyers.

Part 3. Sample Client/Lawyer Agreement

This agreement is entered into by and between ____________________ ("Attorney") and ____________________ ("Client").

Attorney will perform the following services for Client:

(Here specify the services to be rendered.)

Attorney estimates that legal services required by Client will take approximately ____________ to ____________ hours and cost between ____________________ and ____________________ as follows:

(Here the lawyer lists hours and costs for handling different aspects of the case should certain variables occur.)

Disbursement costs (filing fees, deposition and transcript costs, transportation, etc.) will be paid by Client. Attorney estimates that disbursement costs will be as follows:

(Here the lawyer itemizes possible disbursement costs.)

Prior to undertaking work beyond that initially specified, Attorney will provide Client with a written estimate of the additional time, fees and disbursements involved and receive written permission from Client to undertake the work.

Attorney agrees to explain the laws pertinent to Client's problem, the available courses of action, and the attendant risks.

Attorney agrees to notify Client promptly of any significant developments and consult with Client in advance on any significant decisions.

Attorney agrees to send Client copy of all pertinent written materials sent or received by Attorney pertaining to Client's case. Client agrees to reimburse Attorney out-of-pocket costs for the reproduction of those materials.

Or:

Attorney agrees to make available to Client for reading in Attorney's office all written materials sent or received by Attorney pertaining to Client's case. At Client's request, Attorney will provide copy of any material to Client at Attorney's out-of-pocket costs.

Attorney agrees to make all reasonable efforts to answer Client's inquiries promptly.

Client agrees to pay Attorney as follows:

(Here describe agreed-upon fee arrangement.)

Client may terminate this agreement, with or without cause, on written notice to Attorney. Attorney shall return Client's file immediately on Client's terminating this agreement. Termination shall not affect Client's responsibility to pay for legal services rendered up to the date of termination. Attorney may terminate this agreement for reasons permitted under the ____________________ (state) Code of Professional Responsibility.

Nothing herein contained shall be interpreted to limit or restrict the Attorney's professional obligations under ____________________ (state) Bar's codes or canons.

____
Attorney

____
Client

Part 4. Draft of a Fee Manual for In-office Use*

FEE MANUAL

TABLE OF CONTENTS

I. INTRODUCTION

"We Lawyers must take time to study and apply the disciplines of the businessman, if we are to fare as well financially.

"Many lawyers work sixteen hours a day, charge for eight and get paid for four. It is no wonder that while the number of unhappy lawyers in private practice is increasing, the number of sole practitioners is decreasing.

"We are among the best trained and the worst paid in America. And, as the saying goes, something ought to be done about it. But only we can do it."

This manual is one attempt to "do something about it."

This manual is prepared to guide lawyers in all aspects of setting, billing and collecting fees. We can continue to provide the highest quality of legal services only if we are compensated adequately for the work we do. Experience has proved that good business, such as practice in setting fees and billing, is essential to good client relations.

The policies and procedures adopted in this manual have proved effective. They are based on our experience and the experience and advice of many other practicing lawyers.

II. BASIC POLICIES FOR DETERMINING FEES

A. GENERAL POLICY

Our general policy is only to accept work where:

1. We can perform the work with the highest degree of legal skill;

2. It is reasonably certain that we will be compensated adequately for the services rendered;

3. It is reasonably certain that we will be paid promptly. It is not our function to finance a client's business or personal obligations. We are paid for legal services, not for the financing of them.

*This fee manual is not complete and is intended as an example. Readers should adapt their own fee manuals according to their firms' needs, using this as a guide.

B. SPECIFIC RULES

The following rules have been adopted in an attempt to ensure that the general objectives are achieved:

1. The fee must be discussed as early as possible in the attorney-client relationship, preferably at the first meeting. The longer you wait to discuss fees, the more likely it is that you will do work for nothing or experience some problem with the client over a billing. A client is entitled to a fee discussion at the first opportunity.

2. An agreement as to fees must be reached as early as possible. All fee agreements should be in writing. No litigation will be accepted without a written-fee agreement and a substantial advance payment.

3. Agreed fees must be in line with office rules and the office fee schedule.

4. Retainers should be obtained in advance when the work is to be performed for a new client. This is the best time to collect the fees.

5. Retainers *must* be obtained:

   a. Where it is anticipated that we will have to advance costs;
   b. In all litigated matters;
   c. Where the work is of a rush or high-priority nature (the more the urgency, the higher the retainer);
   d. Where the client is not known to us;
   e. Where the client's credit or ability to pay is suspect.

6. An estimate of the total fee and the amount involved in the case must be entered on the blue filing and billing memorandum at the time that files are opened.
7. The work must be of a type we perform. We do no personal injury, divorce or criminal (except tax fraud) work. If you have any questions on what type of case you can accept, consult the managing partner.
8. In most cases, bills must be submitted monthly to clients. Obvious exceptions are contingent fees. Other exceptions are not obvious and must be justified on the blue billing and filing memorandum and to the managing partner.
9. A premium of at least 25 percent over chargeable time will be added for work of a rush or crisis nature. A rush job means increased costs and causes other clients' work to be delayed.
10. A delinquent clients list will be distributed monthly. No new work will be accepted from a delinquent client without the approval of the managing partner.

These rules apply immediately to all new clients and new work for existing clients. Efforts are to be made to bring existing client relationships up to these basic standards. Any variation from these rules must be approved by the managing partner.

III. TIMEKEEPING AND BILLING RATES

A. TIME RECORDS

Every writer and speaker on law-office economics tells us that lawyers who do not keep time are throwing money away. So are lawyers who keep time but do not record it promptly and accurately.

Time slips must be maintained by all lawyers and legal assistants, by client and matter. Time must be recorded daily and time slips must be turned in each week. The date (including year) the work was performed, the lawyer and a brief description of the work must be indicated on the lawyer's time slips. The amount of time to the nearest tenth of an hour is recorded on the slip. In addition to the individual time slips for chargeable items, lawyers should prepare daily time slips showing the time for the recognized categories of nonchargeable time. (See the office manual for instructions in coding time slips.)

Time slips that do not have a description of the work performed are of little value and cause embarrassment when discussing bills with clients. Describe what is done for the client on the time slip.

Many clients have more than one billing matter and the time slips should correctly identify the specific matter to which the time is to be charged. Correct matter numbers can be obtained from the green computer run of numbers that is supplied to each person who may be coding time slips.

Time slips and other relevant accounting information must be turned over to the Accounting Department no later than 10:30 A.M. on the Monday following the week to which they apply. Delays in turning time into the Accounting Department cause loss of income and reduce the effectiveness of the operation of the office. Each Monday the Accounting Department reports to the managing partner who has and who has not turned in their time.

B. BILLING RATES

A schedule of the billing rates of each attorney and legal assistant is shown on the following page. Billing rates are determined by the individual lawyer's skill, experience and reputation. Billing rates also are set high enough to ensure that the firm obtains a reasonable return on its investment.

The billing rate is multiplied by the hours recorded for a particular matter to determine the value of billed time. A report of unbilled time is distributed monthly to the billing partner. It is anticipated that the billing partner promptly will bill all matters on a monthly basis. Billing rates are merely guides for determining fees and it is common that fees are written up and written down depending on the circumstances. Therefore, billing rates also are a measure of productivity and profitability of both client accounts and lawyers.

Our costs continue to increase and consequently we have found it necessary to increase our billing rates in the past and we expect to find it necessary to continue to increase our billing rates in the future. If billing rates are discussed or disclosed to clients or if fee agreement is made to charge "standard rates," care should be taken to provide that our rates are reviewed periodically and are subject to increase without notice.

Billing rates should not be disclosed to a client unless the fee arrangement is one in which the client is to be billed on an hourly rate and the client specifically asks what the hourly rate will be. In any case, where the fee is on an hourly basis the billing must be done monthly.

C. SPECIFIC TYPES OF MATTERS THAT SHOULD NOT BE HANDLED ON AN HOURLY BASIS (to completed by reader)

IV. CHARGES BY TYPE OF WORK

A. GENERAL

A fee arrangment will vary depending on the type of work and nature of the matter.

B. MONTHLY STATEMENT

There are some cases where a fee arrangement will not be discussed with a client in an initial interview. In those cases, the blue billing and filing memorandum will indicate that fees have not been discussed with the client. In all such cases, the office assigns an accounting matter designation of .40 to such accounts. Those accounts are to be billed monthly at regular billing rates. The statements sent to the clients will be itemized by services rendered.

The itemized monthly statement will be used for any type of matter where billing is not discussed with the client. Monthly billing also is recommended if the matter is not covered by a specific rule laid down in this manual and if no other fee arrangement is appropriate.

While the monthly statement does not necessarily provide for recovering a premium over and above our chargeable time, experience has proved that it is far better to bill frequently in small amounts at regular rates rather than to wait a long period of time to bill in the hope of obtaining a premium. Those few cases where a premium would otherwise be recovered will be more than offset by those cases where there is loss because of a delay in billing. It also will more than compensate for the fact that deferred billing means that we are financing a client's legal business.

When monthly statements are submitted, the lawyer should explain to the client that we have minimum charges for telephone calls or letters of .2 of an hour.

In order for the monthly billing to be effective, the work must be performed promptly.

C. ARRANGEMENTS OTHER THAN MONTHLY STATEMENTS

1. General Standards (Sections can be added to cover general matters that must be taken into account in setting fees.)

2. Minimum-Fee Schedule The San Francisco Lawyers Club minimum-fee schedule may be used by attorneys in discussing fees and setting fees. Before using the minimum-fee schedule, you should read the material in Section 4 of the supplement on minimum-fee schedules. As the supplementary material points out, great care should be used when setting a fee by using a minimum-fee schedule. Under most circumstances, you should not disclose that you have used a minimum-fee schedule. The danger is that a client who knows of a minimum-fee schedule may expect to pay the minimum fee whether or not it is appropriate in his or her case. Some clients may feel abused if they felt that we would perform the same services to someone else for less.

The San Francisco Lawyers Club minimum-fee schedule appears in Section 5 of the supplement. The foreword to the schedule should be read before you use the schedule.

Bibliography

ARTICLES

Cleveland, A. L. "You've Got Your Lawyer's Bill? Here's How You Can Analyze It." 9 *National Law Journal* 18 (Nov. 17, 1986).

Cook, A. I. "Hourly Billing: A Thing of the Past?" 10 *National Law Journal* S-1 (Nov. 23, 1987).

Couric, E. "Smart Money Methods to Setting and Collecting Fees." 71 *ABA Journal* 66 (July 1985).

Doherty, W.E. "Toward the Law Library as a Profit Center" 26 *Law Office Econ. & Mgt.* 108 (Spring 1985).

Dombroff, M. A. "Helping Clients Understand the Billing Process." 10 *National Law Journal* S-8 (Nov. 23, 1987).

Furlonger, G. "Time for Business Lawyers to Stop Billing Time?" 27 *Law Office Econ. & Mgt.* 171 (1986-87).

Hildebrandt, B. W. "Understanding the New Economics of Law Practice." 9 *Legal Economics* 48 (August 10, 1987).

Hochdorf, R. S. "Billing for Technological Overhead." 6 *Legal Administrator* 26 (Summer 1987).

Iezzi, J. G. "Automating Lawyers: Does It Help the Bottom Line?" *Law Office Management & Admin. Report* (Issue 87-11, Nov. 1987).

Loeb, A. L. "Hourly Charges in Divorce Cases Are Archaic." 1 *American Journal of Family Law* 133 (Spring 1987).

Miller, J. D. "Pros and Cons of Alternative Fee Structures." 11 *National Law Journal* 15 (March 14, 1988).

Reed, R. C. "It's Time to Think About Billing." 13 *Legal Economics* 28 (September 1987).

"Report on Alternative Billing Practices Survey, December 1985" 16 *Lawyer's Brief* 14 (Nov. 30, 1986).

Roberts, K. "The Hourly Fee System is a Devilish Creature." 10 *National Law Journal* S-4 (Nov. 23, 1987).

Schlein, C. L. "Selection of a Billing System Requires Planning, Goal Setting." 9 *National Law Journal* 25 (Nov. 17, 1986).

Smith, L. "Avoiding Line Item Review: Emerson Electric's Approach to Litigation Budgeting." 6 *Of Counsel* 4 (Nov. 16, 1987).

Sugarman, A. D. "A Universal Format for Legal Billings." 7 *National Law Journal* 12 (July 15, 1985).

Tolman, J. L. "Billing by the Hour Should Be Banned." 41 *Washington State Bar News* 22 (July 1987).

BOOKS

Aronson, R. H. *Attorney-Client Fee Arrangements: Regulation and Review.* Federal Judicial Center, 1980.

Altman, M. A. and Weil, R. I. *How To Manage Your Law Office.* Bender. Chapter 4: Legal Fees.

Gutglass, J. L. *Attorneys' Fees and Law Office Management: A Selected Bibliography.* Washington University Law Library, 1982.

How To Set and Collect Attorney Fees in Criminal Cases. American Bar Association, 1985.

Law Office Economics & Management Manual. Callaghan. Chapter 24: Fees.

Legal Fees & Representation Agreements. ABA Section of Economics of Law Practice, 1983.

Relative Values: Determining Attorneys' Fees. Shepards/McGraw-Hill, 1985.

About the Editor

Richard C. Reed is Chairman of the Board of Reed McClure Moceri Thonn & Moriarty in Seattle, Washington. He is a Past Chairman of the American Bar Association's Section of Economics of Law Practice and is also an active member of the Washington State Bar Association and the Seattle-King County Bar Association. Mr. Reed has written extensively for legal periodicals including *Legal Economics*, *ABA Journal*, and the *National Law Journal*, and his writing has been included in books published by Prentice-Hall, the State Bar of Arizona and the American Bar Association. In addition, Mr. Reed has lectured at the Institute of Law Office Administration in Minneapolis, Denver and Chicago, the American Bar Association, the Canadian Bar Association, the Law Society of Upper Canada and the Washington State Bar Association. Mr. Reed received has A.B. and J.D. from the University of Chicago and now lives in Bellevue, Washington.

Order Form

Quantity	Title	LPM Price	Regular Price	Total
______	Access 1991–1992 (511-0297)	$29.95	$34.95	______
______	Action Steps to Marketing Success (511-0300)	29.95	34.95	______
______	Anatomy of a Merger (511-0310)	44.95	54.95	______
______	Basics for Writing Your Law Firm Brochure (511-0223)	14.95	19.95	______
______	Beyond the Billable Hour (511-0260)	69.95	79.95	______
______	Fast Forms with Macros (511-0269)	99.00	109.00	______
______	From Yellow Pads to Computers, 2nd ed. (511-0289)	64.95	69.95	______
______	How to Start & Build a Law Practice, 3rd ed. (511-0293)	32.95	39.95	______
______	Identifying Profits (511-0259)	14.95	19.95	______
______	Improving Accounts Receivable Collection (511-0273)	39.95	49.95	______
______	Keeping Happier Clients (511-0299)	19.95	29.95	______
______	Law Office Staff Manual (511-0307)	79.00	89.00	______
______	LOCATE 1992–93 (511-0311)	64.95	74.95	______
______	Making Partner (511-0303)	14.95	19.95	______
______	Managing Partner 101 (511-0272)	19.95	29.95	______
______	Marketing Your Practice (511-0215)	44.95	54.95	______
______	Practical Systems (511-0296)	24.95	34.95	______
______	The Quality Pursuit (511-0268)	74.95	84.95	______
______	A Short Course in Personal Computers (511-0302)	14.95	19.95	______
______	Winning with Computers (511-0294)	89.95	99.95	______
______	Win-Win Billing Strategies (511-0304)	89.95	99.95	______
______	WordPerfect in One Hour (511-0308)	9.95	14.95	______
______	Writing Your Law Firm Newsletter (511-0216)	14.95	19.95	______
______	Your New Lawyer, 2nd edition (511-0312)	74.95	84.95	______

*HANDLING

$2.00–$9.99	$2.00
10.00–24.99	3.95
25.00–49.99	4.95
50.00 +	5.95

**TAX

DC residents add 6%
IL residents add 8.75%
MD residents add 5%

SUBTOTAL: $ ______

*HANDLING: (see table) ______

**TAX: (see table) ______

TOTAL: $ ______

☐ Check enclosed (Payable to ABA) ☐ Visa ☐ MasterCard ☐ Bill Me

Account Number ______- ______- ______- ______ Exp. Date ______

Signature ______

Name ______

Firm ______

Address ______

City ______ State ______ ZIP ______

IMPORTANT:
A phone number will speed your order if we must contact you: (______) ______

Return to: American Bar Association, Order Fulfillment 511, 750 N. Lake Shore Drive, Chicago, IL 60611

To FAX order: (312) 988-5568.

BOOK

CUSTOMER COMMENT FORM

ABA

Section of Economics of Law Practice

Title: ______________________________

We've tried to make this publication as useful, accurate, and readable as possible. Please take 5 minutes to tell us if we succeeded. Your comments and suggestions will help us improve our publications. Thank you!

1. How did you acquire this publication:

☐ by mail order ☐ at a meeting/convention ☐ as a gift

☐ by phone order ☐ at a bookstore ☐ don't know

☐ other: (describe) ______________________________

Please rate this publication as follows:

	Excellent	Good	Fair	Poor	Not Applicable
Readability: Was the book easy to read and understand?	☐	☐	☐	☐	☐
Examples/Cases: Were they helpful, practical? Were there enough?	☐	☐	☐	☐	☐
Content: Did the book meet your expectations? Did it cover the subject adequately?	☐	☐	☐	☐	☐
Organization and clarity: Was the sequence of text logical? Was it easy to find what you wanted to know?	☐	☐	☐	☐	☐
Illustrations/forms/checklists: Were they clear and useful? Were there enough?	☐	☐	☐	☐	☐
Physical attractiveness: What did you think of the appearance of the publication (typesetting, printing, etc.)?	☐	☐	☐	☐	☐

Would you recommend this book to another attorney/administrator? ☐ Yes ☐ No

How could this publication be improved? What else would you like to see in it?

____

____

____

Do you have other comments or suggestions? ______________________________

____

____

Name ______________________________

Firm/Company ______________________________

Address ______________________________

City/State/Zip ______________________________

Phone ______________________________

Firm Size: ______________ Area of specialization: ______________

We appreciate your time and help.

Fold

NO POSTAGE NECESSARY IF MAILED IN THE UNITED STATES

BUSINESS REPLY MAIL

FIRST CLASS PERMIT NO. 16471 CHICAGO, ILLINOIS

POSTAGE WILL BE PAID BY ADDRESSEE

American Bar Association
Publications Planning & Marketing
750 N. Lake Shore Drive
Chicago, Illinois 60611

Fold